The Complete Book of Movie Making

The Complete Book of Movie Making

Tony Rose

Fountain Press   London
Morgan and Morgan   New York

Fountain Press
46/47 Chancery Lane,
London WC2A 1JU.

Morgan & Morgan Inc.
400 Warburton Avenue,
Hastings-on-Hudson,
N.Y. 10706 USA.

First Published, 1971.
Second Impression January 1972.
Third Impression April 1972.
©Fountain Press Limited, 1971.
ISBN 0 852 42083 8

Printed by photo-lithography
and made in Great Britain at
The Pitman Press, Bath.

AUTHOR'S NOTE

Some of the material in this book was originally published as a series of articles I wrote for *Movie Maker* under the general title, 'Teach Yourself Movie Making'. This series brought me a great deal of stimulating correspondence from readers, some requesting information on topics that I had not covered and others kindly suggesting that the articles might be converted into a book. What follows is the result.

To call this *The Complete Book of Movie Making* may be accounted presumptuous, for who can claim to have a complete knowledge of any subject — least of all movie making which involves so many diverse and specialised skills. I can only say that I have tried to make it complete within the limits of my experience and to put into it all that I have learned during the past twenty years or so when movie making has been for me not so much a hobby but more a way of life.

ACKNOWLEDGEMENTS

The cover of this book incorporates three strips of movie film each representing one quarter of a second of screen time. The closeup of the eye is from *The Body* and is reproduced by kind permission of Kestrel Films/EMI-Anglo Amalgamated. The other two strips are from *Images*, produced by James Archibald and Associates for Kodak Limited, and are reproduced by kind permission of Kodak Limited.

Special photographic illustrations are by Philip Jenkins FRPS, Anthony Brian Grant, Roy Mathers, Clifford Ling, Caroline Rose and the author.

Film stills from *Grand Prix* and *Doctor Zhivago* by courtesy of M.G.M. and from *McClintock* by courtesy of United Artists.

Frame enlargements from *Watering the Gardener — Then and Now* by courtesy of the National Film Archive, T & R Films and Kodak Limited, from *Good Clean Fun* by courtesy of T & R Films and Kodak Limited, and from *A Place to Call Your Own* by courtesy of T & R Films and Mediterranean Villas Limited.

CONTENTS

Chapter One

SUPER 8 OR WHAT

Right at the beginning, let's be practical.

Before you get interested in the craft of movie making, you need to know the facts about film and equipment — what you are going to need and how much it is going to cost. You may have already decided that the first essential is a camera but, logically, you ought to budget for a projector as well because it's not much good being able to shoot a film unless you can see it — and borrowing a friend's projector every time you want to look at your pictures soon becomes wearisome.

This need to own *two* items of equipment accounts for the fact — or so I fancy — that movie making is still a minority occupation, compared, say, with still photography. Despite the strenuous efforts of the manufacturers to make it easy, nobody plunges into it without thinking.

You can go into a shop and buy a still camera on impulse. If you don't like it, you can sell it and buy another. If the second camera takes a different size of film from the first, no matter! You simply have to remember that in future you must ask for size 120 instead of 127. In fact, you don't even have to remember that; you can hand your camera to the man behind the counter and ask for 'a film to fit this, please'.

In the case of movies, however, the situation is different. When you buy a camera that takes a certain size of film — or gauge as we call it — then obviously you need a projector that accepts the same gauge. Later on, when you buy editing equipment, that will have to fall into line too.

This explains why the amateur movie maker tends to be extremely 'gauge conscious'. Once having picked his gauge and built up a stock of films in it, he is not likely to change in a hurry and may, indeed, easily convince himself that his gauge is superior to all the others.

Hence it is important to choose the gauge that is going to suit you best in the first place.

Is There Anything Else?

Now I have no doubt that many people in the photographic trade would say that I am making an undue fuss about this gauge question at the outset. They would argue that for the newcomer to movies in this day and age, there is only one sensible choice: super 8.

I am not going to deny this.

The vast majority of new movie cameras and projectors on the market today are designed for super 8 film. The range of equipment is such that however much — or however little — you want to spend, you will almost certainly find something to suit your pocket.

The film itself is relatively inexpensive and is supplied in a light-proof plastic cartridge which can be dropped into the camera in broad daylight without any danger of fogging. The super 8 'system', which I shall describe presently, enables you to use the same type of colour film indoors or out and to get technically acceptable results with a minimum of technical know-how. Few of us, you may think, could ask for anything more.

Nevertheless, other gauges do exist and they all have their devotees. As you are bound to encounter them sooner or later, you might as well know about them now so that you can consider their advantages and disadvantages quite dispassionately. In the end, you may well decide to follow the majority and settle for super 8 but at least you will lose nothing in the process and you may even save yourself disappointment or regret.

For the sake of clarity, I am going to deal with them in chronological order.

35 mm is the standard gauge of film used in the commercial cinema. (Nowadays some of the more lavish productions are filmed in 70 mm but that is by the way.) It was used quite extensively by amateurs in the nineteen twenties before the narrower gauges

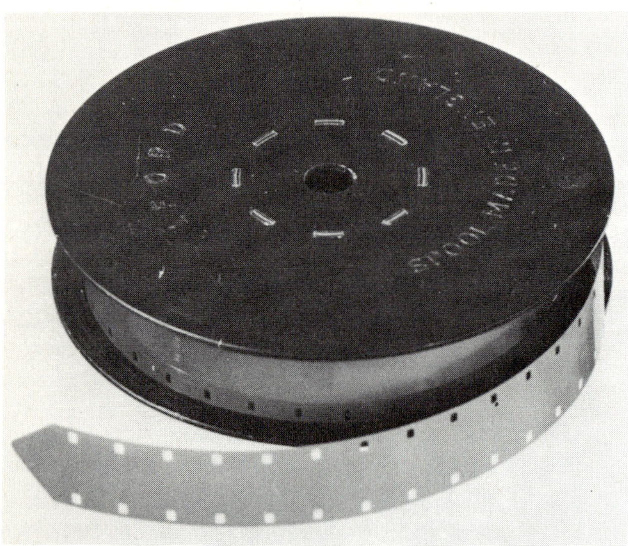

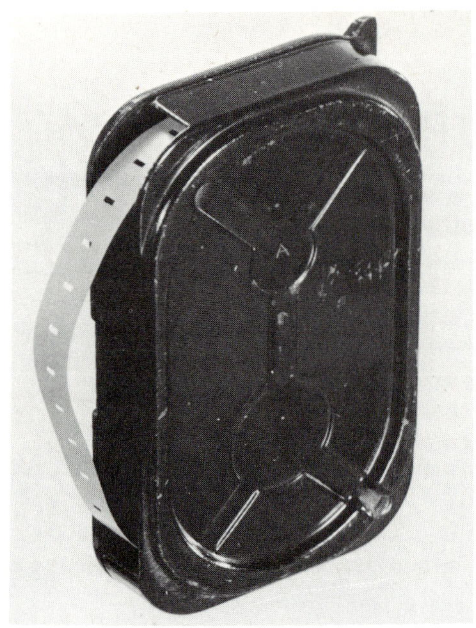

16 mm is the gauge for the ambitious (and/or wealthy) amateur. It is also widely used by professionals in television as well as the industrial and educational fields. In fact the gauge is now regarded as exclusively professional by H. M. Customs and Excise and, as a result, Purchase Tax has been removed from 16 mm equipment.

The film is normally sold on 100 ft spools like the one illustrated above. There are 40 frames to the foot and 100 ft runs for approximately 3 minutes at the normal sound speed of 24 frames per second (4 minutes at the silent speed of 16 f.p.s.).

Most modern cameras will take either the double-perforated or single-perforated film, as illustrated below. Some amateurs prefer to use the single-perforated film so that a magnetic stripe sound track can be added on the non-perforated side, the original then being used for projection.

There is a very large choice of 16 mm film stocks in both colour and black and white, reversal and negative. One special advantage of the gauge is that good quality copies can be made; another is that professional sound facilities are available.

9.5 mm is generally regarded as an obsolete gauge in the retail trade and equipment for it is now only manufactured in France. Nevertheless, it is kept going by a few specialist dealers and a vociferous band of loyal users.

The film is normally sold in H-chargers like the one illustrated above. This holds about 26 ft of film and gives a running time of just over a minute at 16 frames per second. The perforations are in the middle of the film (see illustration below) and between the frames of course. Hence the frames can occupy almost the complete width of the film and are not very much smaller than those on 16 mm. There are just over 40 frames to the foot.

Film is available (from the specialist dealers mentioned above) in both colour and black and white. In addition to the chargers, it can be supplied on 50 and 100 ft spools and these are used in some of the later cameras made in France.

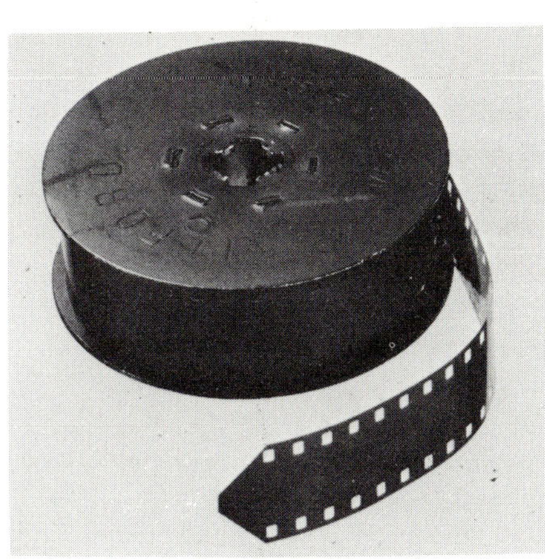

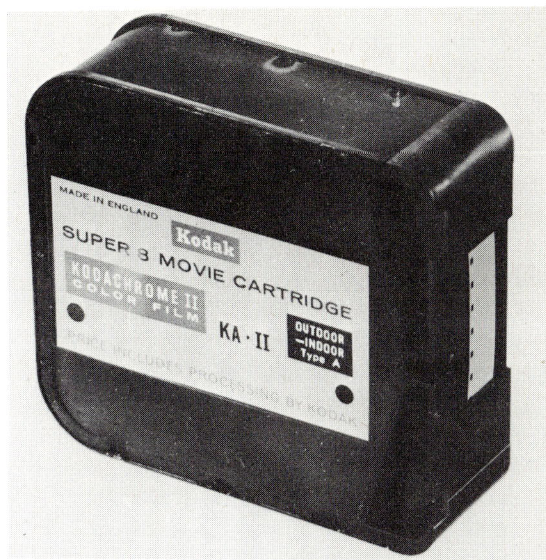

Standard 8 mm was easily the most popular amateur gauge until super 8 arrived in 1965. It is still the most economical and is widely used, although standard 8 mm cameras are now only manufactured in Russia. Many current projectors are dual-gauge models, taking both standard and super 8. So users who switch to the new gauge can still project their old films on the one machine.

The film is normally sold on 25 ft double-run spools like the one illustrated above. It is 16 mm wide but has 8 mm perforations down both edges and is run through the camera twice. The first run exposes one side of the film and the other side is exposed on the second run. After processing, the film is split down the middle at the laboratory and joined end to end. So the customer gets back a 50 ft length of 8 mm film for projection. (See illustrations below.)

There are 80 frames to the foot and at the normal silent speed of 16 frames per second, 50 ft runs for approximately 4 minutes. Film is available in both colour and black and white.

Super 8 is the obvious choice for the newcomer to movie making and the vast majority of new cameras on the market are made to take this gauge.

The special advantage of super 8 is that the film is sold in a light-proof cartridge as illustrated above. So the camera can be loaded easily and quickly and, even in bright light, there is no danger of fogging the film. Additionally, the picture area is slightly larger than standard 8, this being made possible by the fact that the sprocket holes (or perforations) are smaller, as you can see from the illustration below.

The cartridge, containing 50 ft of film, is cut open by the processing laboratory and the film is returned to the customer on a spool ready for projection. There are 72 frames to the foot and at normal speed — which is 18 frames per second for super 8 — 50 ft runs for 3 minutes.

An alternative to super 8 is Single 8. The film and sprocket holes, in fact, have identical dimensions so it is interchangeable as far as projection is concerned. It is sold, however, in an entirely different type of cartridge and can therefore only be exposed in a special Single 8 camera.

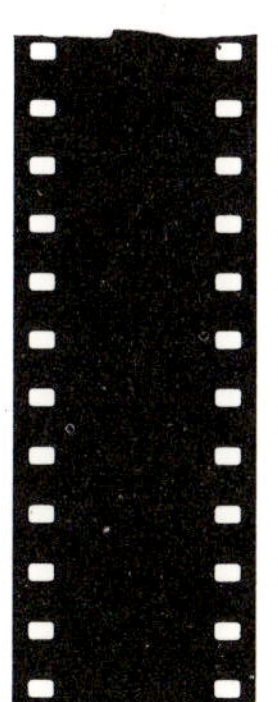 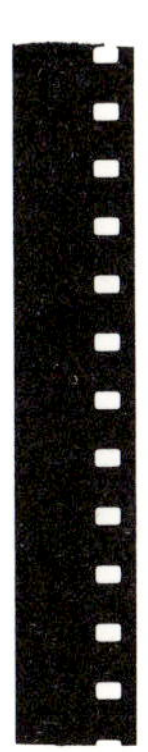

became available. But today it is virtually unknown for an amateur to shoot on 35 mm, owing to the high running costs and bulkiness of the equipment. The only exception I have encountered in recent years was an animated 'short' that consumed a very small amount of film stock in relation to the 'man hours' of labour involved.

16 mm was originally designed specifically for amateur use, although it has now been largely adopted by the professionals — particularly in the television and industrial film fields.

Being the widest of the amateur gauges, it naturally yields the best picture quality and is also the most expensive; the film costs more than twice as much as super 8 for an equivalent running time. Because of its relatively large picture area, it can be projected to fill a screen of ten feet or more in width without appreciable loss of definition. This makes it suitable for showing to public audiences in fairly large halls — and indeed several London cinemas are equipped for 16 mm as well as 35 mm projection.

Technically speaking, there is nothing to prevent a 16 mm amateur film being transmitted on television, whereas the smaller gauges can only be shown with difficulty and by using non-standard equipment.

Perhaps the most important advantage of 16 mm film is that good quality copies can be made from it. Normally, the amateur uses 'reversal' film in his camera and this is processed to form a positive image so that the same film can be used for projection — and is so used until eventually it wears out. In the case of a personal home movie which is always going to be shown on the producer's own projector, this procedure is fair enough; film is tough and with reasonable care will last for years. But when it comes to a more ambitious production that is destined for wide circulation, then clearly some safeguards are required — and this is where the 16 mm user comes into his own.

No matter whether he shoots on reversal or negative film, he can have a cutting copy made from it immediately after processing. This cutting copy will then be subjected to the wear and tear of editing and repeated projection, while the original camera film is preserved intact. When he is satisfied with his editing, he can cut the original very carefully to match the cutting copy. Finally, of course, 'show copies' are made from the edited original which is still never projected but held as a source of any further copies that may be required.

Needless to say, this whole process — which is standard practice among professionals — costs money. But it does give results that are not obtainable in any other way and 16 mm is the only amateur gauge that makes it a practical proposition. The smaller gauges *can* be copied but the loss of quality — particularly where colour is concerned — is immediately noticeable on the screen. So there is not much demand for the service except when the subject matter has unique sentimental value as, for example, in the case of a wedding film.

Sound is also a factor to be considered. Here too the 16 mm user can enjoy certain special facilities for editing and mixing sound that makes the job easier and yields more polished results — but again at a price.

When it comes to equipment, the choice of new cameras is fairly restricted. Those that are available are in the professional or semi-professional class; no doubt the manufacturers assume that anyone who can afford the film can afford an expensive camera too. There are, however, some good and dependable bargains to be picked up on the second-hand market, some of them dating back to the time when 16 mm was regarded as a purely amateur gauge. These may look crude by present day standards but they were built to last and they do.

In the projector field the picture is very much the same, except that a sound projector with facilities for magnetic recording and playback (see Chapter Thirteen) is an expensive item anyway — new or second-hand.

To sum up, 16 mm has advantages all along the line but two major disadvantages: the equipment is comparitively heavy and bulky and the running costs are high. Only the very wealthy would consider using it for personal family films to be shown in the home. But if you are going in for film making on a group basis or for a sponsor or in a school (most schools are equipped with 16 mm projectors), then it is certainly well worth considering.

Few ordinary photographic shops carry stocks of 16 mm apparatus but there are specialised 16 mm dealers up and down the country who will stage demonstrations, offer advice and provide servicing facilities.

9.5 mm was the most popular amateur gauge in pre-war days but has suffered a sharp decline — mainly perhaps because it never gained a foothold in the world's largest market: the U.S.A.

In fact, several years ago, Pathescope Ltd. — the sole British distributors of 9.5 mm equipment — went out of business. With supplies thus cut off, the gauge appeared to be dead so far as Britain was concerned and suitably worded obituaries appeared in the photographic press.

These proved to be premature. A few thousand British amateurs, who had been using 9.5 mm for many years and had become emotionally attached to it, clubbed together in an effort to keep it going. Impressed by their vociferous loyalty, one or two dealers began to import film and equipment direct from France — where 9.5 mm originated — and other parts of Europe.

Hence, although it has virtually disappeared from the shops, the gauge survives in Britain today, thanks to a modestly flourishing mail order business.

What is it exactly that attracts users of 9.5 mm? Well, the special virtue that has always been claimed for the gauge is that the picture area is exceptionally large in relation to the overall width of the film. Whereas the sprocket holes in 16 mm and 8 mm are placed along the edges of the film, those in 9.5 mm are positioned in the centre, one between each individual frame or picture. Consequently, the frames themselves can occupy almost the entire width of the film and, other things being equal, the larger the frame, the better the quality of the picture on the screen.

In fact, the 9.5 mm picture area is not much smaller than 16 mm but unfortunately the price of the film is not much less either and until this situation changes, 9.5 mm users are likely to remain a minority.

For obvious reasons, the choice of new cameras and projectors is restricted but it is only fair to add that they are very reasonably priced, while second-hand models are almost ridiculously cheap. Hence anyone wishing to start movie making for the smallest possible capital outlay, might well decide to give 9.5 mm a try.

Standard 8 mm was first launched by the Eastman Kodak company in 1931. At first it was derided as 'the bootlace gauge' and those amateurs who were already using 16 mm or 9.5 mm regarded 8 mm cameras as mere toys. But the situation changed rapidly.

As film emulsions improved, 8 mm picture quality became more acceptable. Soon more and better cameras and projectors flooded onto the market. In the immediate post-war years, 8 mm enjoyed a tremendous boom. Thanks to the low price of film and equipment, movie making became for the first time a hobby that almost anyone could afford and millions did.

In 1965 super 8 arrived but even now a large proportion of amateurs throughout the world are still using standard 8 mm. The equipment is no longer being manufactured — except possibly in Russia — but the supply of film will no doubt continue as long as there is a reasonable demand.

The film is sold on 25 foot double-run spools which means that you get a 25 ft length of 16 mm film that runs through the camera twice. On the first run, pictures are recorded down one side of the film only. Then you switch over the spools in the camera and, on the second run, the other half of the film is used.

Now you send the film away for processing and after it has been processed, it passes through a machine that slits it down the middle. The two ends are then joined so that you get back a spool of film that is 8 mm wide and 50 feet long ready for projection.

When originally conceived, the double-run idea was a clever one. Because the sprocket holes were the same size as those in 16 mm film, there was no need to re-equip the laboratories. Ordinary 16 mm machines could be used for processing. And, of course, the customer got good value for money, paying only about one third as much as the 16 mm user for each minute of screen time.

There were snags, however. Those large sprocket holes didn't leave too much room for the pictures and 8 mm projector designers were constantly up against the problem of concentrating enough light on the tiny frame area to provide adequate screen illumination. Improved lamp design went a long way to solving this and 8 mm films can now be shown satisfactorily to audiences of up to 200 people. On the small screen at home, of course, even the least efficient projectors give sufficiently bright pictures.

A snag that is more troublesome to the average family movie maker is the necessity at the shooting stage of switching over spools at half time — especially as this has to be done in subdued light to avoid the danger of fogging the film. Care and patience are the only solutions to this one.

Now we come to the question: is there any point at all in starting your movie career with standard 8 mm equipment, knowing that the gauge is destined to extinction in the long run? Some people seem to think there is for standard 8 cameras — particularly the better class makes and models — are still in brisk demand on the second-hand market.

The arguments in favour of starting with standard 8 run as follows:

● The film is cheaper than any other guage and supplies are likely to continue indefinitely because the market is so vast.

● For a given sum of money you can get a better camera — better in terms of versatility, lens quality and so on — than you would in any other gauge.

● Although there are no new cameras on the market, there *are* new dual-gauge projectors which take both standard and super 8 film. So even if you decide to change over to super 8 later, you will still be able to show your standard 8 movies.

Super 8 as the name suggests, is an improved version of standard 8 — improved because the film is supplied in a light-proof cartridge that makes loading extremely simple, while the danger of fogging is removed completely.

Super 8 was introduced — again by Eastman Kodak — in 1965 and its arrival caused a considerable stir to say the least. Manufacturers throughout the world had to decide quickly whether to resist the change or abandon their existing production lines and design new cameras and projectors to suit the new gauge. Almost without exception, they chose to follow the lead of Kodak.

Distributors and dealers had to clear their existing stocks of standard 8 equipment to make room for the new lines. In many cases they cut prices in order to do so. Amateurs who were already using standard 8 had the uneasy feeling that their apparatus — some of it costly — was in imminent danger of becoming obsolete. Initially at least, their resentment caused a degree of sales resistance for they were in no hurry to change over to super 8 themselves and in no mood to recommend it to newcomers.

Nevertheless, super 8 is now firmly established and seems likely to become more and more popular as time goes on. The film is still 8 mm wide, the larger picture area having been achieved by reducing the size of the sprocket holes. Hence the double-run idea is no longer viable and has been abandoned. You simply buy a 50 foot length of 8 mm film, sealed in a cartridge, and run it through the camera once. You then send it to the processing laboratory where the cartridge is cut open and the film processed. Finally, it is returned to you on a spool ready for projection.

There is no threading of the film into the camera and no half-way change over of spools; indeed there are no camera spools. Which makes life very easy.

There is more than this, however, to the super 8 system. For the designers have taken steps to ensure that your pictures will be properly exposed — without you having to do a thing about it. True, there is nothing new about automatic exposure control; many standard 8 cameras incorporate this feature. But the snag is (or was) that some types of film are more sensitive to light than others. The sensitivity — or 'speed rating' to use the technical term — of a film is measured in ASA numbers and before the automatic exposure control system on a standard 8 camera can do its job, you have to set a dial to the appropriate ASA number of the film in use. Not very arduous perhaps but it is something you have to remember if you ever use more than one type of film.

Super 8 dispenses with the dial setting in a very cunning way. The film cartridge has a notch in it and the size of this notch varies according to the speed rating of the film. A sensing arm inside the camera 'reads' the notch and automatically sets the exposure control system to suit the film.

So, providing your camera has automatic exposure control — and nearly all super 8 cameras have — you don't even have to think about ASA numbers.

One other feature of the super 8 system is worth noting. It relates to colour film and once again is designed to save the customer thought and worry.

Normally, there are two main types of colour film: one which is 'balanced' (as the technicians put it) for daylight and one balanced for artificial light. If you use the daylight film in artificial light, you get excessively red pictures. If you use the artificial light film outdoors, you get excessively blue pictures — I mean blue in colour, of course.

It is possible, however, to convert the artificial light film to daylight use by placing an amber filter (Wratten 85) over the camera lens. The devisers of super 8 have taken advantage of this fact: all the colour film supplied in super 8 cartridges is of the artificial light type and all the cameras have built-in conversion filters. So you get correct results in daylight.

When you are half way through a film, you may

decide to go indoors and finish it off by artificial light. Then all you have to do is turn a switch or press a key in the camera (the actual method varies a little from one make to another) and the filter is pushed out of the way.

So there you have super 8 — a film gauge linked to a virtually foolproof system of cinematography that leaves you free to concentrate on the subject and on the craft of movie making that we shall be dealing with in the ensuing chapters. Its advantages are obvious but what about the disadvantages?

Well, the film costs more than standard 8, though less of course than 16 mm and 9.5 mm. Colour is freely available but, owing to the small demand, black and white can only be obtained by special order and then — by the time you have paid for the processing separately — it is more expensive than colour.

A fairly minor technical snag is that the design of the cartridge will not permit you to wind the film back in the camera. So you can't superimpose titles on action scenes or create other double-exposure effects that are possible with the other gauges.

Some film libraries have complained that the small sprocket holes render the film more liable to damage during projection.

Finally, it must be said that although the increased picture area does make for better definition on the screen, the difference is not sensational. It does not, for example, make super 8 a rival to 16 mm. The gauge is intended, as was standard 8 before it, primarily for showing in the home, which, of course, is where the majority of amateurs operate.

Single 8 is not really a different gauge but rather a variation on a gauge. The dimensions of the film and the sprocket holes are exactly the same as super 8, so it can be shown on the same projector. But Single 8 film is supplied in a different type of cartridge.

This calls for an explanation.

As I mentioned earlier, when Kodak introduced super 8, nearly all the equipment manufacturers in the world followed suit and produced cameras to take the Kodak cartridge. Nearly all but not quite. The Fuji Company in Japan claimed to have a better idea and they proceeded to illustrate it by producing their own single 8 cameras. Into the cameras they put their own single 8 cartridges and into the cartridges they put their own colour film — Fujichrome.

At that time, Fujichrome was not exactly a house-hold name in Britain and many of our trade pundits forecast a short, not particularly happy life for Single 8. Yet today it is still going strong — thanks mainly to success in the sizeable Japanese home market where Fuji film (black and white as well as colour) is relatively cheap and extremely popular. Indeed, other Japanese manufacturers find it worth while to design cameras around the Fuji cartridge.

In Britain about half the photographic retail shops stock Single 8 film. In other words, it is less readily available than super or standard 8 but much more readily available than either 9.5 mm or 16 mm.

The Single 8 cartridge is tall and slim compared with the squarish 'chunky' look of its super 8 equivalent. This is due to the fact that the film coils inside it are placed one above the other, instead of being side by side — an arrangement which does permit the back-winding of the film for superimposition effects.

Another point worth noting is that Fuji film has a Mylar base which is exceptionally thin, so that a fifty foot length occupies less space than fifty feet of any other film stock. This, plus the design of the cartridge, accounts for the compact and elegant appearance of most Single 8 cameras.

The Mylar base, however, has a minor disadvantage: film cement, used for joining other types of film stock, does not work on it. This snag may well be overcome in due course by the development of a new type of film cement but meanwhile transparent adhesive tape has to be used for editing.

The technical differences between super 8 and Single 8 are not, indeed, very striking, both systems being devised to give maximum ease of use. The choice of Single 8 cameras is more restricted, of course, but those that are available are sensibly priced and good value for money. There is no difference in the price of the film and Fujichrome is well liked by many who use it. But it seems likely that super 8 will continue to attract the majority of the new customers in Britain at least — if only on account of the deserved popularity of Kodachrome II, backed as it is by perpetual publicity.

One other matter should be mentioned here, since it may have a bearing on your choice of gauge, and that is the availability of professional films for home or club projection. Here is a brief assessment of the situation, gauge by gauge:

16 mm is best served by the libraries. There are

several large 16 mm libraries, specialising in modern feature films (and modern means that the 16 mm prints are issued within a few months of cinema release), others which deal mainly with silent or early sound classics, and others again which are devoted in the main to sponsored documentaries. The features, of course, tend to be expensive (as much as £26 for a widescreen epic in colour) and there are stringent regulations to prevent you from setting up as a rival to your local cinema. The sponsored documentaries, on the other hand, can often be had on free loan.

The 'package' side of the business — the outright sale of films or film extracts — has dwindled in recent years so far as 16 mm is concerned.

9.5 mm was once *the* gauge for home entertainment and hence still has much to offer the collector of vintage movies. Indeed the sale and exchange of survivals from the old Pathescope Library has become a minor hobby in itself. Current library business is relatively small.

Standard 8, ironically enough, is attracting more library business now than when it was a going concern. The reason seems to be an increase in the sale of 8 mm sound projectors (including dual-gauge models that will accomodate super 8 as well). While nearly all 8 mm projectors in use were silent machines, a modern library service was hardly justified. Instead, the 8 mm user had to be content with package movies — usually bits of vintage slapstick or visual sequences lopped out of talkies or specially produced 'glamour' films. These are still available of course, but now there are libraries as well offering reasonably modern and sophisticated full-length features with sound on magnetic strips.

Super 8 and Single 8, as I mentioned earlier, are identical when it comes to projection. Most of the package movies, originally issued in standard 8, are now also available in super 8 but there seems to be a strong reluctance to put out super 8 versions of library films. The library managers say that the smaller sprocket holes increases the danger of print damage but this may be only a temporary scare.

Chapter Two

THE LANGUAGE OF FILM

Nobody buys a typewriter — or even a ball-point pen — unless he intends to do some writing. He may not be a professional author but it is fairly safe to assume that he knows how to spell simple words like 'cat' and 'dog' and that he can put such words together to form an intelligible sentence.

Yet each day hundreds of people buy movie cameras — and quite expensive ones at that — without having the slightest intention of ever making a film.

It's not that they don't want to make films. It's just that they don't know how to do it. Moreover, they are modestly but mistakenly convinced that a film comes into being by means of some mysterious process that is far beyond their grasp.

Everybody who goes to the cinema or watches television — and this includes many who have never learned to read and write — can *understand* the language of film. But when it comes to *using* the language, this is a different matter. This is assumed to be a secret practice exclusive to professional technicians and possibly a few 'dedicated amateurs'.

In the course of my work I see several hundred 'films' exposed by amateurs each year. Because these are entries in national competitions, it is fairly safe to say that they are above average in terms of accomplishment. But even in this relatively small body of work, there is much that can only be classified as illiterate — the visual equivalent of what a two-year-old child might tap out on a typewriter.

Believe me, I am not out to mock the makers of these non-films. On the contrary, I simply want to emphasise that just as a child can learn the language of words, so any one of them — and that means you too — can learn the language of moving pictures.

To be a great film maker, to be an artist if you like, calls for some inborn talent. But all of us can become craftsmen; we can learn to express ourselves clearly and concisely in terms of film. And the aim of this book is to help you do just that.

I want to make it clear that the job can't be done without your active participation. What you are going to do with your cameras after reading these pages is

far more important than any words of mine.

What I am going to say is, I think, generally accepted as true but this does not mean that it must be accepted by everyone. The language of film is a living language and it is constantly being altered and extended. So if, at the end of this book, you decide to reject half of my suggestions and start making films in your own way, I shall be perfectly content.

Frame = Letter

Let's begin by looking at the components of film language — what you might call the parts of speech.

The smallest component is a frame — one of the many still pictures recorded on a length of movie film. On standard 8 mm film there are eighty frames to every foot. On super 8 there are seventy-two frames to the foot; on 16 mm and 9.5 mm there are forty.

Irrespective of gauge, sound films are projected at the rate of twenty-four frames per second and silent films at the rate of sixteen (or eighteen) frames per second. Normally, of course, the shooting speed is the same as the projection speed but this can be varied if a slow or quick motion effect is required.

The frame can be likened to a letter of the alphabet which means very little unless it is seen as one of a series of letters making a word. When we read a book we scan the pages too quickly to be aware of individual letters, taking in whole words and sometimes whole sentences at a glance.

Similarly, when we watch a film, the frames flashing onto the screen at the rate of sixteen or more per second, are not seen as individual units. They pass too quickly and, thanks to a little human weakness known as 'persistence of vision', they merge together producing the illusion of movement on which our whole craft is based.

Shot = Word or Sentence

The smallest unit that can be apprehended — and it's a very significant one — is the **shot**. Normally, a shot is

MAKING A CONNECTION between one shot and the next is one of the prime essentials of movie making. There are many different ways of doing this but the most common is based on the law of cause and effect exemplified here. Shot 1 shows a cause — the boy firing his catapult — and Shot 2 the effect — a broken window. This in turn becomes the cause of Shot 3 — the boy's dismayed reaction — and so on. By alternately arousing and then satisfying audience curiosity in this way interest can be sustained right through the film.

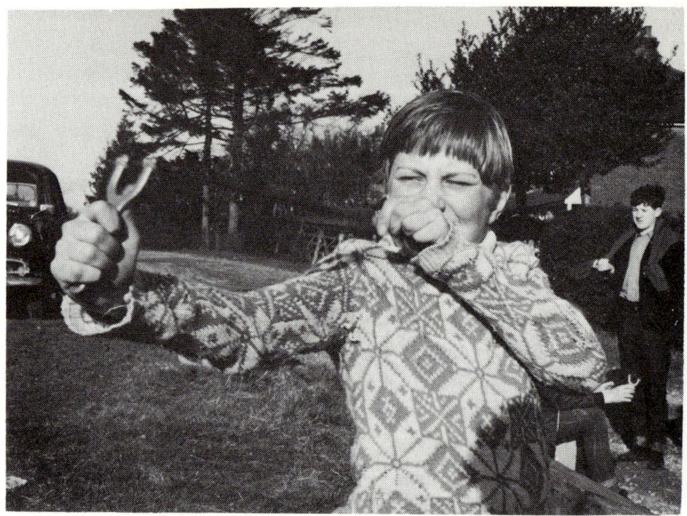

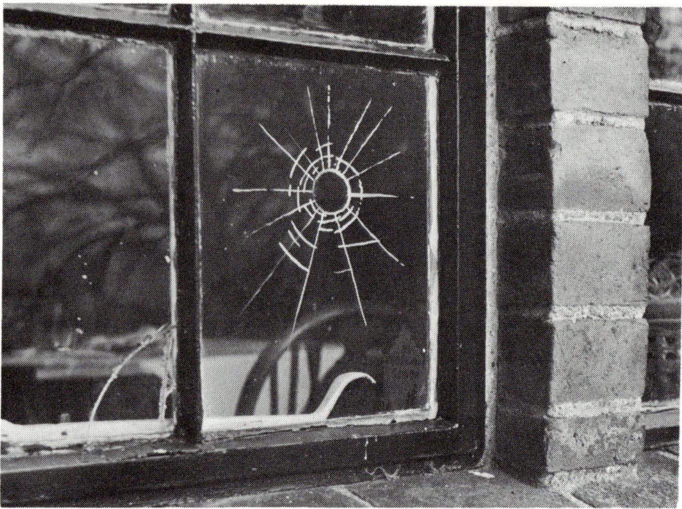

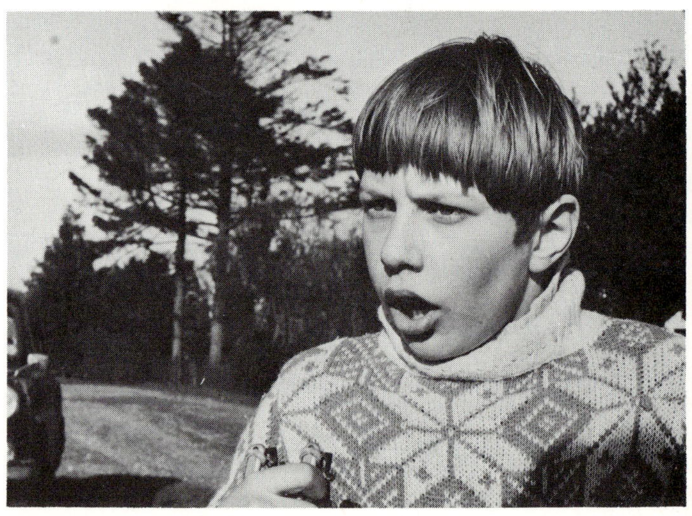

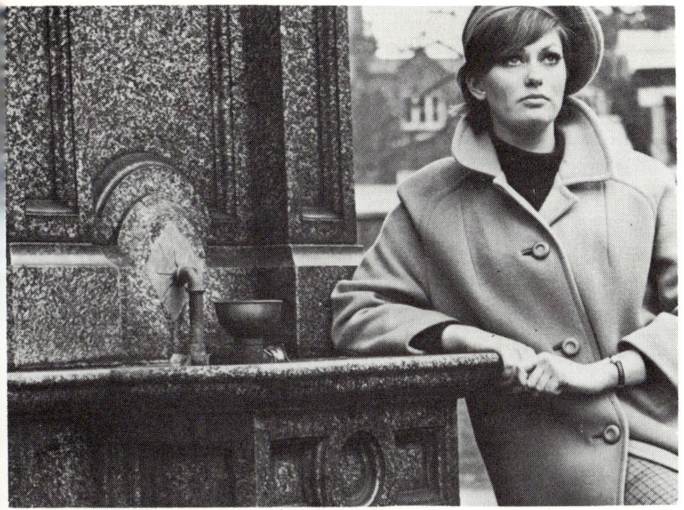

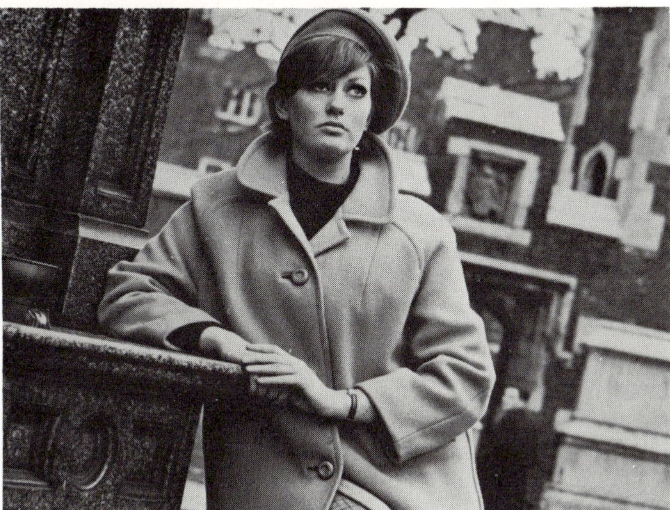

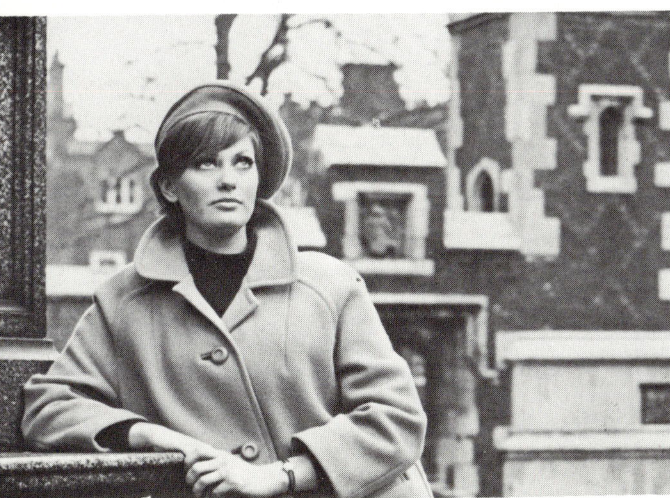

FRAMING THE PICTURE is critically important. Whereas the still photographer can make adjustments by masking his negative or cropping his prints, the movie maker has to do all his composing in the viewfinder. Here we see three attempts at framing the same subject. The first one is obviously careless: the girl is jammed up against the edge of the frame and part of her head is cut off at the top. The second attempt is slightly better but in order to make the figure vertical the cameraman has inadvertently tilted his camera, thus giving the unfortunate impression that everything else is toppling over to the right. The third attempt is the best: more space has been allowed on the right and top of picture because the girl is looking in that direction and only a small amount of the dark stonework on the left has been included in the frame so that it does not destroy the 'balance' of the shot. With a little more care still, the cameraman might have avoided the suggestion that a tree in the background is 'growing' out of the girl's head.

the length of film you expose each time you press the start button on your camera and it is taken with the camera motor running continuously. (The main exception to this rule is that in animation work a shot is taken one frame at a time but we need not worry about that for the moment.)

A shot may vary in length from, say, a quarter of a second (six frames at sound speed) to thirty seconds or more. But the extremes are unusual. Most of the shots in a silent film — or perhaps I should say a non-talking film — are between three and ten seconds in length. In a dialogue picture they tend to be longer because picture plus speech can sustain interest longer than picture alone.

In its simplest form, the shot is equivalent to a word. It may, for example, be just a picture of a man or a bird or a car or a house. But usually there is some development of action within a shot that makes it do the work of a phrase or sentence. Thus a statement such as 'man hesitates on edge of pavement, then crosses street' could quite easily be accomodated in a single shot.

Sequence = Paragraph or Chapter

Now the point is that, no matter whether the shot is equivalent to a word or a sentence, it can never stand alone. It will always be seen as one of a series and its meaning will always be judged in relation to what comes before and what follows. That is an inescapable characteristic of the film medium.

Suppose that you take a shot of a girl looking out of a window and then a shot of a boat at sea. Suppose also that the shots are projected in that order. Anyone watching the screen will inevitably conclude that the girl is looking at the boat and therefore that the window is overlooking the sea.

Maybe you didn't intend to convey that impression. Maybe in actual fact the window overlooked the gas-works and was situated a hundred miles from the coast. Maybe you took the shot of the boat after a six month interval during which your camera had been put away in a cupboard and maybe you had forgotten all about the girl in the window. No matter. The audience can only judge from the evidence on the screen and that evidence will always show that the girl looks out of the window and sees the boat at sea. It may not be true in fact but *it is true in the film* — even if only by accident.

When we read a book or a newspaper or a personal letter, we naturally expect that word will follow word and sentence will follow sentence in a logical, coherent order. Similarly when we watch a film, we instinctively seek a connection between one shot and the next and no matter how weak the link, our minds fasten on it.

If there is no link at all, we are baffled. Very soon we become bored and irritated and this, of course, accounts for the great universal joke about home movies: they are boring and should be avoided like the plague.

This joke is well known to every reader of *Punch* and to everyone who looks at the cartoons in the national newspapers. It is a bit stale by now but the very fact that it is repeated so often shows that it is soundly based on bitter human experience.

The vast majority of amateur films are boring just because they are a collection of shots that have not been arranged in any kind of logical order. Having to look at them is like being compelled to read a book by an author who has selected his words at random from the dictionary without any reference to their meaning. Individually, the words may be beautiful — just as the individual shots in a bad film are often very nicely photographed — but unless they make sense, all other refinements are a waste of time.

I am stressing this point because I think it is of overriding importance. Once you have realised the need to link your shots together and form them into a sequence, you will have crossed the barrier of filmic illiteracy. You will be on your way to lucidity and self-expression. From this point you will start to communicate with your audience and you will find that the niceties of technique can be acquired with relative ease.

So we have arrived at the sequence — the third unit in the language of film and perhaps the most difficult to define. The sequence can be compared to a paragraph in a letter or, at its most ambitious, to a chapter in a book. Normally it is a series of closely related shots dealing with a single topic and often confined to one time and place.

Thus in a holiday film we might refer to the 'bathing sequence' or the 'fishing sequence'. Quite commonly a sequence is designated by its setting: the 'market sequence', the 'bedroom sequence' and so on. A chase sequence, on the other hand, would probably involve several different settings.

In a well-constructed fiction film or documentary,

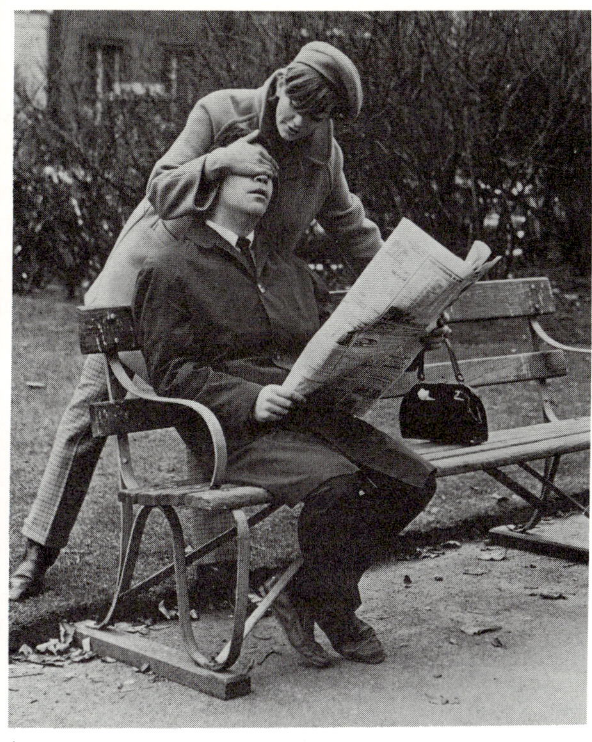

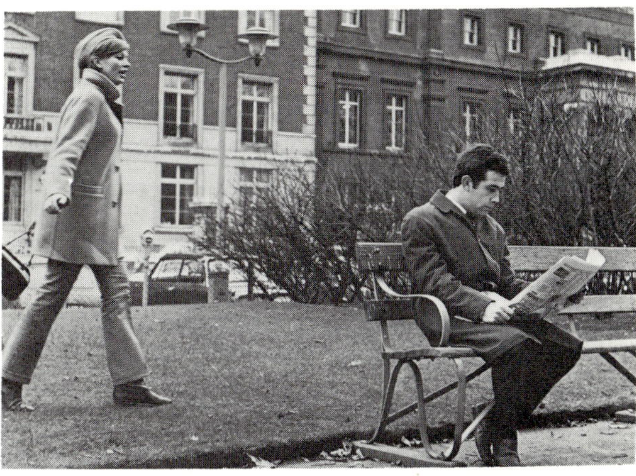

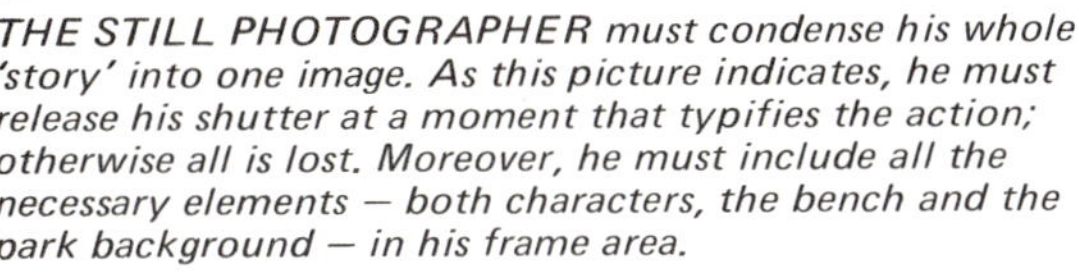

THE STILL PHOTOGRAPHER *must condense his whole 'story' into one image. As this picture indicates, he must release his shutter at a moment that typifies the action; otherwise all is lost. Moreover, he must include all the necessary elements — both characters, the bench and the park background — in his frame area.*

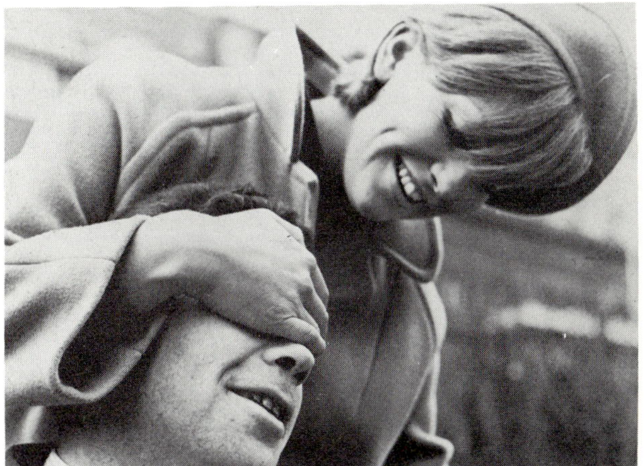

THE MOVIE MAKER *must cultivate an entirely different approach to the subject. His story can be — in fact, must be — spread out in time. In order to exploit this extra dimension, he must first build up anticipation for what is about to happen (Shot 1). Then he must show what happens, possibly emphasising the climax by moving his camera in close (Shot 2). Finally, he must reveal the consequence or aftermath of the action (Shot 3). This approach has been summed up in the classic advice: 'Always tell the audience what you are going to do. Then do it. Then tell them that you have done it.'*

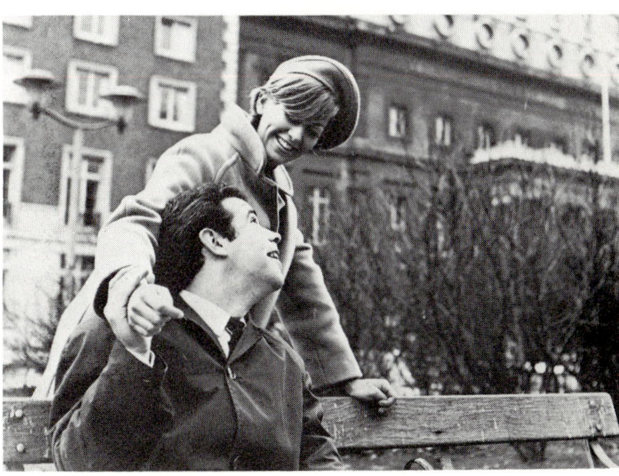

the sequences are closely knit together and the transitions from one to another smoothly arranged. In a personal travelogue or family film they tend, quite naturally, to be more loosely linked rather in the manner of a diary and that is quite acceptable. Each one could almost be considered as a little film in itself.

To sum up in reverse order then, we have a film made up of sequences, a sequence made up of shots, and a shot made up of frames.

Punctuation Marks

Before we leave this introduction to film grammar, a word should be said about punctuation.

Basically, there are two visual indications of a pause or time lapse in film narrative. These are the fade and the dissolve and they are sometimes called 'opticals' because in professional circles they are produced in the laboratory on an optical printer. Amateurs usually make them in the camera for economy reasons.

In a fade the screen image becomes progressively darker until it is completely obscured; this part is known as a 'fade-out'. The next shot begins in darkness and becomes progressively lighter until normal brightness is reached; this part is called a 'fade-in'.

At one time it was considered almost obligatory to start each sequence with a fade-in and end it with a fade-out. But nowadays there is a tendency to use fades sparingly or dispense with them completely, employing more subtle ways (which we shall discuss in a later lesson) of indicating the passage of time.

The dissolve — sometimes called a 'mix' — may be described as a fade-out overlapped on a fade-in. The effect on the screen is that the outgoing shot becomes progressively darker while the incoming shot becomes progressively lighter so that the two images are momentarily mixed or superimposed.

By its nature the dissolve is a less definite form of punctuation than the fade. It is commonly used to suggest that, although time has passed between the outgoing and incoming scene, there is nevertheless a strong narrative connection between the two. Thus we might dissolve from a shot of a woman admiring a hat in a shop window to a shot of her walking home already wearing the hat.

Currently, however, there is a tendency to dispense with the dissolve in straightforward situations like this.

For the sake of pace and economy, many transitions in time are made by means of a straight cut, one image being replaced instantaneously by the next.

This is, of course, largely a matter of taste and fashion there is also the question of mood to be considered. The straight cut is snappy and vigorous, whereas the visual effect of a dissolve is more slow and soothing.

Finally, for the sake of completeness, I ought to mention three other forms of punctuation that are seldom encountered but may be required for special effects.

The **wipe** introduces a new scene by sliding it in from the side, top or bottom of frame and at the same time 'pushing out' the old one. In the case of a 'crash wipe' the new scene explodes like a rapidly expanding star from the centre of the frame, pushing the old one out at the edges. This is clearly a very obtrusive effect and is probably best reserved for advertising films and TV commercials. Incidentally, it is virtually impossible to produce in the camera.

In the case of a zip pan the camera appears to move suddenly and rapidly away from the old scene, producing a blurred image until it comes to rest on the new one. This is quite easy to produce and, in fact, the blurred section of film can simply be cut in between the two normal shots. But again it's rather a flashy effect which at one time was almost flogged to death in the television film series, *The Man from Uncle*.

The focus transition is perhaps the most useful of the three. Here the old scene is thrown out of focus until the image becomes unrecognisable. The next shot starts with the image out of focus and become sharp. In an appropriate story situation this could serve the same purpose as a dissolve and is quite easy to produce in camera, given a long focus lens.

Your First Movie Shot

Let's conclude this chapter by considering the problems that face you when you take your first movie shot.

If you are accustomed to still photography, and most people are to some extent, you will find the technical requirements surprisingly simple. We shall be dealing with exposure and focus controls in Chapter Five but for the moment it's sufficient to say that anyone who can take an acceptable snapshot can take an equally acceptable movie shot — and probably with greater ease because there's no need to tell the people in the picture to stand still!

When the manufacturers tell you that with most modern movie cameras all you need to do is point and shoot, they are technically correct.

The difficulty crops up on the artistic side: that is deciding what to point the camera *at* and how much of it to include in the picture area. Still photographers don't have to make a final decision at the time of shooting; they can enlarge portions of their negatives or trim their prints with scissors until they have what is known as a pleasing composition. Movie makers, on the other hand, must do all their composing in the viewfinder. They must decide *now* what is to be shown and what is to be left out — and this is exactly what defeats many of them right at the start.

The normal lens on a movie camera gives a rather narrow angle of view compared with a still camera. So the beginner's natural feeling when he first looks through the viewfinder is that he wants to get more into the picture. And he does this by moving the camera from one part of the subject to another while shooting, sometimes covering the entire landscape as if he were spraying it with a hosepipe. The result, as he soon discovers, is a blurred mess. By trying to show everything he has shown nothing clearly.

Movement, to be sure, is the first essential of a good movie but this means movement of the subject, not the camera. And the effort to get everything into one shot is totally wasted because, as we have seen, a film does not consist of one shot but a series. All that needs to be shown can be shown in good time, a separate shot being devoted to each important aspect of the subject.

The still photographer who comes to movies with artistic pretentions may not be plagued by 'hosepiping' but he may well waste a lot of time on carefully contrived static compositions. The eye is seldom guided to the centre of interest in a movie shot by converging diagonals — or any of the other devices well known to photographic pictorialists. The eye is guided by movement which is such a dynamic element that it overrides everything else.

To begin with, therefore, it is sensible to think of composition in terms of the most effective way of presenting movement, and this can be determined simply by looking through the viewfinder. You will see at once, for example, that a subject moving towards or away from camera is presented more effectively than one moving straight across the field of view.

It is a pity, in a way, that movie making is derived from photography and so closely associated with it. The rules and conventions of the earlier craft can be misleading and inhibiting.

The photographer strives to distil the whole essence of his subject into a single picture. Seizing just the right moment to release the shutter and freeze the action is all important.

The movie maker's approach is entirely different. He composes his picture in time, expanding and elaborating. For him there is not just the pregnant moment but also the before and after. He must build up to his climax and then show its consequence.

Chapter Three

THE CAMERA VIEWPOINT

In the very early days of the commercial cinema it was the custom to shoot an entire movie from one camera viewpoint. The camera was set up and the actors performed in front of it and the cameraman kept on cranking until the 'story' had run its course or until there was no film left. Thus the finished production often consisted of just one shot.

Furthermore, it was considered essential that any human figures should be shown from head to toe. A chalk line on the studio floor warned the actors to keep their distance. If they ventured over this, their feet would be cut off and it was feared that audiences would complain they were not getting full value for money.

Very soon this rigid system was abandoned as directors came to realise that any incident could be portrayed much more clearly and vividly by means of a series of shots from different viewpoints, sometimes taking in the whole scene and sometimes filling the screen with a single face.

Every novice who takes up movie making must go through this evolution of the craft over again in order to discover for himself exactly why it is that the changing viewpoint helps and exactly how the mobility of the camera can be used to full advantage. Fortunately, he need not rely entirely on trial and error but can take a certain amount on trust from the experience of his forerunners.

The Attentive Observer

That oft-quoted sage, the Russian director V. I. Pudovkin, provided the key to understanding long ago when he said that the lens of a movie camera can be likened to the eye of an attentive observer who sees only what he wants to see at any given moment.

Picture yourself then as this attentive observer standing in the middle of a street market. You probably start by taking in the scene as a whole — the market stalls and shoppers milling along the pavement. Then perhaps your attention is caught by an aggressive-looking woman with a large shopping bag elbowing her way through the throng. She pauses and looks off to the right. Immediately you turn your head and glance in the same direction. You see a fruit and vegetable stall topped by a pyramid of glossy red apples. You look back at the woman and follow her with your eye as she thrusts her way to the stall and demands service. Now your attention is transferred to the man behind the stall who begins to weigh out some apples at her request. You notice that he has a crafty expression on his face and, peering more closely, you see that he is tipping the scale by pressing his finger on the side of the apples. So you glance back at the woman to find out whether she has noticed the deception and a look of dawning suspicion tells you that trouble is brewing . . .

Breakdown Into Shots

Now, although you have only been observing the scene for a very short time, you have changed your viewpoint several times. Sometimes you looked to the left, sometimes to the right; sometimes your glance embraced a broad expanse and sometimes it was confined to a tiny detail.

Notice that there was nothing haphazard about your observation. It was the subject itself — the development of the incident before you — that compelled you to change the direction of your glance. Without these changes, you would certainly have missed a great deal but because you were alert and reacted quickly, you were able to follow exactly what was going on.

When we make a movie our job is to show the audience exactly what is going on, and we can do this; by putting the camera in the place of the observer. By pointing the lens this way and that, by moving it closer to the subject or further away, we can make the audience see the action just as the observer would see it in real life.

Thus the street market incident might be broken down into the following shots:

1. Long Shot. Looking down the street, we see a row of market stalls on the right and the crowded pavement on the left.

2. Medium Long Shot. A group of people walking towards camera. The woman with the shopping bag comes into foreground and pauses looking off right.

3. Medium Shot. Fruit and vegetable stall with pyramid of apples prominent in picture.

4. M.S. The woman walks to the right as we pan (swivel) the camera to follow her until she reaches the stall. She points at the apples.

5. M.S. The stallholder puts some apples into a bag which he places on the scales. He begins putting more apples into the bag.

6. Close-up. The stallholder's face. He is looking down at the scales with a crafty expression.

7. Big Close-up. The stallholder's hand steadying the bag of apples on the scales. We see his finger exerting a downward pressure.

8. C.U. The woman's face. She looks down suspiciously in direction of scales.

Now in this short passage we have employed the full range of camera distances from long shot to close-up and we have done this in order to show the audience what the observer would see — or perhaps what he would wish to see — at any given moment. Only the essential parts of the action have been revealed and all distractions have been eliminated.

Varying the Angle

We may decide that the sequence of events can be further clarified by varying the camera angle as well as the distance. Shot 1, for instance, would obviously be more effective if taken from above the heads of the crowd — a high-angle shot. For Shot 7 we would probably take the camera round to a side angle, showing that the man's finger is behind the paper bag from the woman's viewpoint.

In most cases the best camera angle can be chosen on a functional basis — does it show the subject as clearly as possible? But it is worth just mentioning here that the angle can also be varied for emotional effect. Thus, if we wanted to suggest that the woman with the shopping bag is a dominant character, we could shoot her from a low angle and similarly if we filmed the stallholder from a high angle, this would hint at weakness or inferiority.

To a large extent — as I have tried to indicate — each change of camera viewpoint is dictated by the subject itself. When the woman pauses and looks to the right, the observer feels compelled to follow the direction of her glance. But along with this element of compulsion, there is also an element of free will. For it is a fact that no two observers see any incident in precisely the same way. One will be more inquisitive than another, one more excitable and this will affect the duration of his glances as well as the closeness of his scrutiny.

It follows that no two movies makers will ever film an incident with shots of precisely the same length, taken from precisely the same angles and distances. We cannot say that one way is right and all other ways are wrong; there are many possible interpretations. Moreover, when the action is less exciting — less compulsive — the element of free will becomes greater. It is this element that enables you to express your own individuality or, to put it another way, forces you to give yourself away in every film you shoot.

Controlling the Audience

For make no mistake, you are the observer and you are the one who must decide what the audience is to look at next and how closely and for how long. The film medium gives you this unique power to guide their attention from one part of the scene to another, stressing what you consider important and ignoring what you consider irrelevant.

In the case of a stage play the audience can look at any part of the scene within the proscenium arch and the producer must rely on his actors, and possibly on tricks of lighting, to draw attention to significant detail. In a movie you have the opportunity to control their thoughts and emotions very precisely and without uttering a word by the selection and arrangement of your camera viewpoints.

When you come right down to it, this is what movie making is all about. The associated crafts of photography, acting, commentary writing and music are what you might call fringe benefits.

Perhaps you are asking yourself by now: at what stage should this selection and arrangement take place — before you begin shooting, while you are shooting or afterwards on the editing bench? The answer is that it nearly always takes place at all three stages, although the relative importance of each stage is bound to vary from one film to another.

If you are making an instructional film on some cut-and-dried subject like the assembly of a machine, you may well be able to plan every shot beforehand,

FIXED VIEWPOINT. When the movie camera was first invented a film consisted of one shot only, taken from a single, fixed viewpoint. The camera was set up so that the field of view embraced the whole scene and the action was then played out in front of it. The cameraman went on shooting until all his film was used up — or until the 'story' was finished. Witness this sequence of frame enlargements from the first-ever fiction film, Lumiere's Watering the Gardener _— a box-office hit of 1897 now in the National Film Archive._

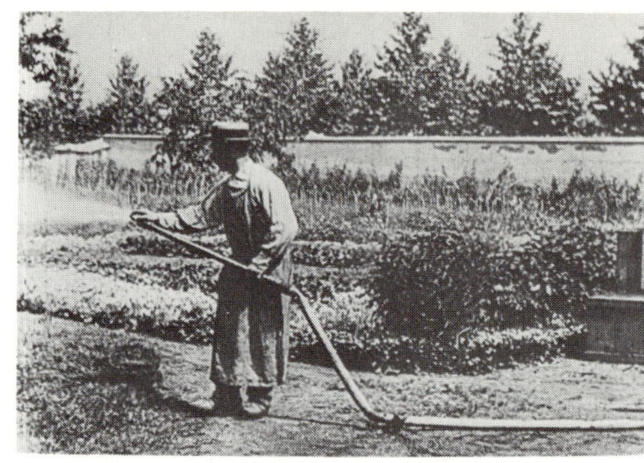

1.   The gardener is seen watering the flower beds.

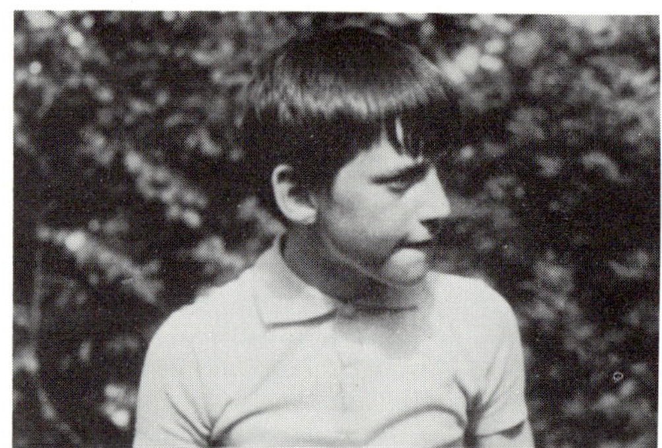

1.   The boy is looking at . . .

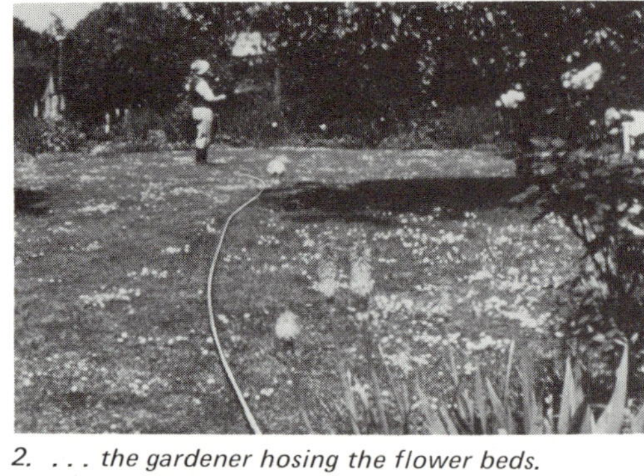

2.   . . . the gardener hosing the flower beds.

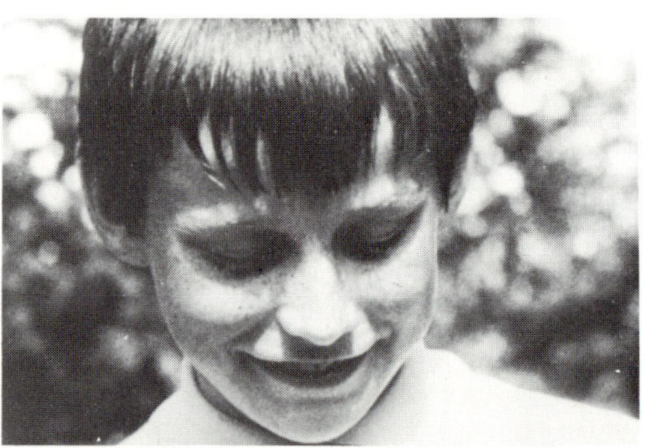

3.   The boy looks down and smiles as . . .

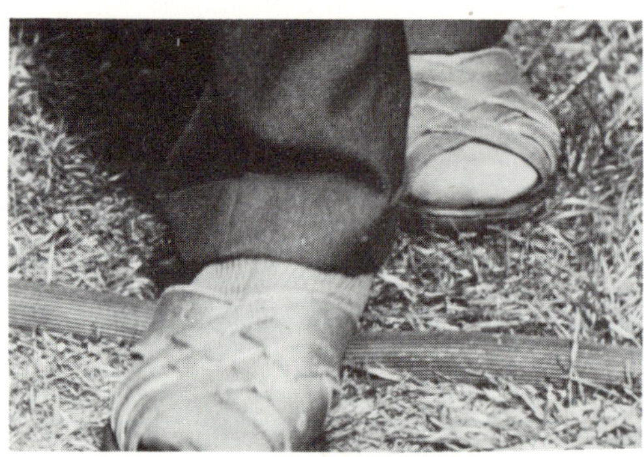

4.   . . . he places his foot on the hose.

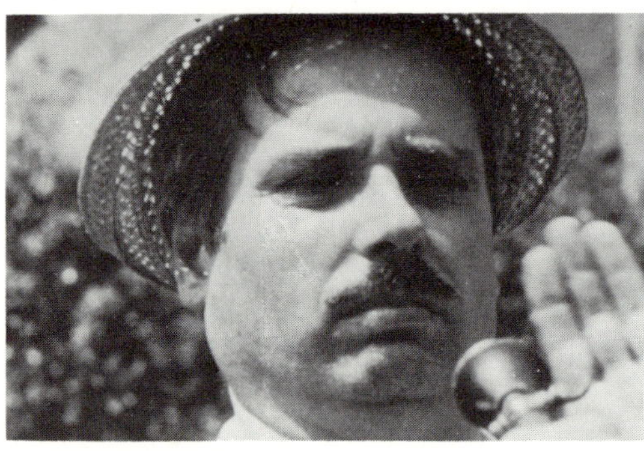

7.   The gardener taps nozzle of hose.

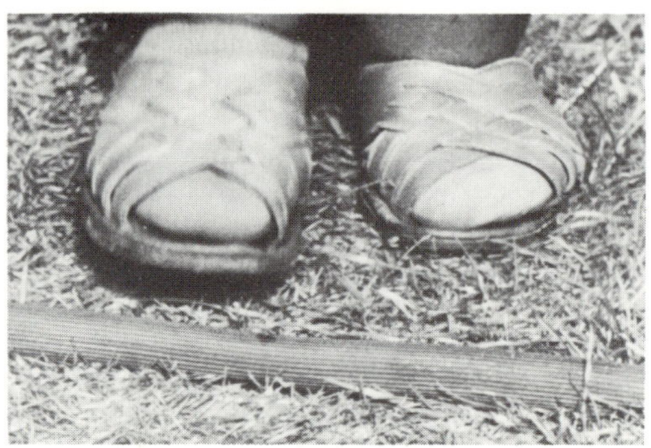

8.   The boy removes foot from hose.

18

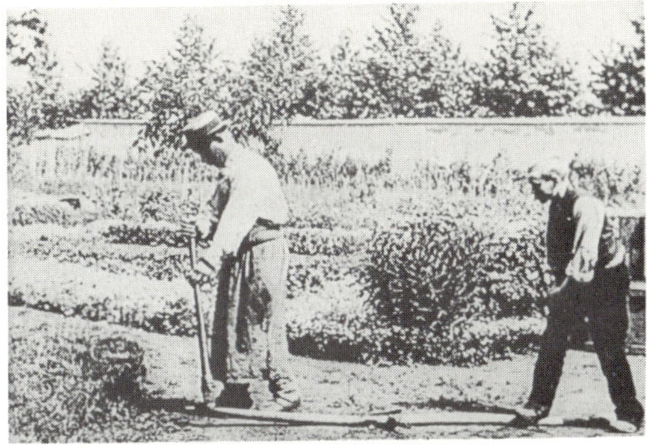

2. *Boy enters frame and places foot on hose. Water stops flowing and gardener looks at nozzle.*

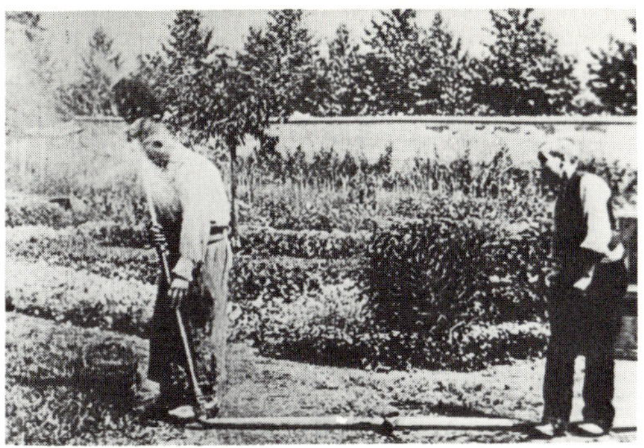

3. *Boy removes foot from hose and water hits gardener in face.*

CHANGING VIEWPOINT. It was soon realised that any incident could be shown more clearly and vividly by taking a series of shots from different viewpoints, then joining them together in sequence to give the impression of continuous action. In this way salient points in the action could be emphasised and the characters brought alive by inserting closeups of their facial reactions. Hence the 'editing principle' which is the whole basis of film narrative as we know it today. Witness this sequence of frame enlargements from Watering the Gardener — Then and Now, *an updated version of the Lumiere film produced by T and R Films for Kodak Limited.*

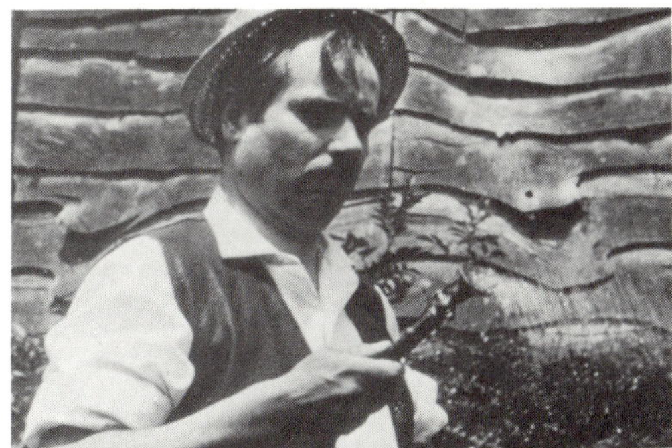

5. *The water stops flowing and gardener is puzzled.*

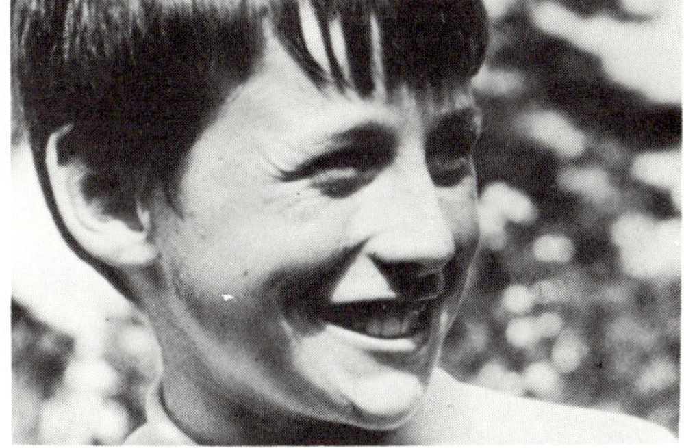

6. *The boy watches him, amused.*

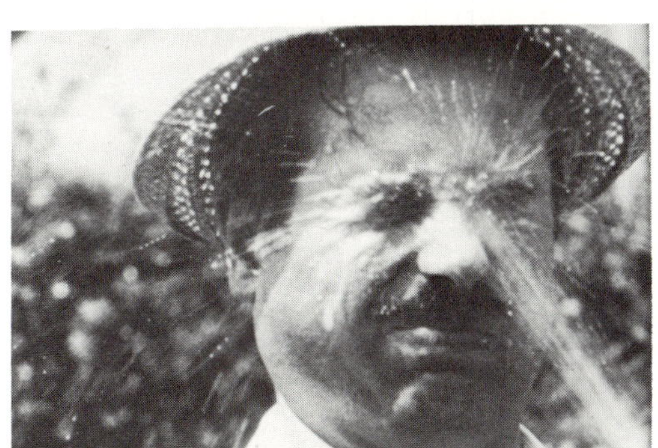

9. *Water hits gardener in face.*

TYPES OF SHOT. In shooting scripts, as well as in conversation among technicians, the shots in a film are usually designated in terms of distance: long shot, medium shot, closeup and so on. These terms, however, really refer to image size, rather than the actual distance between the camera and the subject which varies according to the size of the subject and the focal length of the lens in use. It is convenient to define the terms as they apply to the human figure — as illustrated here.

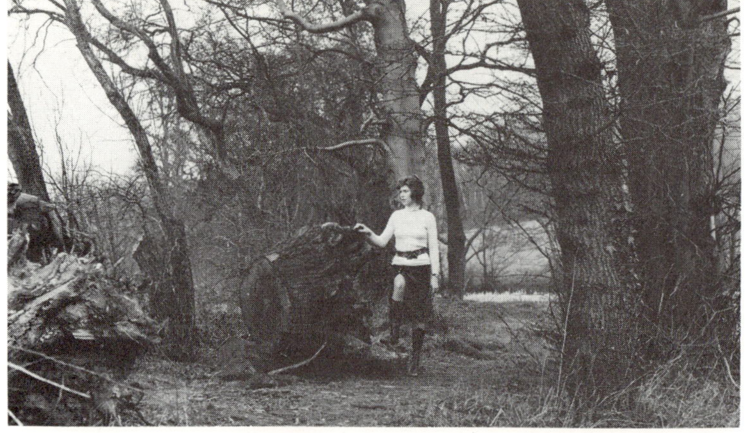

LONG SHOT

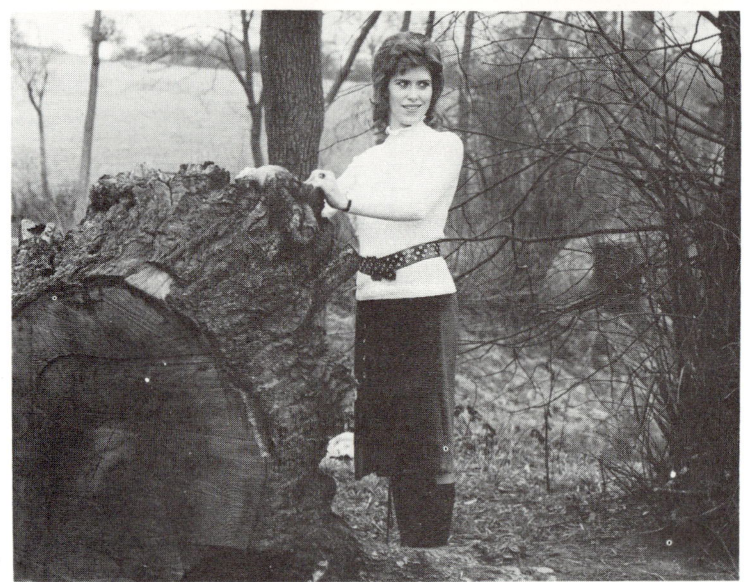

MEDIUM LONG SHOT

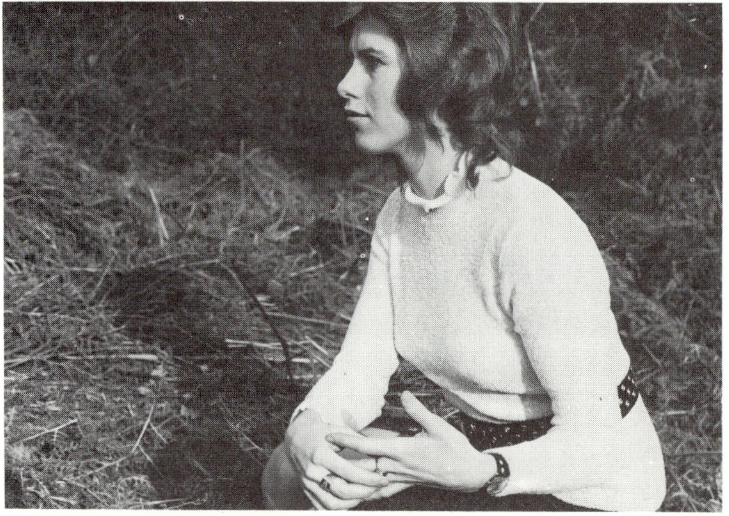

MEDIUM SHOT

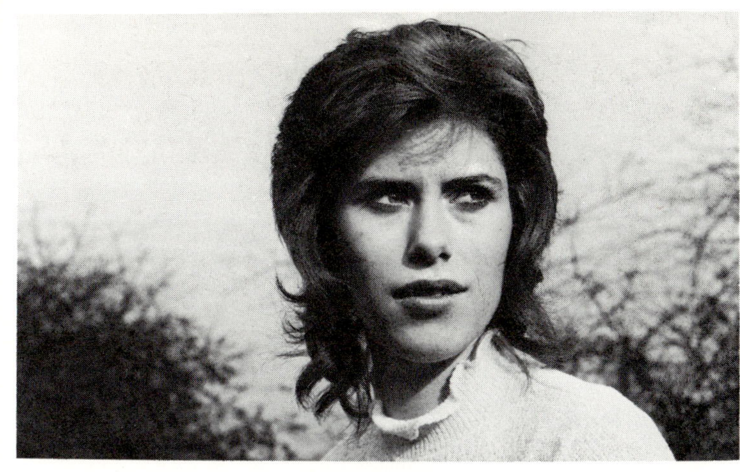

*MEDIUM
CLOSEUP*

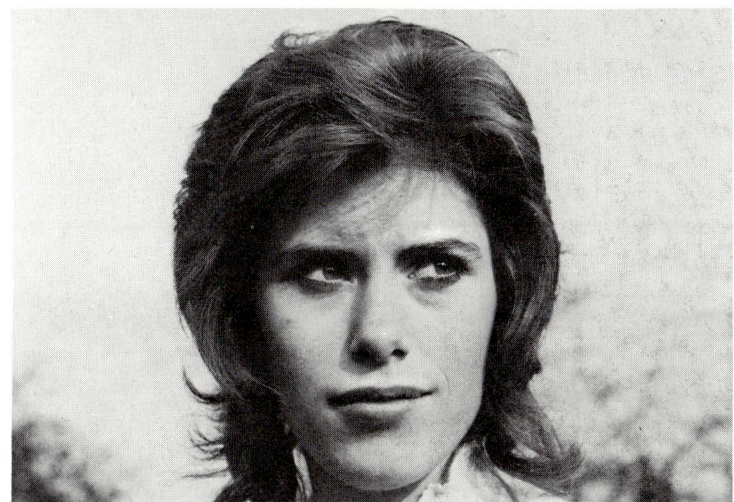

CLOSEUP

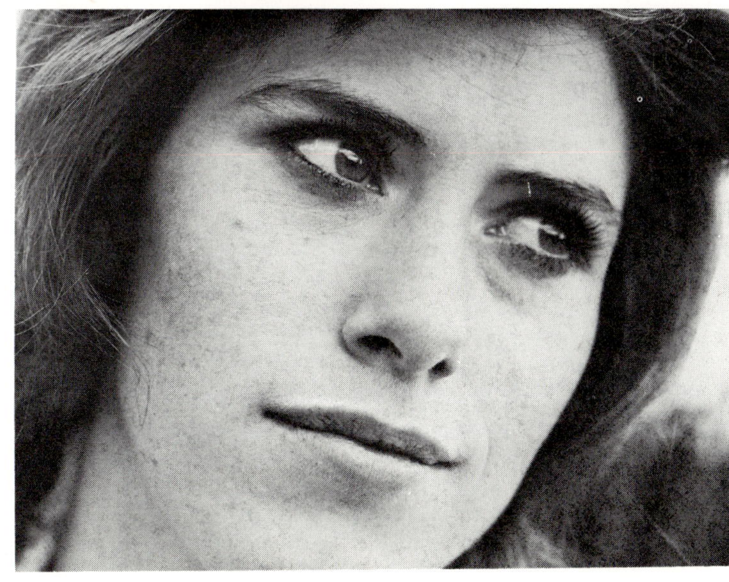

BIG CLOSEUP

CAMERA ANGLES (1)

When the camera is placed higher than the subject the result is usually described as a 'high-angle shot' and when it is placed lower than the subject, the result is called a 'low-angle shot'. Such variations in camera angle may be used functionally as here to suggest the physical whereabouts of the characters. The establishing shot (1) shows that the man is higher than the girl. So logically the closer shot of him (2) is taken from a low angle, approximating to the girl's viewpoint. Similarly, the closer shot of the girl (3) is taken from a high angle, approximating to the man's viewpoint.

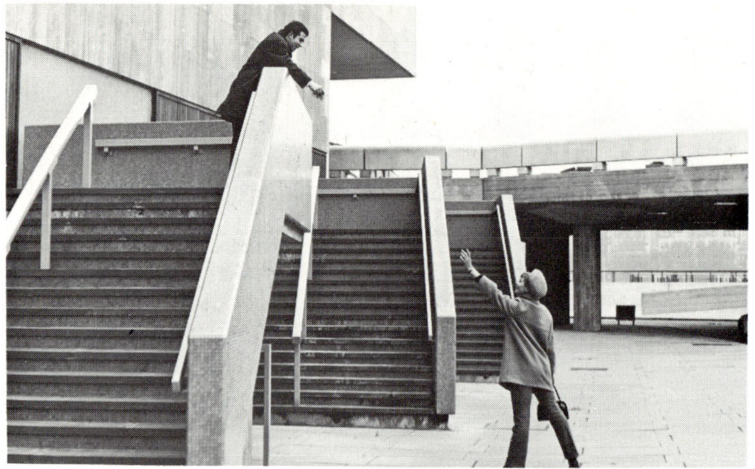

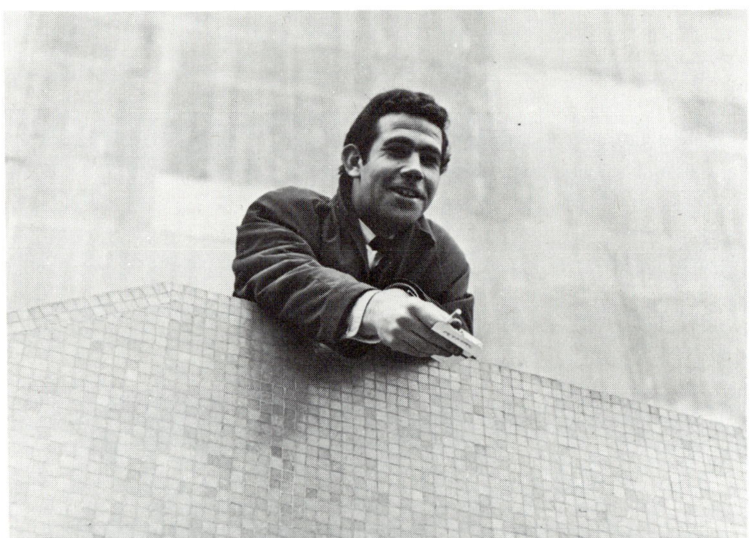

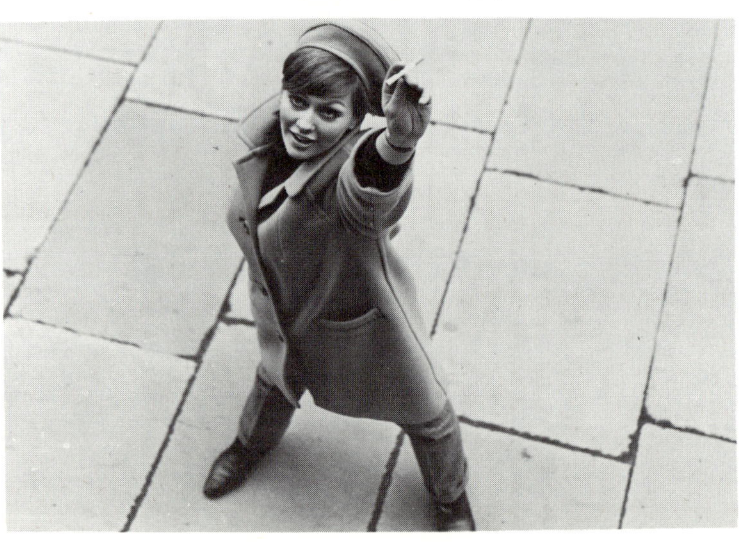

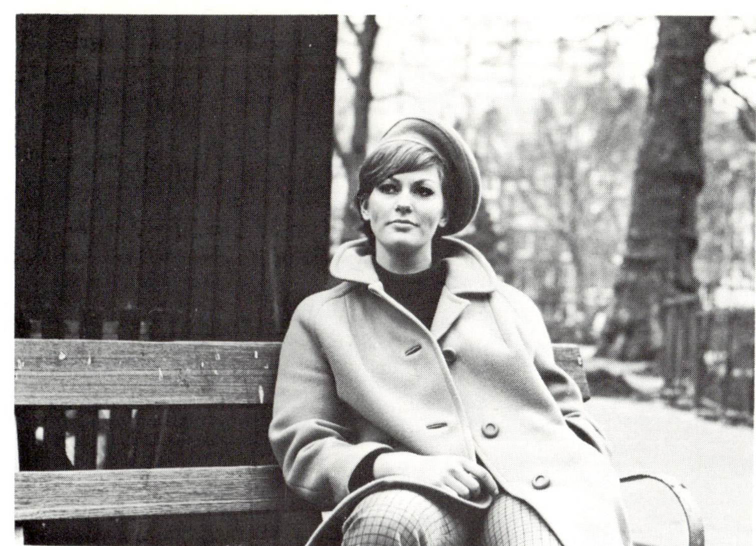

CAMERA ANGLES (2)

Variations in camera angle may also be used to create an emotional effect. Shot 1 here is taken from eye-level and is therefore neutral. Shot 2 is taken from a low angle and makes the man appear to be a commanding and dominating figure. On the other hand, Shot 3, taken from a high angle, makes him look lonely and subordinate — an impression that is helped, of course, by taking the camera back so that the figure is small and in one corner of the frame.

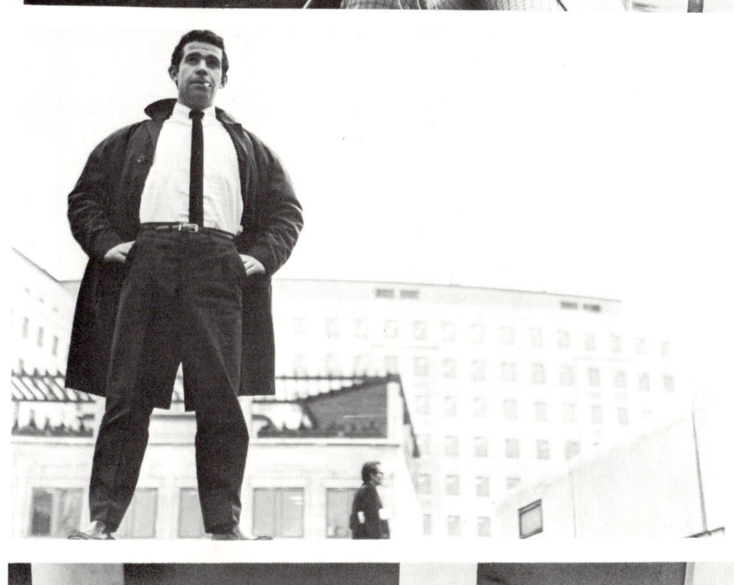

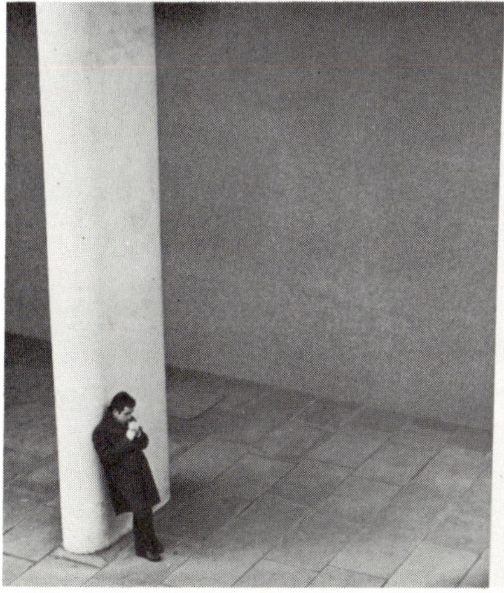

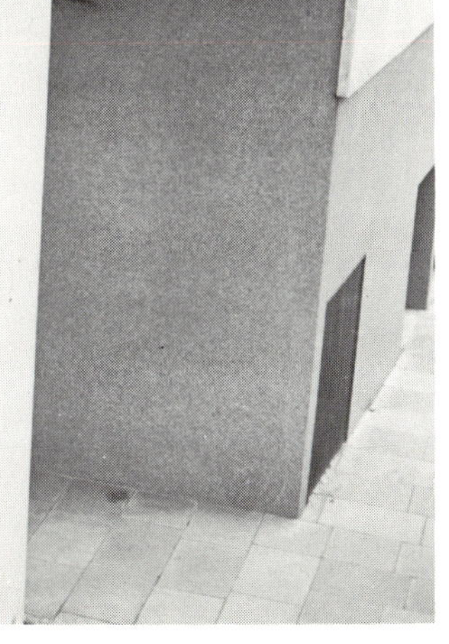

knowing that the procedure will always be the same. Then the actual filming and editing will be simply a matter of following the shooting script as a carpenter follows a blueprint.

In the case of an actuality event such as a wedding or a football match, you can only script those parts of the action that conform to a set pattern. You will know, for instance, that the kick-off is going to take place in the centre of the pitch but you won't know which side is going to score the winning goal. So more work will have to be done at the shooting stage and more thought devoted to the editing.

Some subjects, like fires and earthquakes, don't permit any advance planning at all and leave you very little time for thought at the time of shooting. It is then a matter of filming everything in sight and doing the creative work on the editing bench.

When you can anticipate the action or when you have it under your control, as in the case of a fiction film, it is obviously a good idea to write a thorough shooting script because it is far cheaper to make your mistakes on paper than film. On the other hand, a script is not a sacred document and you will probably find ways of improving on it when you actually come to look through the viewfinder. Again when you look at the processed film, you will almost certainly see ways in which the shots can be re-arranged slightly to give a more lucid or telling result.

As long as you ask yourself at every stage 'What would the observer wish to look at next?' you will not go far wrong.

Now comes the realisation that scripting, shooting and editing are not really separate functions; they are three steps in the same process of pictorial story telling. This is why any film director worthy of the name wants to exercise control over the script and editing as well as the shooting. It also explains why the lone amateur can often obtain more artistic satisfaction from his work than the professional who is bound to a rigid departmentalised system.

Chapter Four

CONTINUITY

When movie makers discovered the advantage of shooting a film in short pieces and changing the cameras viewpoint after each shot, they also discovered the problems of continuity.

Now that the camera was not running continuously the action could not be continuous either. In between takes, people and props could change position, actors could stub out cigarettes and even change hats. Yet it was vitally important that the action should still *appear* to be continuous on the screen; in other words, continuity had to be maintained.

When we watch a well made film in the cinema or on television we are scarcely aware that the camera viewpoint is constantly changing. Certainly the ordinary filmgoer would be surprised to learn that, in the course of an average feature film, the action is interrupted about 500 times while the camera is moved to a new position — and that sometimes weeks may elapse between the moment when a character opens a door and the moment when he comes through on the other side.

We accept the changes of viewpoint without question because they correspond with our own natural way of observing a scene in real life. Just as we begin to wonder what the reaction of a particular character will be to a given situation the film cuts to a close-up of that character and our curiosity is satisfied.

Ideally, in fact, we only notice the intentional 'shock cuts' — the sudden close-up of the fire alarm bell ringing or the sub-machine gun poking through the window — that the director uses knowingly to take us by surprise.

Preserving continuity, in the broad sense, is a matter of telling the story in a logical manner and avoiding awkward breaks or discrepancies. In the narrower technical sense, it is a matter of observing certain 'rules' regarding the placement of the camera in relation to the subject. These need to be learned and understood even if, later on, you decide to break them.

Continuity of Movement

Because movement is the most dynamic element in a movie, continuity of movement should be your first consideration.

Here then is rule number one: when a moving subject is portrayed in a series of shots, keep the direction of movement *on screen* consistent — left to right or right to left.

Suppose, for example, that you take a series of shots of a girl walking through the park. If she crosses screen from left to right in the first shot, she must cross from left to right in all subsequent shots — unless, of course, she is actually seen to turn around in picture. This means in practice that the camera must always be on her right side.

If, for the sake of a more pleasing composition, you switch the camera to her left side, her *screen direction* will be reversed and the audience will get the disturbing impression that she has suddenly doubled back on herself — even though her geographical direction has never changed.

Unless the audience happens to be very familiar with the location, actual geography is of little importance in a film. Your girl could walk either way through the park but so long as her general direction relative to the camera did not change, the movement would appear to be consistent on the screen.

Notice I say *general* direction relative to the camera because there is nothing to prevent you from changing your camera angle so long as you don't cross the invisible line of movement along which the girl walks. You could, for example, take a shot of her walking from left background to right foreground and another from left foreground to right background. In each case the direction of movement across screen would be left to right, so the continuity would remain unbroken.

The girl walking in the park is a simple example but the same rule applies to more complicated action.

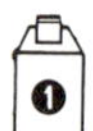
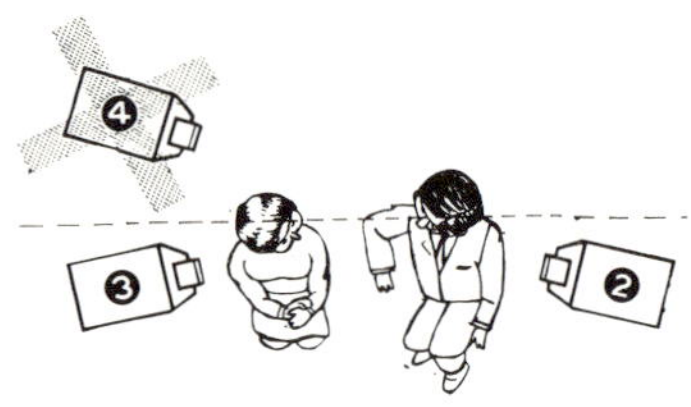

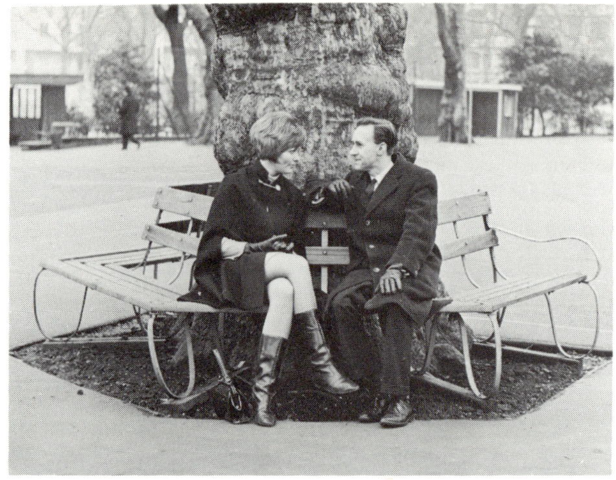

1

DIRECTION OF LOOKS. The direction in which people look relative to the camera must be consistent from shot to shot. Otherwise there is a danger of confusing the audience. Here Shot 1 establishes that the girl is on the left looking right and the man on the right looking left. These positions and the direction of the looks remain constant in the ensuing closeups (Shots 2 and 3). For, although the position of the camera has changed drastically, it has not crossed the invisible line between the eyes of the two characters who are looking at each other. Shot 4, however, is out of continuity because it was taken from the wrong side of the line and thus makes it appear that the man is looking in the opposite direction.

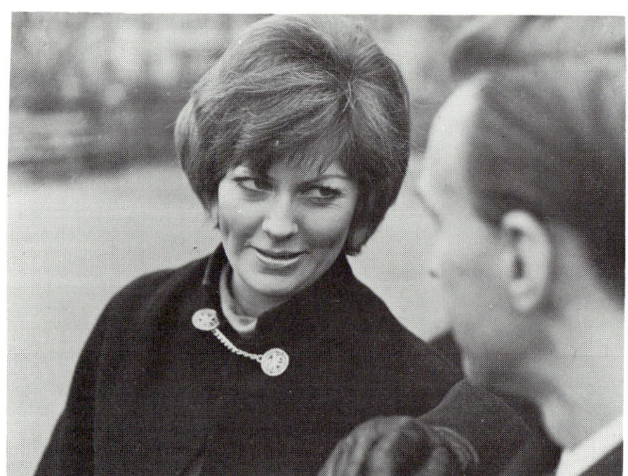

2

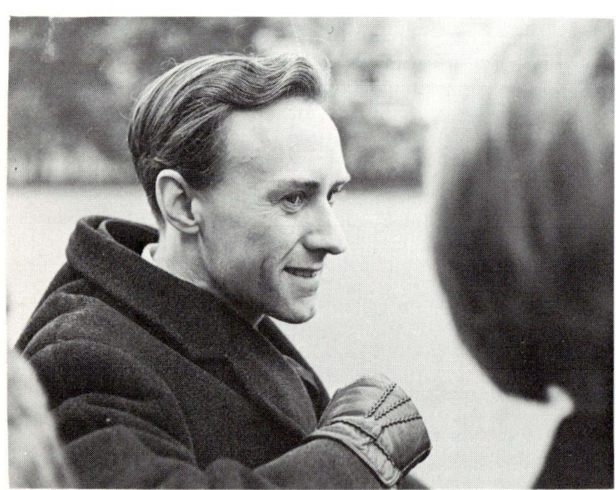

4

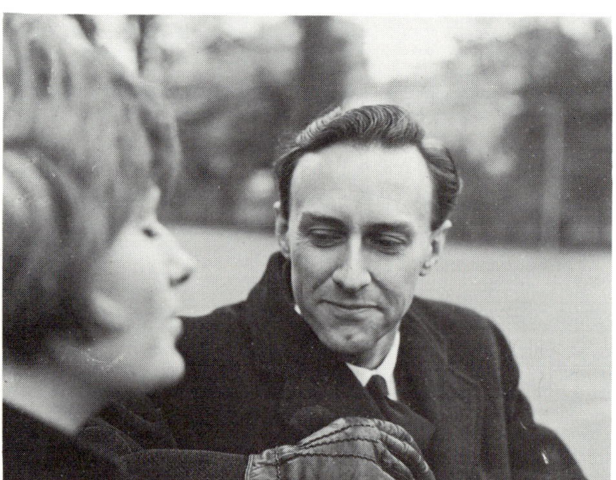

3

Suppose you have a sequence of a man chasing the girl. Then the shots of him must also be taken from the same side. Otherwise his screen direction will be right to left and, when the shots are joined together, instead of running away from him, it will appear that the girl is rushing to meet him.

Similarly, if you are filming a motor race, it is important to keep the camera on the same side of the track for every shot to ensure that the cars always move in the same direction — a point that may easily be overlooked in the heat of the moment.

It sometimes happens that a group of amateurs join forces to film some local event such as a gala procession or an athletics meeting. If film from the various cameras is to be cut together successfully, the camera positions must be planned in advance to keep the direction of movement consistent.

But what if it should prove physically impossible to secure vantage points that are all on the same side of the processional route or the athletics track? Then the solution is to take what is known as a 'buffer shot' in which the direction of movement is directly towards or directly away from camera. Better still would be to shoot across a corner or bend in the track so that the subject enters frame heading one way and exits heading the other way. A shot of this kind can be used as a bridge between left-to-right and right-to-left movement.

One other solution is worth mentioning. Suppose you take a shot looking across a race track with runners passing from left to right in foreground and spectators on the far side. Now if you cut to a close shot of these same spectators which excludes the foreground action (this could be staged afterwards), the following shot can legitimately be taken from their viewpoint and show the runners passing from right to left.

Continuity of Position

Almost as important as the direction in which people move in relation to the camera is the direction in which they look.

As we have seen, the camera cannot cross the line of movement without reversing the direction of the movement and similarly it cannot cross the line of a look without reversing the direction of the look.

If that seems complicated, consider a straightforward example. Let's say that you start a sequence with a shot of a man and a girl sitting on a park bench. This would be called an establishing shot because it establishes the positions of the characters relative to each other and the background; it shows that the man is on the right looking left and the girl on the left looking right. Now you want to move your camera in for a close-up of the man and to show his expression clearly you decide to make it a full-face shot. So you shoot him over the girl's right shoulder and he is still looking slightly to the left of picture.

So far so good. You have not crossed the line — an imaginary line, if you like, drawn between the eyes of the two characters and extending in either direction from the backs of their heads.

You are now free to move your camera round within 180 degrees and take a close-up of the girl over the man's left shoulder. She will still be looking marginally to the right of picture, thus maintaining continuity. But once you cross the line — if only by a few inches — the direction of the look will be changed and the audience may well lose their bearings or get the false impression that one of the characters has suddenly lost interest in the other.

Now you don't have to tell me that this rule against crossing the line is not enforcable by law and that experienced professional film makers sometimes break it knowingly. As a matter of fact, there is a striking example in Joseph Losey's film, *Accident* — a sequence in which a husband and wife (played by Dirk Bogarde and Vivien Merchant) talk to one another while sitting in deck chairs. Losey shoots this from the front so that Bogarde is on the left of picture and Merchant on the right. Then he cuts to a shot taken from behind them so that Bogarde appears on the right and Merchant on the left.

As if to prove that this is not the accident mentioned in the title of the film, opposing shots of this kind are intercut several times. The effect is vaguely jarring and Losey means it to be; he uses this visual device to suggest the growing emotional hostility between the two characters.

But before you try to 'do a Losey', notice how careful he is to avoid confusing the audience. He never once uses a close-up which would isolate a character from the surroundings. Everything is taken in medium shot to include both people and a clearly identifiable sharp-focus background so that we never lose our sense of geography. Although we jump from one side of the couple to the other, the striking change of

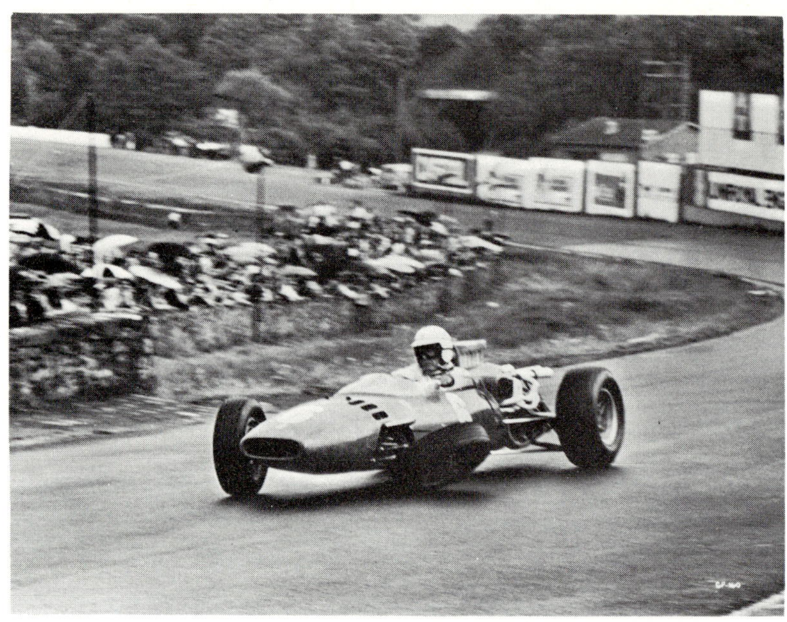

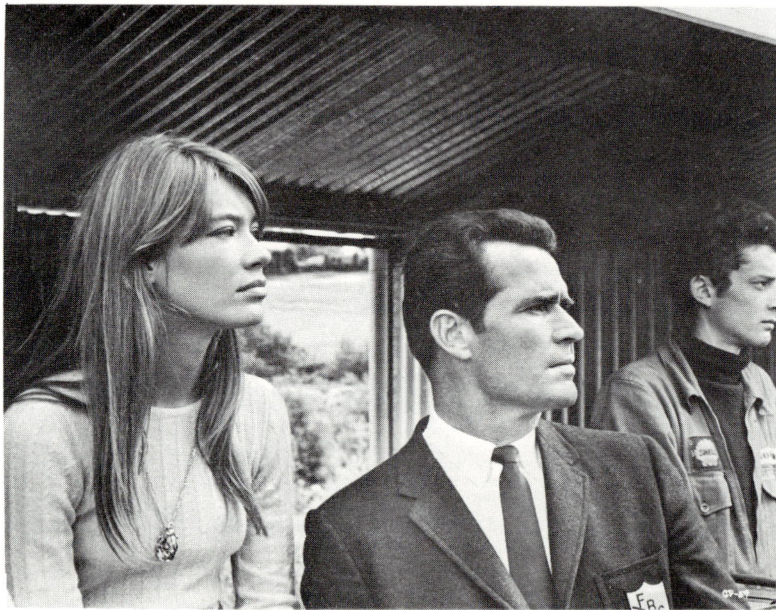

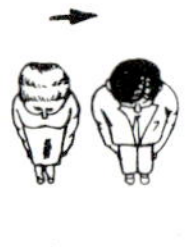

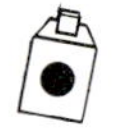

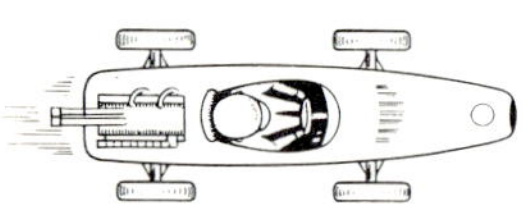

REACTION SHOTS of people watching actuality events such as motor racing are often taken afterwards as a matter of convenience. The question then arises: in which direction should the spectators turn their heads to follow the action? Here, for example, the car is travelling right to left and it might appear that the spectators should also turn from right to left. But this would be wrong; they should actually turn from left to right. The way to remember this is to think of the car as travelling behind the camera — quite logical when you come to consider it. (Stills from *Grand Prix*.)

background tells us immediately in which direction we are looking.

What it all comes down to is this: the 'rules' of continuity exist to help you, not to restrict you. If you break them, nobody will clap you in prison; the worst that can happen is that the audience will lose track of what you are trying to say. Which is sufficient reason for most of us to obey the rules unless we know that a deliberate break with tradition is going to serve some useful purpose.

Photographic Continuity

It goes without saying, perhaps, that the need for consistency applies as much to the actual photographic quality of consecutive shots as it does to the action contained in them.

This is not just a matter of getting the exposure right and, although we shall be dealing with camera techniques and lighting in a future chapter, it is worth noting here some of the regular pitfalls.

In exterior shooting light changes are a perpetual problem. The difference between a shot taken in full sunlight and one taken in cloudy conditions can't, unfortunately, be erased by adjusting the lens aperture. One will contain sharply defined shadows and bright colours; the other won't.

The perfectionist's way of dealing with this situation is to decide quite firmly in advance that all the shots in a given sequence must be taken in sunlight and then just wait for the sun. Which is fair enough if you have plenty of time on your hands. You probably won't have to wait so long in this country if you decide to take all your shots when the sun is behind a cloud; this is the alternative chosen by many professional units nowadays and it is generally agreed that cloudy-bright conditions yield particularly pleasing results on colour film.

What about a compromise if you have to film on a day when the sun is constantly dodging in and out of cloud? My advice in these circumstances is to take your long shots in bright light and close-ups in subdued light. The marked difference in pictorial content makes direct comparison difficult and the absence of well defined shadows on faces is more flattering anyway.

The angle of light on the subject should also be considered. If you are using front and side lighting for the bulk of a sequence, don't stick in one back-lit shot because it happens to look good in its own right. Work around to it gradually if you like or save it for a dramatic moment when the visual shock to the audience will be justified and understood.

Even when realism seems to demand an abrupt change in the angle of lighting, proceed with caution. Going back to our couple on the park bench, if the man is facing directly into the light, close-ups of the girl would logically be back-lit but in very strong light this could result in her features being too dark for expressions to register. The solution is to 'cheat' her position to get some light on to her face, being careful to avoid any landmarks in the background that may give the game away — or, better still perhaps, use a reflector to brighten up her features while keeping a suggestion of back lighting.

Now, a word about the colour temperature of daylight. Gradually and almost imperceptibly, the light gets warmer towards evening so that a shot taken at, say 6 p.m. may look startlingly red when joined to one taken at 3 p.m. The safe way to avoid jarring changes of colour is just not to do any filming after about four o'clock in the afternoon. On the other hand, of course, the warm glow of evening can be very pleasing if you use it consistently through a whole sequence.

As a matter of fact, I can remember one amateur film — *The Day of the Parade* by Peter Wilson — which was shot entirely by evening light and the warmth of the colour plus the long shadows added immensely to the mood of the story. But Mr. Wilson must have exercised tremendous patience to get all his shots at just that hour of the day when the colour of the light matched.

Continuity of Content

Little, I suppose, needs to be said about continuity in the actual content of the picture because this is something that every layman understands.

Some people, in fact, make a game out of 'collecting' continuity errors at the cinema — the girl who gets out of a taxi carrying a white handbag and arrives at the front door in the next shot with a black one, the glass of beer that is almost drained in medium shot and appears miraculously full again in the ensuing close-up. And so on.

While films are made piecemeal over long periods of time mistakes of this kind are bound to happen

JUMPING A CHARACTER from one side of the screen to the other is a very disturbing effect and an easy mistake to make in any sequence involving three people. Here, for example, the girl 'jumps' from the right of picture in Shot 2 to the left of picture in Shot 3 and it looks wrong, even though we know from the establishing shot (Shot 1) that she is still in the centre of the group. This jarring cut could be avoided quite simply by inserting a closeup (Shot 4) between 2 and 3.

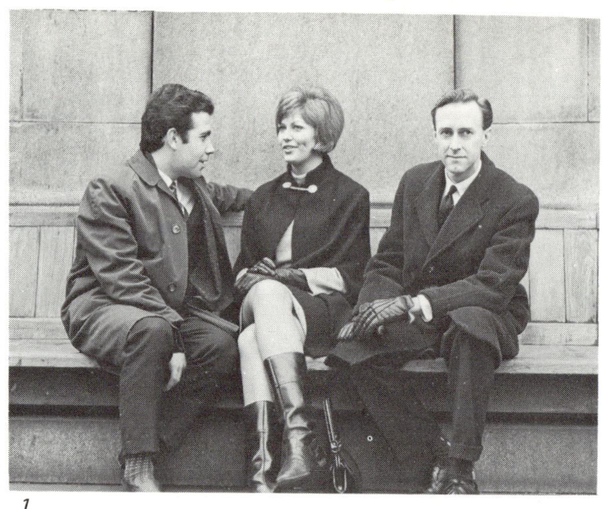

1

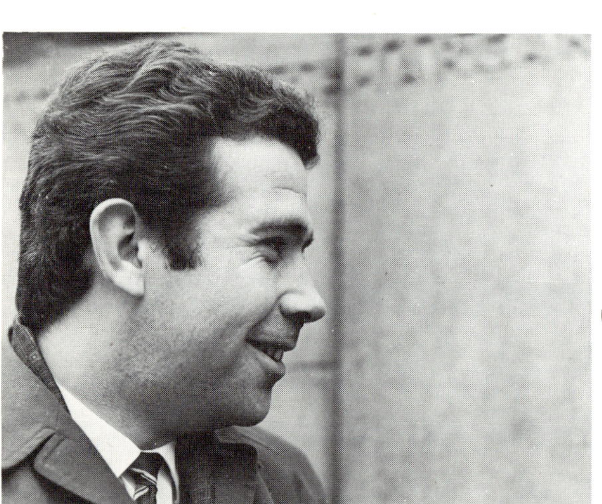

2

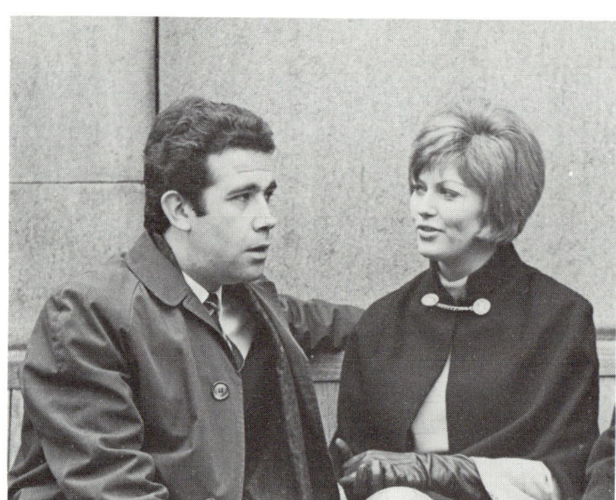

3

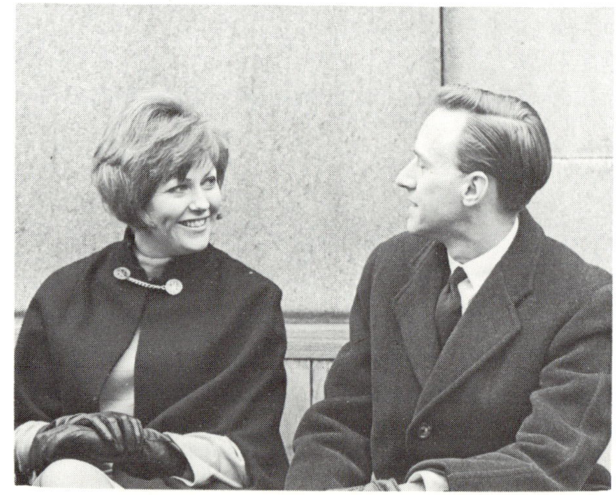

4

occasionally. They happen even among professionals who employ continuity girls as a safeguard against them, although to be fair to the girls, the errors often creep in as a result of revisions made on the editing bench. So how can we amateurs hope to avoid them?

The answer is that we can't avoid them entirely but we can take steps to keep them to a minimum.

The first step is to understand how and why continuity errors arise. The main reason is that, in order to simplify production, a film of any complexity has to be shot out of sequence; that is to say the shots can't be taken in the order in which they are eventually to be shown.

The story may begin, for example, with a sequence at a golf club. Later in the film, the characters may return to the club and at the end of the film they may return to it a second time. Assuming that the location is not near at hand, you may decide quite logically to film all three golf club sequences on the same occasion. But remember that in between these sequences the characters will be appearing elsewhere; they will probably change clothes and have haircuts; they may even grow old and sprout beards. This can get complicated and the complications increase in direct proportion to the number of characters, the number of locations in which they appear and the time span of the film.

A few years ago I made what seemed to be a very simple film indeed, called *Good Clean Fun*, about three children chasing a dog and getting covered in mud. The story began and ended on the back lawn of the children's house but shooting all the lawn scenes together necessitated having two sets of identical clothes: one clean and one dirty. Shots had to be classified: 'before the mud' and 'after the mud'. Moreover, I had to keep the mud 'fresh' by frequent applications of water.

The moral is: unless you have a photographic memory, keep the story line simple and, as far as you possibly can, shoot 'in sequence'.

Finally, I would add: don't let the details of continuity become a fetish. Providing you keep the action flowing in the right direction and keep it lively, you can get away with murder. Most audiences only see a film once and if they have nothing more interesting to think about than continuity errors, it's a sure sign that the movie isn't up to much anyway.

Chapter Five

OPERATING THE CAMERA

Most people begin by buying a movie camera and learning how to operate it.

However, that is not necessarily the most logical way to start. In fact I am inclined to think that it is the hard way. If you start to use a camera before you have any idea what movie making is all about you will probably waste yards of film simply through lack of purpose. Wild and woolly camera movements, for example, are not the result of technical ignorance so much as a vague uncertainty about what the shot is intended to show and what the next shot in the sequence is going to be.

Moreover, if you concentrate all your attention on the camera, there is a danger of becoming over-preoccupied with the quality of the photographic image at the expense of subject matter and movement — which is one fairly certain way of boring an audience to death.

That is why, in this book, I have dealt first with the basics of film narrative and visual continuity. But now that we have 'placed' the camera, as it were, in relation to the whole business of movie making, the time has come to get to grips with the thing itself.

Like racing cars and guns and computers, movie cameras are surrounded by a certain mystique — particularly, of course, the expensive ones. This aura of glamour must be penetrated at once. You will never make a decent movie so long as you regard your camera as an object of adoration; it is simply a tool. A tool with certain functions and certain limitations. In order to get the best from it, you must understand exactly what these are. So let's have a look at the various camera 'features' and see how we can put them to work for us.

Exposure Control

Every movie camera on the market has some form of exposure control, be it manual, automatic or semi-automatic. This is simply a way of controlling the amount of light that reaches the film and it is necessary for two reasons. Firstly the amount of light reflected by the subject varies (notably according to weather conditions) and secondly, some types of film are more sensitive to light than others.

When you take a still photograph, you normally control the exposure by adjusting the shutter speed and the lens aperture. But in a movie camera the shutter speed remains constant unless you alter the running speed of the camera — and as this is only possible on more advanced models we shall be dealing with it a little later on. So there is just one adjustment to make and that is to the lens aperture.

In the case of cameras with manual exposure control, a rotating ring on the lens barrel controls the size of the aperture by means of an opening and closing mask (sometimes called an iris diaphragm) which is normally situated between the glass elements of the lens itself. Round the lens barrel are engraved a set of numerals called f-numbers and by setting a mark on the aperture ring against one of these, you can adjust the exposure to suit the lighting conditions and the sensitivity (or speed) of the film in use.

The usual f-number scale includes f/2, f/2.8, f/4, f/5.6, f/8, f/11 and f/16, each one of these settings letting through half as much light as the one before. In other words, the larger the f-number the smaller is the aperture. Some lenses have an even larger maximum aperture — say f/1.4 — or a smaller one at the other end of the scale — say f/22.

The simplest and most inexpensive movie cameras usually carry a printed chart on the side showing you which f-number to select for any given subject and lighting conditions: Open Landscape with Bright Sun — f/11, and so on. And in the case of super 8 cameras the manufacturers don't have to worry about variations in film sensitivity because at present there are very few different makes of colour film on the market and they all have the same speed rating.

This kind of chart, which you will also find enclosed in most film cartons, is sensible enough and will prevent you from making any gross errors but obviously the system has its limitations. For terms like 'hazy sun'

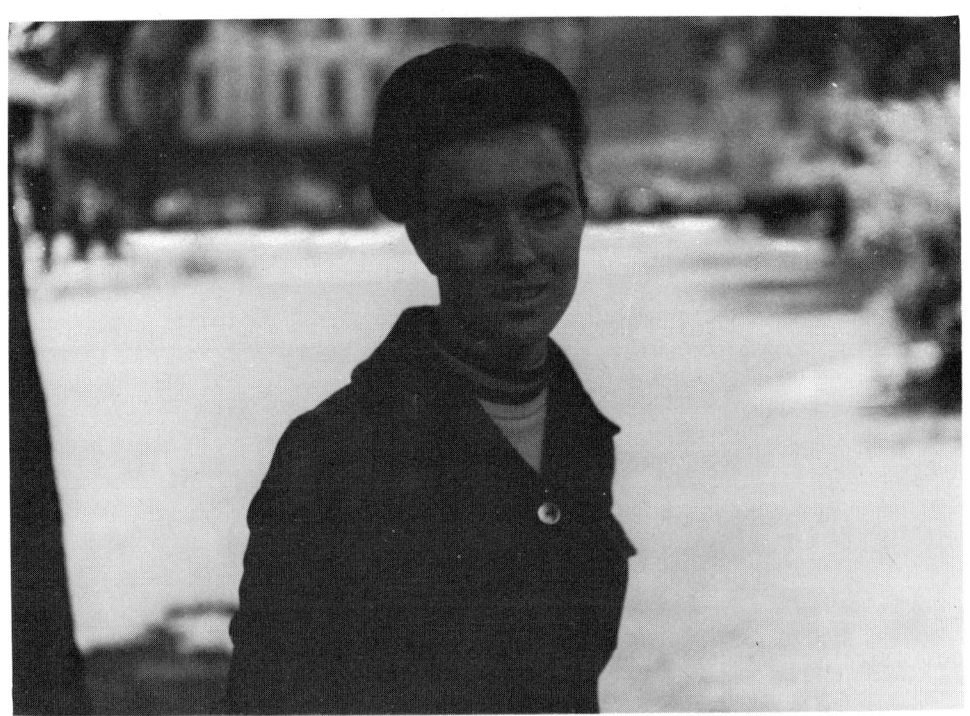

EXPOSURE PROBLEMS. *The automatic exposure control that is a feature of most modern cameras can be relied upon to give pleasing results under normal circumstances. It only fails when the main subject of interest is much darker (or lighter) than the background. Here is a case in point: the girl is standing in the shade of a tree and is therefore much darker than the sunlit background. The camera's exposure system naturally measures the light from the whole scene and the image of the girl is therefore under-exposed. The picture below shows how this can be corrected by using the manual override to open up the lens aperture. Exposure is now correct for the girl and the over-exposed background is quite acceptable; in fact it helps to put the emphasis where it belongs.*

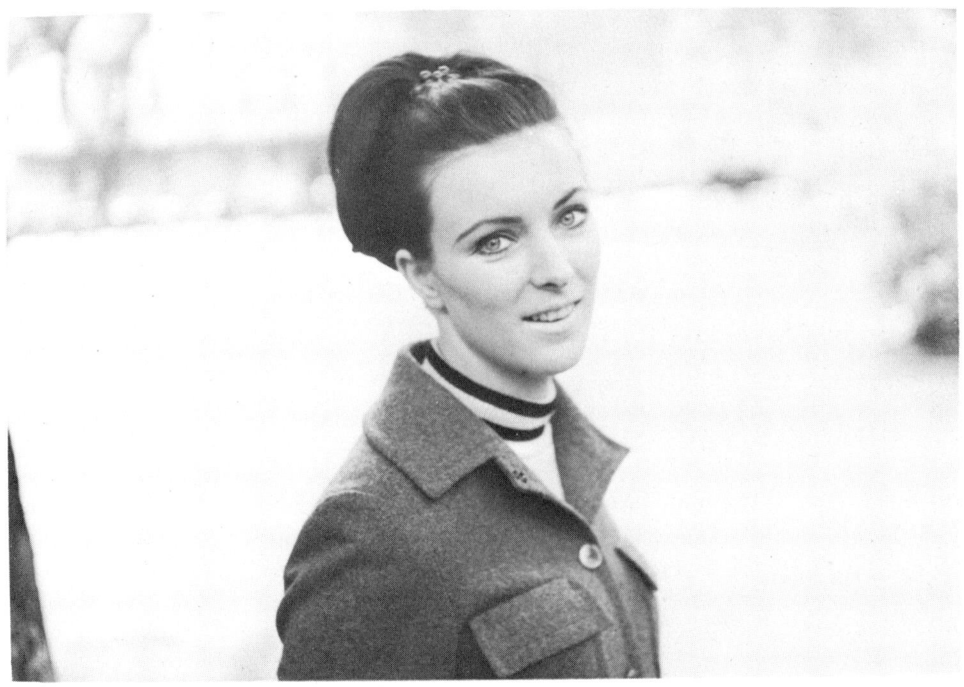

and 'cloudy bright' leave a lot of room for individual interpretation.

Certainly, for precise accuracy of manual exposure setting you need an exposure meter which measures the light reflected by the subject. These instruments vary slightly but normally the method is to pre-set the meter to suit the sensitivity (or speed rating) of your film, then point it at the subject, whereupon a moving needle indicates the required f-number.

In actual fact, the process is not quite so mechanical as that because a degree of intelligence is needed to interpret the subject as well. For example, if you are filming a person against an open sky background, the meter will measure all the light from the sky and indicate a very small aperture which will result in the person being under-exposed. The way to overcome this is to take your meter up close to the person and measure the light reflected by his or her face — assuming you regard that as the most important part of the picture.

Another way, which is probably easier in the case of a long shot, is to point the meter down towards the ground so that you prevent it from 'seeing' too much sky.

Experienced cameramen generally prefer to use a separate exposure meter which perhaps explains why most 16 mm cameras as well as some of the more advanced standard 8 mm models rely on manual exposure setting. This is one feature they have in common with the very cheapest super 8 cameras.

However, there is no doubt at all that the modern trend is towards automatic exposure control — or in other words towards cameras with built-in meters coupled to the iris diaphragm. Such cameras, if they are standard 8, may be semi-automatic which means that you have to adjust the lens aperture by hand until two needles, visible in the viewfinder, are in alignment. The more common system — and super 8 has made this practically universal — is fully automatic which means that the lens aperture is coupled to the meter's photo-electric cell and adjusts itself without any human aid at all.

So if you are starting with a fully automatic camera, you can forget all about f-numbers and indeed all that I have said about exposure control and the chances are that most of the time you will get very nicely exposed pictures. Nevertheless, it is worth remembering the basic principles, if only because they will help you to understand an occasional failure —

usually the result of expecting the camera to do your thinking for you.

If you remember nothing else, remember that the built-in meter is bound to measure the light from the *whole* of the scene in front of it. You can't expect it to know that you are only interested in the white flower in foreground and that you *want* the dark wall in the background to be under-exposed.

Being just an electro-mechanical device, the meter will always work on the assumption of average subject matter. If you want to rely on it completely, you will just have to stick to average subjects — which incidentally still gives you quite a lot of scope. If not, then you will have to pay a little more for one of those cameras which makes provision for manual override of the automatic system when the circumstances demand it.

Focus Control

Strictly speaking, if a lens is focused on a certain distance, only subjects at that distance will be rendered as sharp images on the film. Fortunately, however, there is a range of distances both behind and in front of the focused distance within which all subjects are still rendered acceptably sharp.

This zone of tolerance in focusing is called 'the depth of field' and it increases as the lens-to-subject distance increases. It also increases as the lens aperture is made smaller and finally it varies according to the focal length of the lens in use.

There is quite a lot to learn about these variable factors and I shall be dealing with them in detail in the next chapter which is devoted entirely to the use of lenses. For the moment, however, it is sufficient to know that the depth of field phenomenon has proved a boon and a blessing to camera manufacturers the world over because it has enabled them to produce inexpensive and easy-to-use cameras with what are called 'fixed focus' (or 'universal focus') lenses. A fixed focus lens is permanently focused on one set distance and no adjustment is possible — an ideal arrangement for the casual movie maker who can't be bothered with technicalities.

In the case of standard 8 mm, for example, a lens focused permanently at 10 feet will give acceptably sharp pictures of any subject from just over 4 feet to infinity while the aperture is set to f/5.6. And even if you open the aperture to f/2.8 you can still film as close as 6 feet from the subject without losing sharpness — a more than sufficient range of tolerance for most home movie requirements.

The obvious snag is that you can't take big close-ups. Some manufacturers compensate by offering supplementary close-up lenses which can be attached to the front of the normal one but this is something of a compromise solution. A proper focusing lens has no such limitations and will give even sharper results at all distances, providing of course that it is set accurately.

Up to now I have been talking in terms of one lens of standard focal length, but some of the more advanced cameras can also be fitted with wide-angle and tele-photo lenses.

Because it embraces a broad field of view, a wide-angle lens is useful for filming in small rooms; it has a short focal length and therefore yields even greater depth of field than a normal lens. A telephoto is just the opposite; it has a narrow angle of view and is therefore useful for taking close-ups of small or distant subjects; it has a long focal length and there-fore a restricted depth of field which means that it must be focused very accurately.

The modern thing, of course, is a zoom supplied as an integral part of the camera. This is a lens of variable focal length or, if you like, it is the equivalent of a wide-angle, normal and telephoto lens all in one. The convenience value is obvious: you can select the view you want and then adjust the zoom until the framing is just right without having to change your camera position. You can also zoom from, say, a medium shot to close-up while actually shooting, although this effect is best reserved for very special occasions.

Only the more expensive zoom lenses will give you the extremes of short and long focal lengths that you would expect from three separate lenses. Focusing, of course, is most critical when the zoom is on telephoto setting.

Viewfinding

An important adjunct to the lens is the viewfinder. This is usually mounted above or alongside the lens and gives a representation of the field of view which is accurate enough for most shots. In the case of close-ups, however, the fact that the viewfinder is slightly off-centre will produce what is called a 'parallax error'. Some finders can be adjusted to compensate for this; others are simply marked to indicate the approximate allowance to make for parallax when filming very close to the subject.

More accurate is a reflex viewfinder which allows you to see almost exactly the same picture as the lens. This was once regarded as an exclusive feature but is now to be found on quite moderately priced cameras — particularly those with zoom lenses. Still an expensive feature, however, is reflex focusing which allows you to see in the viewfinder just when the picture is sharp as you adjust the focusing ring.

Camera Speeds

As we already know, the standard projection speed for silent films (including those with tape accompani-ment) is 16 or 18 frames per second. So it is quite logical that the simpler cameras should be made to run only at one of these speeds; in the case of super 8 it is 18 f.p.s.

More elaborate models offer a range of running speeds which may include 8, 12, 16, 24, 32, 48 and 64 f.p.s. These enable you to produce a number of special effects. For example, by shooting a scene at 8 f.p.s. and projecting it at 16, you double the speed of the action on the screen. Conversely, if you shoot at 32, 48 or 64 f.p.s. you 'stretch' the action over a greater length of film and thus achieve slow motion.

If your films are going to be projected at the standard sound speed of 24 f.p.s., then of course it is essential to have a camera that runs at this speed. From the point of view of sound quality, you may not think this very important — quite presentable tracks can be recorded and played back on an 8 mm stripe projector running at 18 f.p.s. It *is* important, however, if you are working on 16 mm and plan to use profes-sional services for having a track recorded optically. Professional recording equipment will only run at 24 f.p.s.

Moreover, if you should aspire to having a film shown on television — not an impossible goal these days — it is worth remembering that any sound-on-film track recorded at less than 24 f.p.s. will be useless.

Needless to say, increasing the running speed of the camera also increases the shutter speed so that each frame of film is exposed to the light for a shorter time. Therefore, you must remember to compensate for this by using a larger aperture; if the running speed is doubled, the aperture must be opened by one f-stop.

Some cameras with automatic exposure systems make provision for automatic compensation when the running speed is altered. However, as you may imagine, this poses quite a problem for the camera designers. So it is not surprising that most fully automatic cameras only have one running speed and even the most expensive models have a limited range of speeds.

Backwind

As its name suggests, the backwind is a device that enables you to wind back any given length of film in the camera in order to expose it a second time. This is commonly used for superimposing titles on a moving background or for making dissolves.

You will not find the backwinding facility in super 8 cartridge-loading cameras because the design of the cartridge only allows the film to run in one direction.* But it is quite a popular, if expensive feature, where the other gauges are concerned and, incidentally, one of the advantages claimed for Fuji's single 8 system is that the cartridge *does* permit backwinding.

In order to make a successful superimposition, however, you must be in a position to check exactly how much film has been wound back before starting on your second exposure. This means that the normal type of footage counter is not good enough. Instead, the camera needs to be fitted with a frame counter which shows how many frames have been exposed when the mechanism is running normally and subtracts frames when the backwind is in operation. Naturally, all this adds to cost.

Camera Movement

Now if you are a newcomer to movie making and have followed me this far, you may be thinking that the movie camera is a terribly complicated instrument. Well, of course, it can be if you want all the possible refinements — and in an effort to be comprehensive I have tried to describe most of them. Yet the fact is that the majority of models on the market are very simple indeed and can, as they say, be operated by a four-year-old child.

If yours is one of the majority with a single lens, a single running speed and only one visible control — the starting button — don't lose heart. You can make good movies with *any* camera, so long as you understand its limitations. And what I am going to say now applies to everyone, four-year-olds included.

As I mentioned in Chapter Two, the beginner is always tempted to move the camera around while shooting in a mistaken attempt to get more into the picture. Having seen the result of this 'hosepiping', he may well swear off camera movement completely for a while, which is not a bad idea

It takes a little time just to realise the importance of holding the camera absolutely steady while allowing the subject to do the moving. The ideal aid to steadiness is, of course, a tripod and for shots taken with a telephoto lens (or a zoom lens on telephoto setting) it is pretty well essential as any slight tendency to wobble will be exaggerated frantically on the screen. With a normal or, better still, a wide angle-lens, you may be able to get away with hand holding the camera, particularly if there is plenty of foreground movement in the subject. Even so, it is always advisable to take advantage of any natural support that offers; resting the camera on a wall or leaning your back against a tree while filming helps immensely.

When you have mastered the craft of taking good static shots, it will be time to think of ways in which you can use *controlled* camera movement to advantage.

There are three main types of camera movement to consider: panning (swivelling horizontally), tilting (swivelling vertically) and tracking (moving the camera bodily forwards, backwards or sideways in relation to the subject). Panning is by far the most commonly used and its main purpose is to follow a moving subject: a running figure perhaps or racing car.

A pan shot of this kind can be very effective and, providing that you keep the subject in the same position in the frame throughout, the fact that the background is blurred will add to, rather than detract from its impact. But beware of panning over an empty landscape; this way you will tend to get the blur without the centre of attraction unless you pan very slowly indeed.

As a matter of fact, a pan shot of a static subject is hardly ever worth taking — except perhaps to suggest the viewpoint of a character carefully surveying a street

---

*Since this was written, one manufacturer has found a way of providing limited backwind — sufficient to accommodate a dissolve.

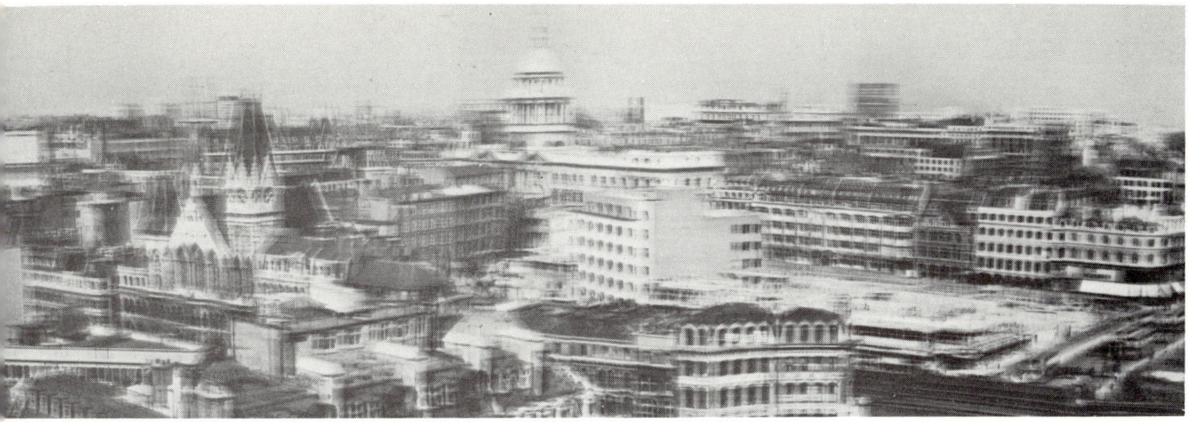

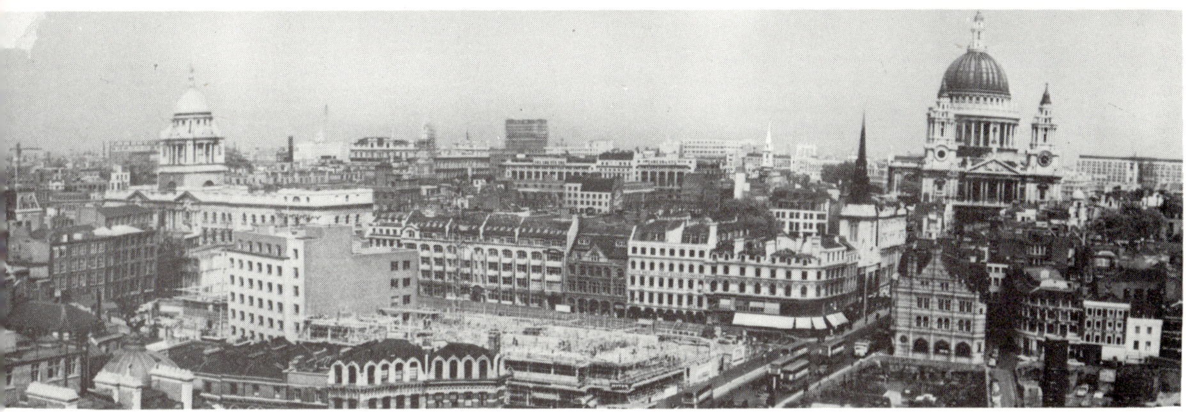

PANNING ON A STATIC SUBJECT should generally be avoided. The tendency always is to move the camera too fast which gives a horrible, blurred result as indicated by the top picture. For an acceptable panning shot (lower picture), the camera must be mounted on a tripod and moved very slowly indeed.

PANNING WITH A MOVING SUBJECT is effective so long as it's done with care. The speed of the pan must, of course, be matched to the speed of the subject so that it remains in the same position relative to the sides of the frame — ideally with a little more space in front than behind. The background is blurred but that helps the effect of speed.

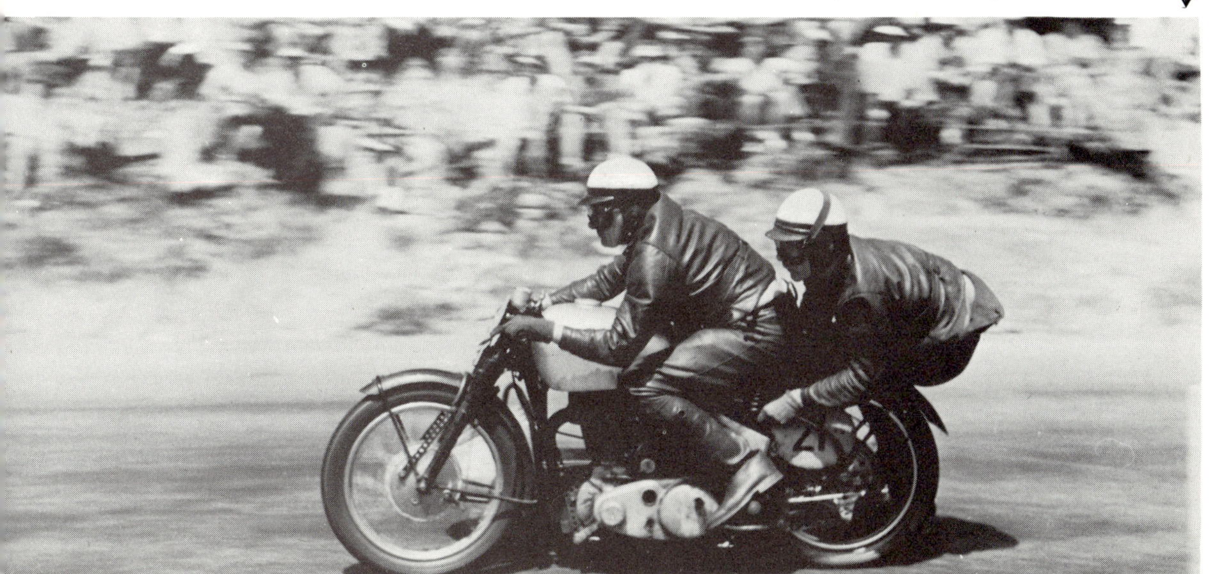

or building. Then you should start the shot with the camera stationary, move it gradually to a pre-determined point and let it come to rest before taking your finger off the button.

The same rules apply to tilting which may be used, for example, to follow a man climbing a ladder or a parachutist descending to earth.

Tracking shots are more of a rarity in amateur films because of the physical difficulties involved. Professionals use a special vehicle known as a camera dolly with solid rubber tyres running in grooved metal tracks to ensure silky smooth movements. You and I must be prepared to settle for something simpler and only use tracking shots when the circumstances are favourable. A boat on the river makes a good dolly, for instance.

Tracking shots from a car can be quite good, providing you take suitable precautions. The first essential is a flat road surface and the second is a wide-angle lens (or the wide setting of a zoom) which renders bumps less noticeable and also exaggerates the impression of speed so that a shot taken at about 15 m.p.h. looks quite fast. Ideally you need some form of rigid camera mounting which bolts the camera to the chassis of the car but, failing this, try shooting at a slower than normal speed — say 32 f.p.s.

Chapter Six

USING LENSES

When a beginner walks into a photographic shop to buy himself a movie camera, you can bet your life that his heart is set on a zoom lens. That is the way of the world; yesterday's luxury is today's necessity.

If the beginner were to ask himself *why* he wanted a zoom, I suspect the honest answers would be something of this order:

A. Because a zoom lens looks impressive on the front of a camera and the people next door have one.

B. Because it's fun to look through the viewfinder while working the zoom lever and watch everything getting bigger or smaller.

C. Because it saves you having to walk about with the camera; you can just stand in one place and frame the picture as you want it by adjusting the zoom.

The third answer makes a bit more sense than the other two but, even so, it's inadequate. If you only want a zoom to save your feet, the chances are that you'll make better films without one.

Let's be absolutely clear about this right at the start: you can make very good films with a single prime lens of standard focal length. I am not saying that there is any virtue in limiting the scope of your equipment — only that you can progress a very long way in film making before you really need the extra versatility that a zoom or additional prime lenses can give.

Having established that, let's assume that you are beginning to feel the pinch. You have explored the possibilities of your standard lens and you are ready to extend your filmic vocabulary.

Focus Effects

We have already touched on the obvious functions of a wide-angle and a telephoto lens. The wide-angle, with its broad field of view, enables you to 'get more into the picture' when working in a confined space. The telephoto, with its narrow angle of view, enables

you to fill the frame with small or distant subjects and is therefore much favoured by wild-life photographers.

But this is really only the beginning. To appreciate the more subtle characteristics of these different lenses, we must return to the subject of focal length and depth of field.

The depth of field (or zone of acceptable sharpness) increases as the focal length of the lens decreases. So when you are working with a wide-angle (short focal length) lens in reasonably good light you can be sure that everything in the picture — whether it is only a foot or so away or in the far distance — will be sharply defined.

As so many film scenes contain action 'in depth', this might seem therefore to be the ideal lens for movie making. And so it is in a great many cases; notably for example in rough and tumble newsreel work where the camera is right in among the action, and where there is no time to alter the focus setting between shots. If you are filming a street riot, or just a visit to the local market, a wide-angle lens (or a zoom adjusted to its widest setting) is a big asset. But it is not much good if you can't get close to the subject; a cricket match filmed with a wide-angle lens would simply look like a few white dots in a sea of green.

Again for 'realistic' indoor drama where all the action is fairly close to the lens and where you want to show inter-play between foreground and background characters, a wide-angle is the answer. But not all films are realistic and there may be times when you want to put all the emphasis on a foreground face or figure and soften the background by throwing it out of focus. Such 'differential focus' effects are virtually impossible with anything but a telephoto lens — or the extreme telephoto end of a good zoom.

And before somebody pounces on that remark, I ought to explain that I am talking primarily in terms of 8 mm cameras. You see the focal length of a standard lens is related to the size of film. In the case of standard 8 it is usually 13 mm; in the case of super 8 it is usually 15 mm; in the case of 9.5 it is usually 20 mm and in the case of 16 mm it is usually

FOCAL LENGTH — 1. These three shots are all taken from the same camera position with lenses of different focal length. (The same effect could be achieved by using three different settings of a zoom lens.) Progression from wide-angle to telephoto restricts the field of view and gives the illusion of moving closer to the subject. Notice, however, that there is no alteration in the perspective as there would be if the same lens were used throughout and the camera moved physically closer to the subject. Because we expect a change of perspective as we get 'closer' to a subject, the telephoto shot appears unnaturally 'flat', whereas the wide-angle shot has a considerable feeling of depth about it.

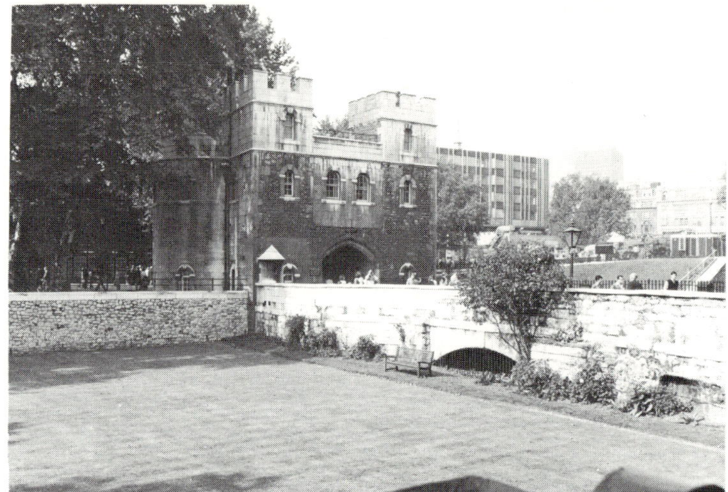

WIDE ANGLE

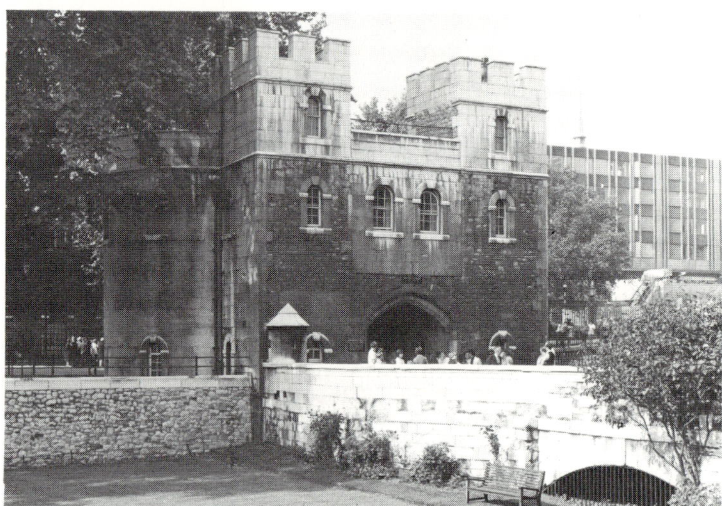

NORMAL

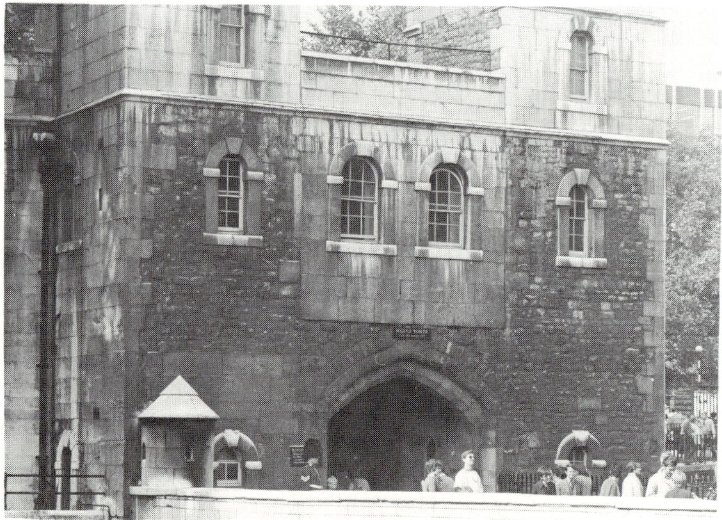

TELEPHOTO

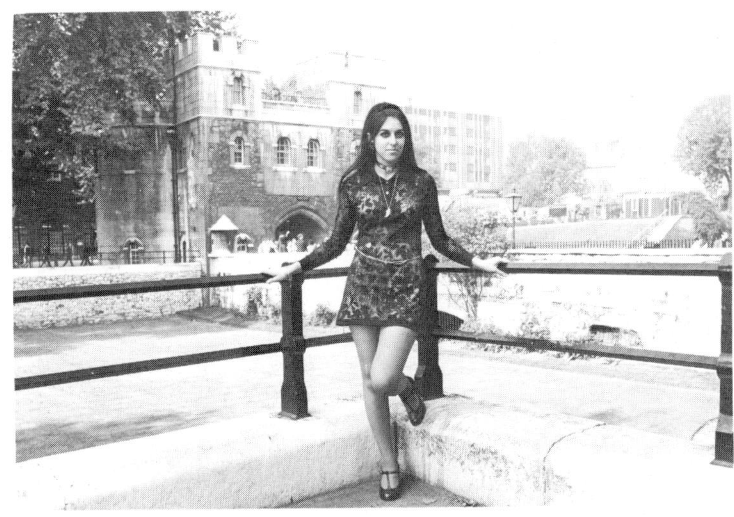

FOCAL LENGTH — 2. These three shots were again taken with lenses of different focal length but this time the camera position was changed also to keep the foreground image of the girl the same size. Notice how this alters the relationship between foreground and background. In the wide-angle shot the girl easily dominates the picture. In the normal lens shot — the camera having moved back — the building in the background has grown larger. In the telephoto shot — the camera having moved back still further — the building in the background has become completely dominant.

WIDE ANGLE

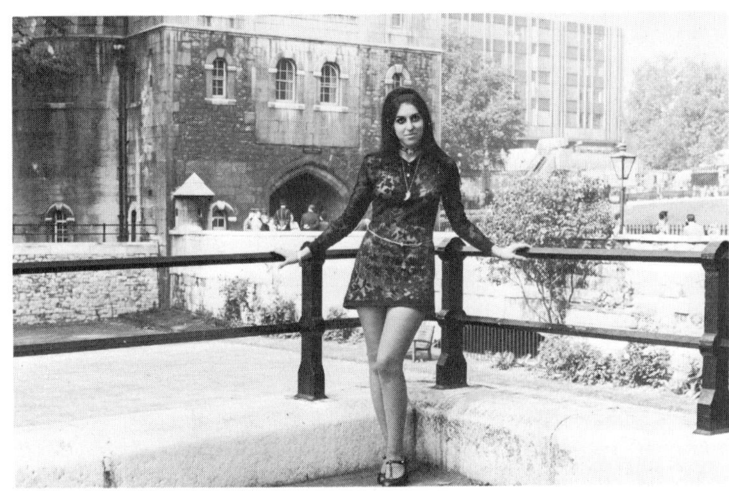

NORMAL

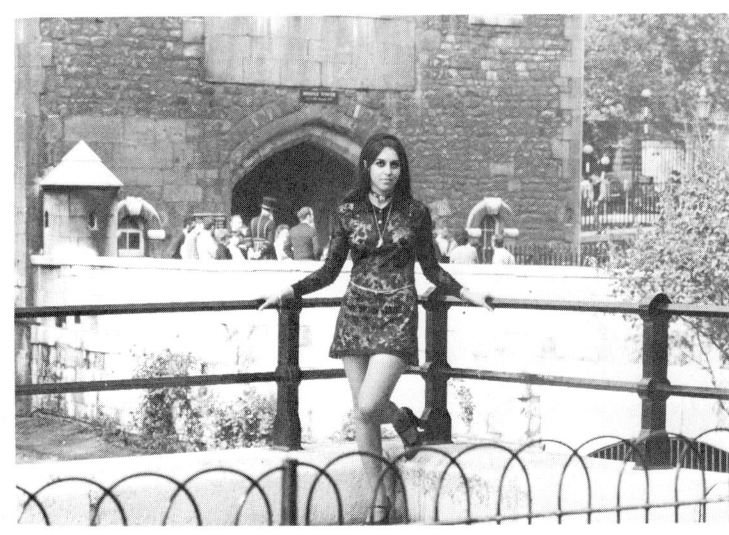

TELEPHOTO

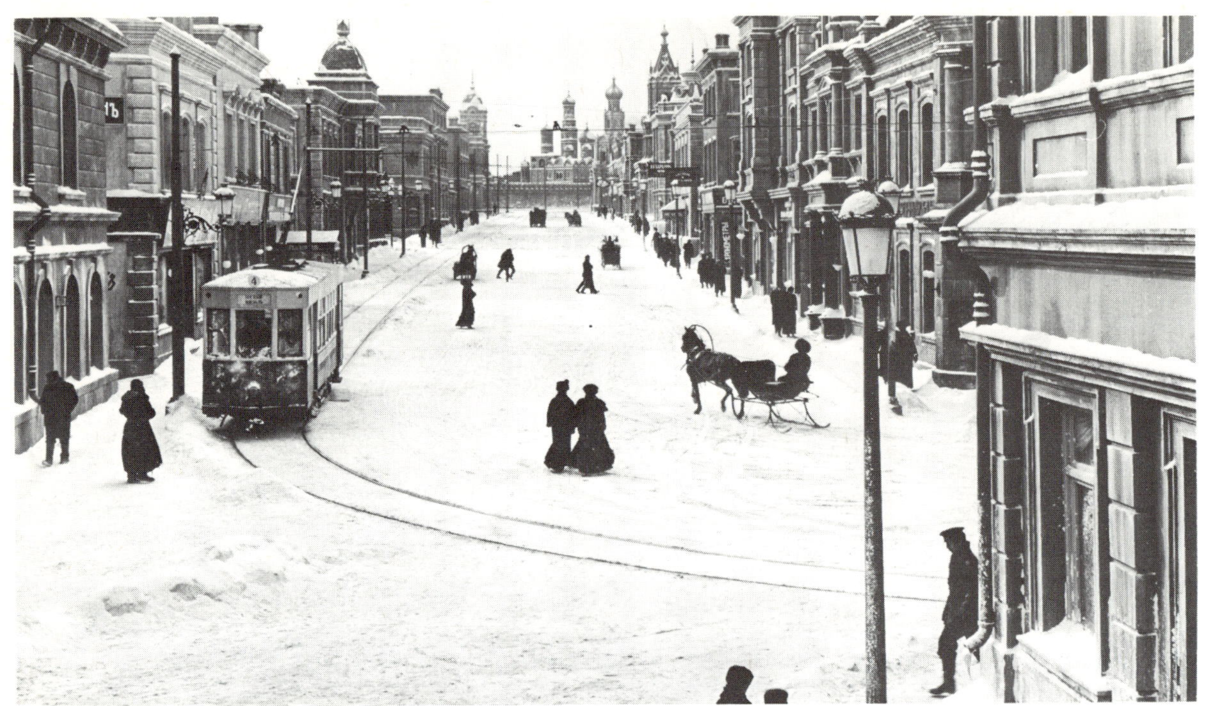

WIDE-ANGLE LENS *gives great depth of field, suitable for any scene containing movement towards or away from the camera as well as scenes in which foreground and background action are of equal importance. In this shot from* Doctor Zhivago *the buildings at the end of the street are almost as sharp as those very close to the camera.*

TELEPHOTO LENS *restricts depth of field and is therefore suitable for scenes like this in which all the emphasis is on a foreground character. Notice how Julie Christie stands out from the soft-focus crowd in the background in this second shot from* Doctor Zhivago. *Incidentally, a telephoto is also more flattering for closeups because the greater distance between camera and subject reduces perspective and minimises the size of the nose.*

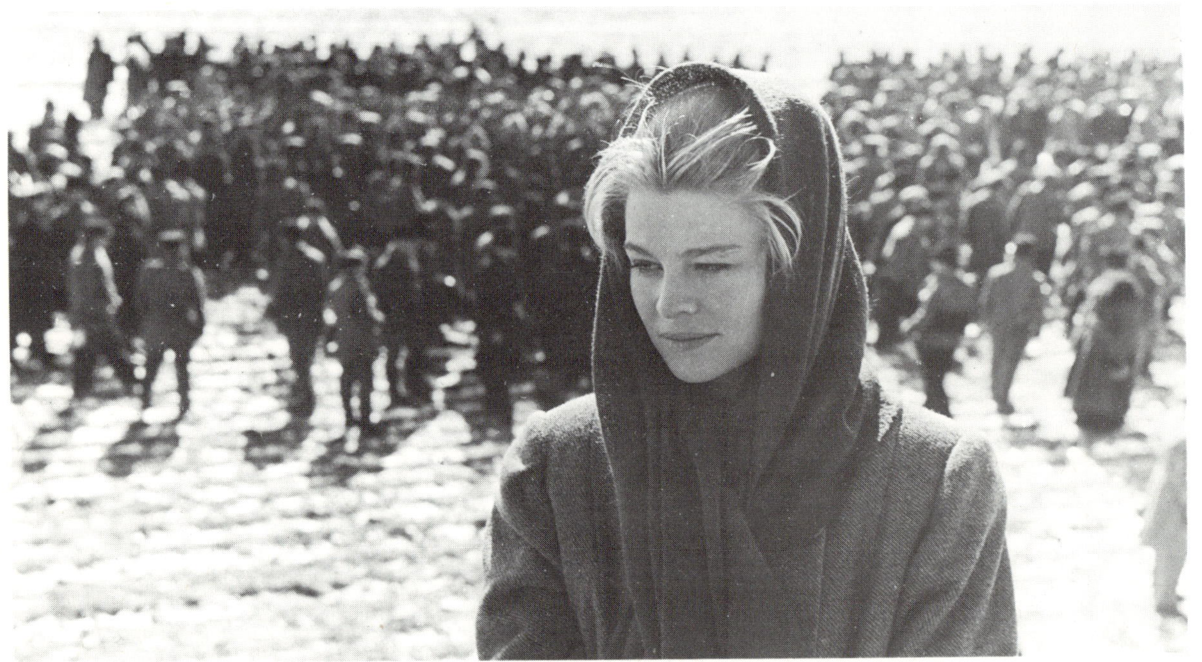

25 mm. As the film format gets larger the standard focal length also increases.

So it follows that the depth of field is much more restricted with the standard lens on a 16 mm camera than it is with the standard lens on an 8 mm camera. In one sense this is a disadvantage for the 16 mm user; it means that he has to take more care over focusing. But it does enable him to get differential focus effects more easily and, of course, to make them even more emphatic by using a telephoto.

Because the discreet use of soft focus backgrounds can add greatly to the visual distinction of a film, it is worth recalling that another way to reduce depth of field is to open the lens aperture. And that, of course, means working in subdued light or if you find it quite impossible to get away from the sunshine — using a neutral density filter.

Perspective Effects

Leaving focus aside for a moment, there is another vital difference between the way a scene is rendered by a wide-angle and a telephoto lens.

The technicians will tell you that the perspective of a scene is not affected by the focal length of the lens in use, perspective being controlled entirely by the distance between camera and subject. Like many technical statements this is both true and thoroughly misleading.

The fact is that if you think of the same subject occupying about the same proportion of the frame area, the camera just *has* to be further away for a telephoto shot than a wide-angle one. So you can take it from me that in practice you have a choice between exaggerating perspective by shooting with a wide-angle lens or minimising perspective by moving the camera back and switching to a telephoto. (The typically 'flat' telephoto look can easily be spotted in newsreel shots of cricket where the players at the near and far end of the pitch are almost exactly the same height in frame.)

Let's consider how this choice of lenses might be used expressively in a film. Suppose you have a medium long shot of a man splitting logs with an axe; a few yards away in the background is a pile of logs waiting to be split. He is full of vigour and, by using a wide-angle lens, you show him as a commanding figure, dominating the scene. You cut away to something else

and come back to him a few moments later but by now you wish to suggest that he is beginning to feel tired. So you move the camera back and use a normal lens.

His figure is still the same size in frame but the pile of logs is now larger and more daunting.

Another cut-away and you come back to him again but this time you move the camera even further away and use a telephoto. The pile of logs looks huge and the man relatively insignificant. Thus by purely visual means you convey the idea that his work is getting on top of him.

It's just conceivable that you could get the same effect in one shot with a zoom lens by tracking the camera back gradually and, at the same time, gradually zooming in. You may like to try this as an experiment, although it would need to be done with enormous dexterity not to look tricky.

Because it exaggerates depth, the wide-angle lens is not very flattering for close-ups; it tends to give a frightening prominence to noses, chins and other protruding features. So if you want to present your leading actress to the best advantage, shoot her with a telephoto and she will come out small featured against a romantically diffused background. In medium close-up she may look a trifle flat-chested as well but you have to take the rough with the smooth.

Focal Length and Movement

This business of focal length and perspective also needs to be considered in relation to subject movement.

Generally speaking, any movement of the subject towards or away from the camera can be presented more effectively with a wide-angle. For one thing there is no problem about holding focus and for another the image size increases or decreases more rapidly, thus adding to the impression of speed. On the other hand, when you are panning with a subject that is moving across your field of view (a racing car, for example) a telephoto is ideal. By moving the camera back, you can hold the subject in frame over a longer distance and stationary objects in the background or foreground will flash through the frame at an impressive rate.

However, some of the most striking effects in film are obtained by standing one of the general rules on

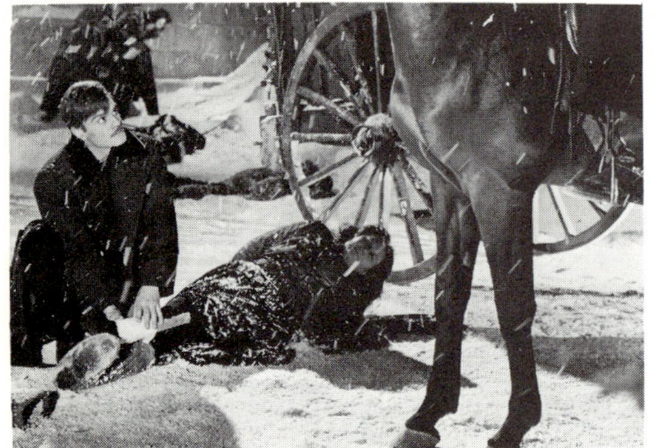

A DIRECT COMPARISON between a wide-angle shot (left) and a telephoto shot (below). The first thing you notice is that the wide-angle gets more into the picture but look again and you see more subtle differences. The camera is actually further away in the telephoto shot and this has flattened the perspective so that the background figures on the left and the wheel are larger in relation to the foreground, separation being achieved by differential focus. Additionally, of course, there is more space between lens and subject and therefore apparently a greater density of snowflakes, those near the lens being rendered as out-of-focus blobs. (Stills from Doctor Zhivago.)

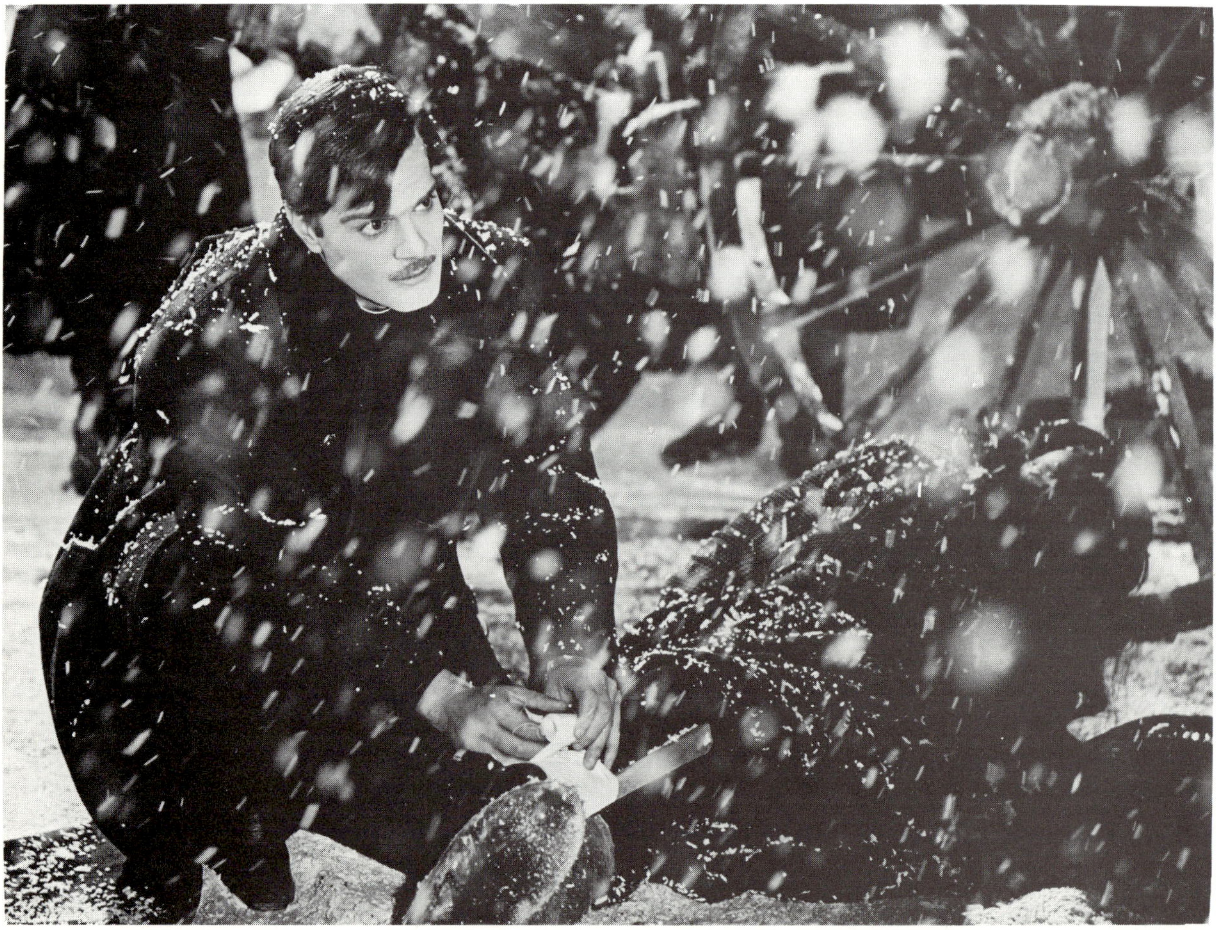

its head. So let's think what it would be like to take a long shot with a telephoto lens of a girl racing towards camera. We would see her legs moving up and down at normal speed but her size in frame would hardly alter so that she would appear to be running very fast and getting nowhere. This could be very good in a dream sequence. Perhaps the girl is escaping from a haunted house but, try as she may, she can't leave the house behind; we see it looming over her in the background.

Now suppose you want to release the girl from her dream and show a return to normality. You could do this by having her run towards camera for several seconds, then turn and run at right angles so that you can pan with her.

Perhaps it is hardly necessary to add that what is true of subject movement is also true of camera movement. Thus tracking the camera into or away from the subject is nearly always more effective with a wide-angle lens which adds to the impression of both speed and steadiness. A parallel track — going along a row of faces for example — can be effective with a telephoto but I should add the warning that you need a rock-steady camera mounting to avoid excessive bumpiness.

In this chapter I have tried to indicate some of the ways — creative as well as functional — in which you can make your lenses earn their keep. Needless to say, I have only been able to scratch the surface of the subject but I hope this will be enough to start you off on a voyage of personal discovery.

Chapter Seven

USING DAYLIGHT

Light is the intangible substance that makes the cinema work. It is light that records the image on the emulsion and light that projects it onto the screen.

When there is not enough light we can't operate and even that modern miracle, the fully automatic exposure system, admits defeat by showing its little flag of truce — the 'Don't Shoot' signal in the viewfinder.

All this should be enough to remind us of the importance of light but because it is so freely available during the greater part of our waking lives, we tend to take it for granted. We assume that when there is light the subject will be revealed and when there is no light the subject will be concealed and that is that. But of course that is not that.

Light has the power not only to define but also to transform everything that we see in the world around us. The appearance of people and things depends on the angle of light as it strikes them, on its intensity and colour, on whether it is direct or diffused or reflected.

Often we only become aware of the endless variety when we start to use artificial light sources indoors. Then the fact that we control the lights compels us to notice their effect but, in truth, the best we can contrive is only a poor imitation of what nature offers day by day, hour by hour and minute by minute. The only real advantage of artificial lighting is that we can take as long as we like to study it and reproduce any given scheme when we want it.

Commercially, this is a considerable advantage. But for the amateur who has time on his side there is much to be said for using natural daylight whenever possible and regarding artificial sources as a last resort. It is a matter of waiting and watching and exercising what control we can.

Indeed, once we have mastered the simple mechanics of operating the camera, there is only one way to progress in photography and that is by making more deliberate use of light. So let's consider some of the variable factors and the ways in which we can determine the kind of pictures we get on the screen by choice or control.

Front Lighting

First of all we can choose whether to film with the sun behind us so that the subject is lit from the front, or to one side so that the subject is cross-lit, or with the sun in front of us so that the subject is back lit. Naturally, there are infinite variations between these three main positions and we can also decide whether to shoot at noon when the sun is high in the sky or towards dawn or dusk when it is much lower.

The most conventional choice, I suppose, is three-quarter front lighting (the sun shining over one's right or left shoulder) and this is what we generally try to simulate with a 'standard' interior lighting set-up when we put the key light 'high up and close to camera'. Certainly it is safe insofar as it provides even illumination of the subject — so that a built-in meter or a separate meter taking an ordinary reflected light reading will result in satisfactory exposures. Yet because the light source is slightly off-centre there will be a rim of shadow on faces and figures to give a degree of modelling and separation from the background.

The photographic text books warn us against dead frontal lighting because it flattens the subject and the characters tend to get confused with the background. This is true of black and white film, not necessarily true of colour for we can often obtain separation by selecting a contrasting background. And it is worth remembering that colours look their brightest when the light is reflected straight back into the lens — often an asset on a dull day.

Side Lighting

Side or cross lighting puts half the subject in shadow and therefore gives an emphatic three-dimensional effect which may add interest to a landscape, to a man's rugged features or a girl's voluptuous curves. It also creates an exposure problem because you have to decide whether to set your aperture to suit the shadows or the highlights or something in between.

If you are working in direct sunlight, the range of brightness may be too great for colour film, resulting in clogged shadows or burned out highlights. And this is where a reflector will help by softening the shadows; you can use cooking foil stuck to a piece of hardboard or an old cine screen or, at a pinch, just a sheet of newspaper.

If the field of view is too large for an artificial reflector to be of much use — and there is a limit to the size of hardboard sheets that we can cart around on location — keep an eye open for natural reflecting surfaces. Light-coloured walls, cliff faces and sand dunes can all be pressed into service.

Back Lighting

Back lighting is generally regarded as a bit arty and rather too 'advanced' for the beginner but, in fact, there is no mystery about using it. Naturally if you point an exposure meter — built-in or otherwise — at a back-lit subject, you will be measuring the actual light source, rather than the very small amount of light reflected by the subject. So the indicated aperture will be small and the subject drastically under-exposed — not much more than a silhouette in fact.

In certain circumstances this may be just the effect you require. For example, if you have a shot of boats sailing into the sunset, you wouldn't expect to see them as anything but silhouettes and any attempt at exposure compensation would merely detract from the colour of sea and sky. For scenes of this kind an automatic camera can be left to its own devices.

On the other hand, there are times when a silhouette is no good. Perhaps it is a romantic medium shot of a young couple sitting on the terrace of a hotel with a sunlit boulevard behind them. You want to show their expressions clearly and use the back lighting simply to add a halo effect. In these circumstances you will have to take your reading from the shadowed side of the subject nearest the camera (possibly brightening it by means of a reflector) and let the background be over-exposed.

When colour cine film first came on the market amateurs were sternly advised not to use back lighting at all on the assumption that colours don't show unless they are lit from the front. What was forgotten was that when the sun is high up as well as to the rear it spills just around the edges of things and gives a bright, jewel-like rim of colour which can be magically effective in a scene that is mainly sombre.

What was also forgotten was that not all subjects are entirely opaque. Many indeed are translucent and reveal their colour and texture more tellingly when the light shines through them rather than on to them: curtains, sails, stained glass, coloured liquids, petals, balloons and smoke to name a few.

Diffused Light

Up to now we have been thinking mainly in terms of direct sunlight which most amateurs still regard as the natural ally of good photography. But diffused sun-light — or what the exposure manuals call 'cloudy bright' — actually yields more pleasing results on colour film and for close-ups where flesh tones are predominant, even dull conditions are acceptable.

In some modern feature films all exterior scenes are deliberately taken when the sun is covered by cloud. And a similar style can be maintained indoors by bouncing the light off reflectors instead of direct-ing it straight onto the actors in the conventional way that always shrieks 'studio interior' even when it is well done. This is a highly recommendable method for amateurs who seldom have the spotlights that are needed for a proper studio lighting job anyway.

Outdoors again, you will find that in addition to clouds there are other natural light diffusers that can sometimes form an attractive part of the picture itself. On a misty morning, for example, you can get shots of sharply defined foreground action against a vague pastel background, bearing in mind that the greater the distance between lens and subject the greater density of mist there is for the light to penetrate.

The Colour of Light

As I mentioned in Chapter One, there are two basically different types of colour film on the market: Daylight Type and Artificial Light Type.

The reason for this is that daylight has a higher 'colour temperature' than the artificial light provided by normal tungsten lamps, and the higher the colour temperature of light, the more it tends to be blue, whereas the lower the colour temperature, the more

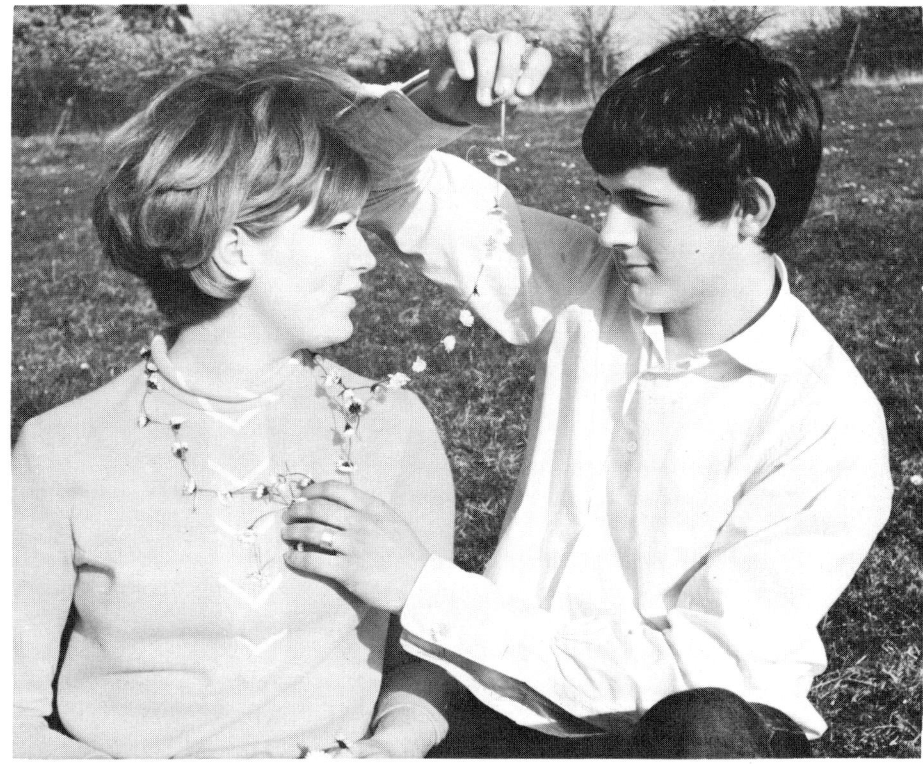

'Light has the power not only to define but
also to transform everything that we see in the
world around us. The appearance of people
and things depends on the angle of light as it
strikes them, on its intensity and colour, on
whether it is direct or diffused or reflected.'

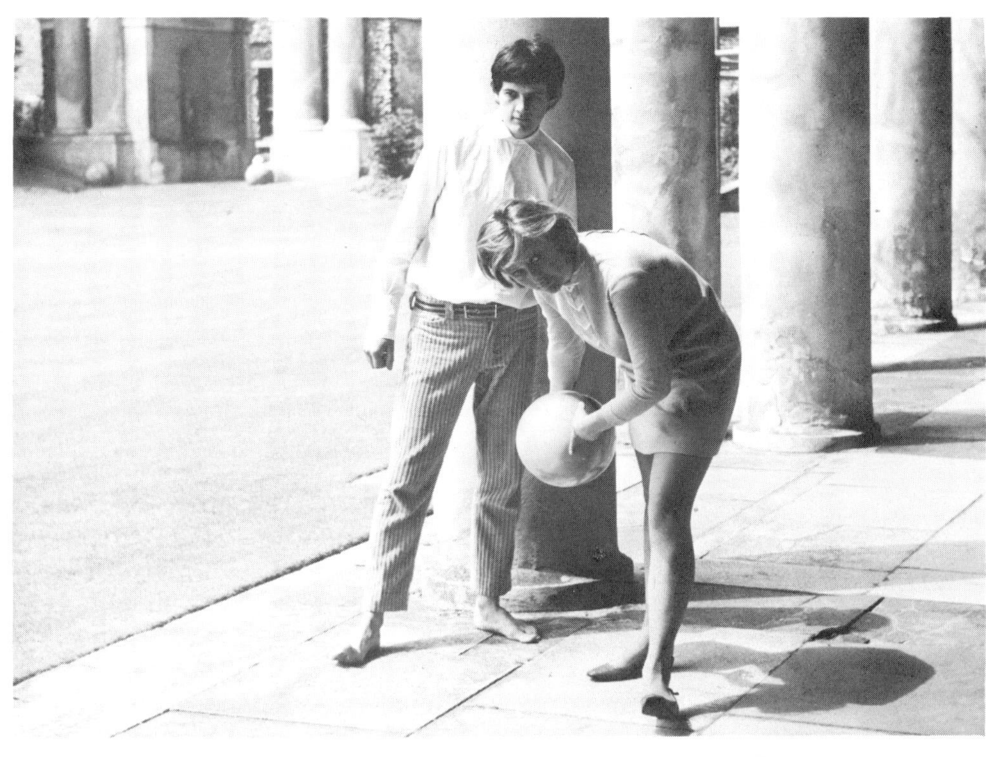

SIDE LIGHTING
emphasises shape (more
necessary in black and
white than colour) and
gives a three-
dimensional appearance
to the scene. Notice
here the definite
'modelling' of the two
figures, the ball and the
pillars. A possible
danger when shooting
in bright sunlight is that
the contrast range will
be too great for colour
film, resulting in burned
out highlights, clogged
shadows, or both. In
this case a certain
amount of light
reflected back from the
stone floor has kept
the contrast range
within reason.

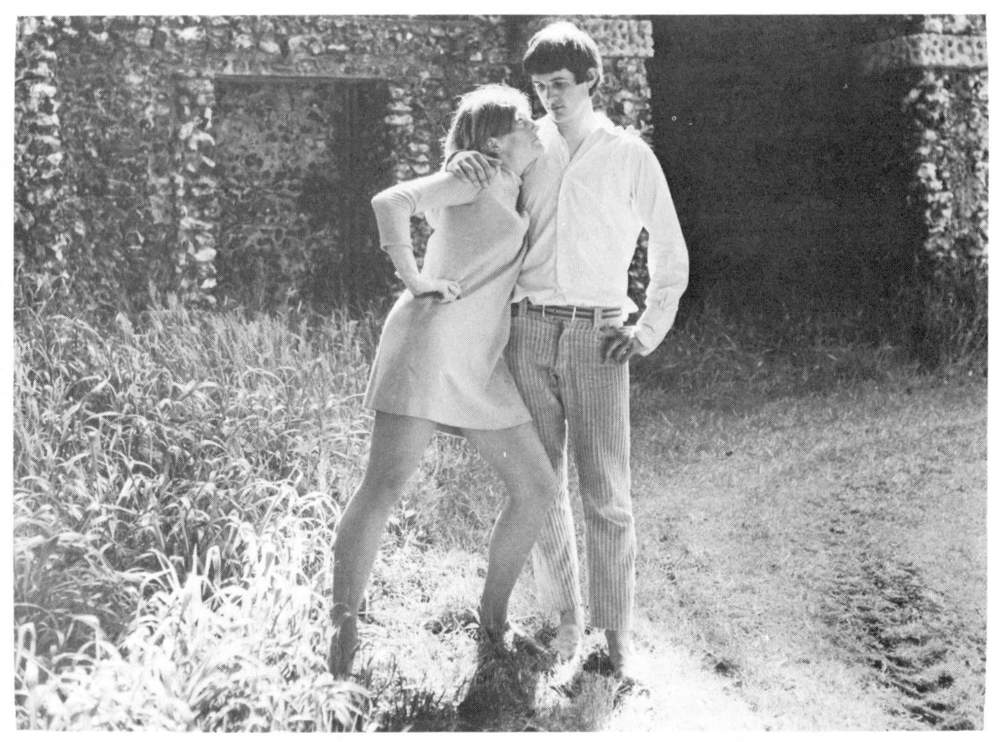

BACK LIGHTING
gives a touch of magic
to the scene and
emphasises the separa-
tion between the
background and the
foreground characters
by surrounding them
with a halo of light.
The danger is that if
you simply point an
exposure meter (or an
automatic camera) at a
scene like this, you may
well measure the light
coming directly from
the sun and therefore
under-expose the
subject. The danger
has been avoided here
by taking a closeup
reading from the front
of the subject which is
in shadow. The small
highlight areas are
burned out but this adds
to the pleasing effect.

49

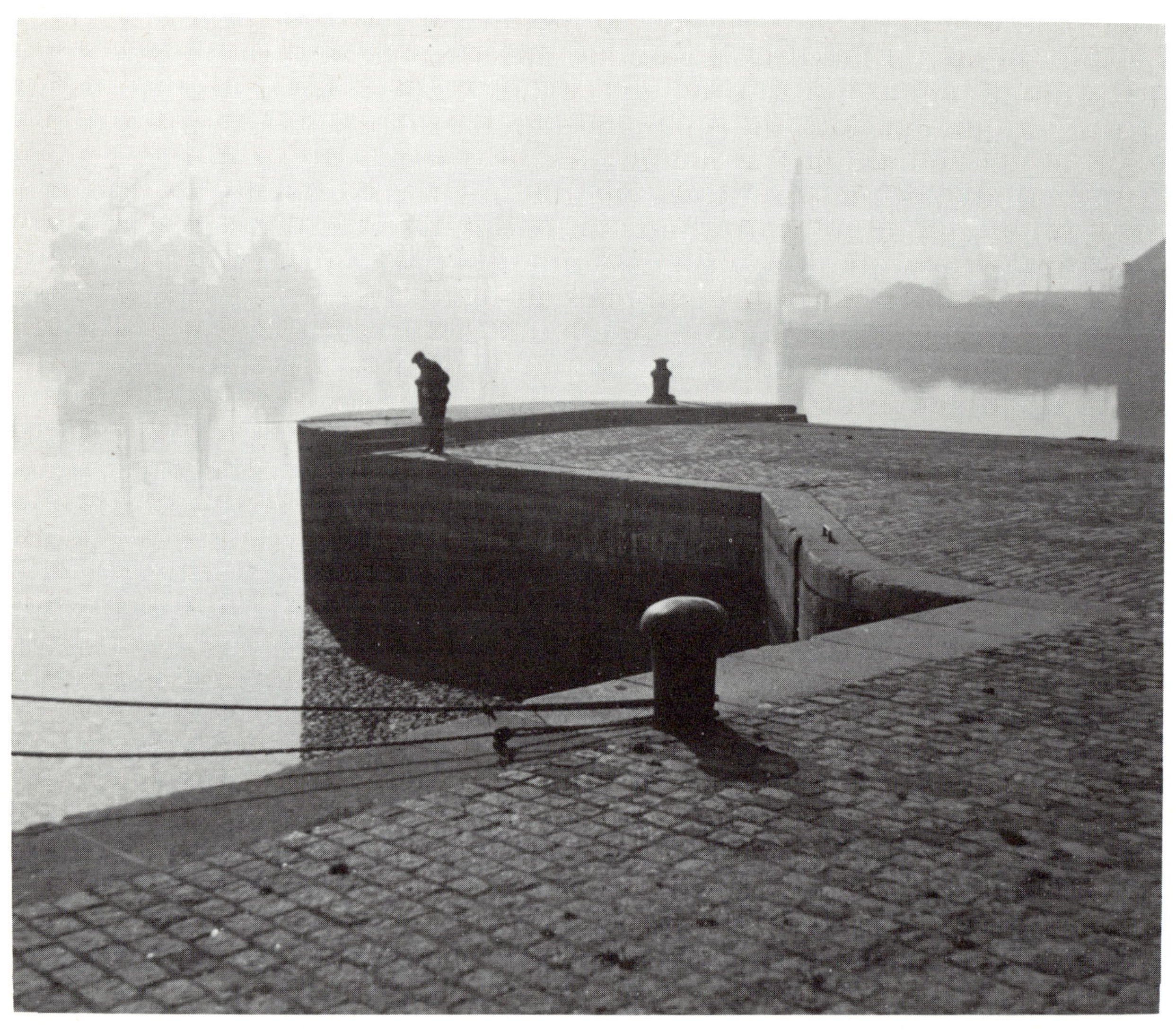

NATURAL LIGHT DIFFUSERS — notably mist — can sometimes be used effectively as an integral part of the shot. Notice here how the density of the mist has given an indistinct, ghost-like quality to the background while leaving the foreground relatively sharp and distinct simply because it is nearer to the lens.

it tends to be red. In order to obtain accurate colour rendering, the appropriate type of film must be used.

It is possible, however, to convert the artificial light film for daylight use by placing an amber filter (Kodak's Wratten 85, for example) over the camera lens. Indeed many 16 mm and standard 8 camera owners prefer to use artificial light film all the while as this saves the trouble of re-loading the camera when moving from an interior to an exterior scene or *vice versa.*

The addition of the filter does, of course, reduce the amount of light reaching the film but as there is usually plenty of light available outdoors, this is no problem. The cameraman simply has to remember to allow for the filter by altering the ASA setting on his exposure meter or on the camera's built-in exposure control system. (In the case of Kodachrome IIA the setting changes from 40 ASA without the filter to 25 ASA with the filter.)

When the back-room boys at Eastman Kodak sat down to devise the super 8 system, they cleverly exploited the conversion filter idea in order to make life easier for the beginner. Hence all super 8 colour film is of the artificial light type and all super 8 cameras have built-in conversion filters. So you get correct results in daylight automatically.

For indoor work you displace the built-in filter — usually be inserting a 'key' in the camera — and this automatically adjusts the exposure control to the new ASA setting. So once again you get correct colour rendering without even trying.

With super 8 there is seldom any need to worry about the technicalities of colour temperature.

Once in a while, however, you may wish to shoot a scene that involves mixing artificial light with daylight. This is always a tricky situation where colour film is concerned, no matter what the gauge, and even in professional feature films you sometimes get a glimpse of a blue-looking exterior scene when somebody opens a door or glances out of a window.

There are two solutions, neither of them very easy. Firstly, you can decide to shoot for daylight (with the conversion filter) and put blue filters over your lamps. The trouble with this arrangement is that the filters reduce the efficiency of the lamps and you may well find that you just can't get an adequate exposure. The method may be useful, however, for close shots when an open door is providing the main light source and the lamps are being used merely to relieve shadows.

The second — and generally more acceptable — solution is to shoot for artificial light (without the conversion filter) and put an amber filter over the windows. Ideally, one would like to have huge sheets of Wratten 85 for this purpose but in practice sheets of gelatin used for stage lighting effects make reasonable substitutes. These are available from Strand Electric of 29 King Street, London W.C.2.

Even if the window itself is not going to appear in the picture area, it's quite a good idea to cover it with gelatins so that you can use the window light to supplement your lamps. Otherwise, of course, you must draw the curtains to exclude all daylight and rely entirely on artificial light — with results that may not be too happy if you want a daytime effect.

One further point needs to be mentioned and this is that the colour temperature of daylight varies quite considerably, being much lower (therefore redder) at dawn and sunset than in the middle of the day. We tend not to notice these changes in real life because our eyes adapt to them but they are, of course, faithfully recorded on colour film. So if you cut straight from a shot taken at noon to one taken at, say, 6 p.m., the colour change will be painfully obvious.

Perfectionists who insist on precisely correct colour continuity from shot to shot use a colour temperature meter (which measures colour temperature in degrees Kelvin) and employ a whole series of filters to make marginal corrections. Most of us, however, are content to settle for a common sense compromise which means that — unless we are deliberately aiming for a dawn or sunset effect — we try to confine our filming to the hours of 10 a.m. to 4 p.m. or thereabouts.

Chapter Eight

USING ARTIFICIAL LIGHT

Insofar as you have more direct control over the results, I suppose it's more satisfying to work with artificial light than daylight. You can shift your lamps around, switch on one at a time and study the varying effects before deciding on the one that suits you best. That is, of course, assuming that you have all the lights you need at your command.

In actual fact, most of us tend to make do with rather sketchy lighting equipment and so have to settle for results that fall short of the ideal. Outdoors we have to work within the limitations imposed by the weather — or wait patiently for the right conditions. Indoors, we must learn to work within the limitations of our equipment. Let's start then by considering the three basic types of lighting unit that are available and see what we can expect from them.

The Photoflood was once the basis for all interior lighting in amateur films and many amateurs still manage with nothing else. It looks just like an ordinary electric light bulb but is over-run with the result that it emits more light and has a correspondingly shorter life.

A No.1 Photoflood is rated at 275 watts and will normally burn continuously for something in the region of two hours, A No.2 is rated at 500 watts and has an estimated life of six hours.

As the name suggests, a Photoflood provides a flood of light in all directions but for maximum efficiency it obviously needs to be concentrated on the subject you are filming. In other words, it should be fitted with a reflector which you can buy or, if you want to save money, make your own from a pudding basin or old biscuit tin.

An alternative is the reflector-type Photoflood — or Photospot as it is sometimes called — which has a mirror reflector actually built into the glass envelope. Naturally, this sort of lamp costs a bit more.

The Movielight is a relatively new arrival on the amateur lighting scene and has the advantage of compactness coupled with long lamp life. It has not,

however, ousted the Photoflood as it was once expected to do — probably because the initial cash outlay is fairly high.

The name 'movielight' is applied loosely to two types of lamp: the sealed beam variety which is similar to a car headlamp and the quartz iodine which consists of a glass-like quartz tube filled with iodine vapour and set in front of a reflector. A typical example of the former is rated at 650 watts and one lamp can be expected to burn continuously for around ten hours.

A quartz iodine type movielight, rated at 1,000 watts will cost more and the lamp life is again in the region of ten hours. However, this type has the special advantage that the lamp burns at the same colour temperature throughout its life. Purists may notice that shots lit by photofloods or sealed beam lamps which are about to expire have a disturbing reddish tinge and this can be a real problem if the shots in question are later intercut with other material filmed when the lamps were new.

One problem with quartz iodine lamps is that they become extremely hot, and, apart from being difficult to handle, may damage the movielight housing if left burning for long periods of time. The better models are therefore fitted with three-position switches so that the lamps can be brought on at half power for rehearsals and only switched to full power when shooting is about to commence; this is an excellent refinement which also helps to prolong the life of the lamps.

The Spotlight tends to be regarded by many amateurs as a needless luxury but, in fact, it is absolutely essential for certain kinds of lighting effect as we shall see presently.

Basically, a spotlight consists of a clear lamp with a reflector behind it and a lens in front of it. This arrangement enables you to direct the entire light output exactly where you want it, and, by adjusting the distance between the lamp and the lens, you can alter the shape of the beam to cover a larger or smaller area.

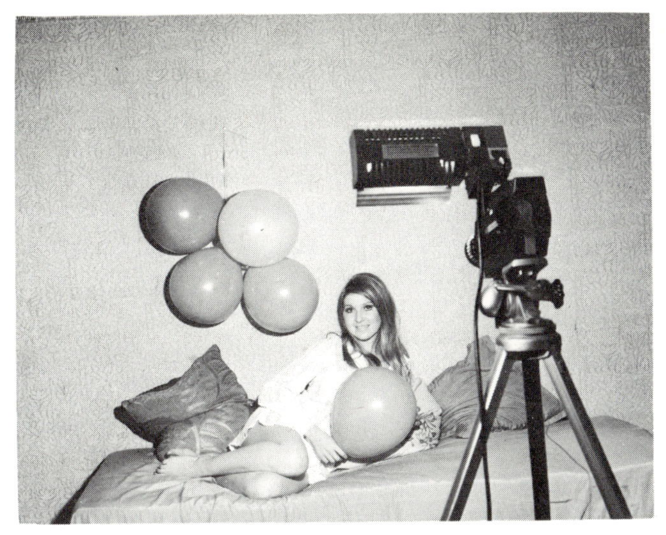

ONE LAMP DIRECT. The very simplest way to use
a movielight is to have it mounted on the camera
and pointing directly at the subject. The lighting is
flat, giving very little sense of roundness or modelling as the shadows are amost directly behind the
subject. Nevertheless, results can be acceptable,
providing that the background wall is close enough
to receive a fair share of the illumination.
(Remember that light intensity depends on lamp-
to-subject distance.) Here the girl is close to a
medium-light toned wall so that illumination is
even over the whole frame area and the camera's
automatic metering system gives correct exposure.

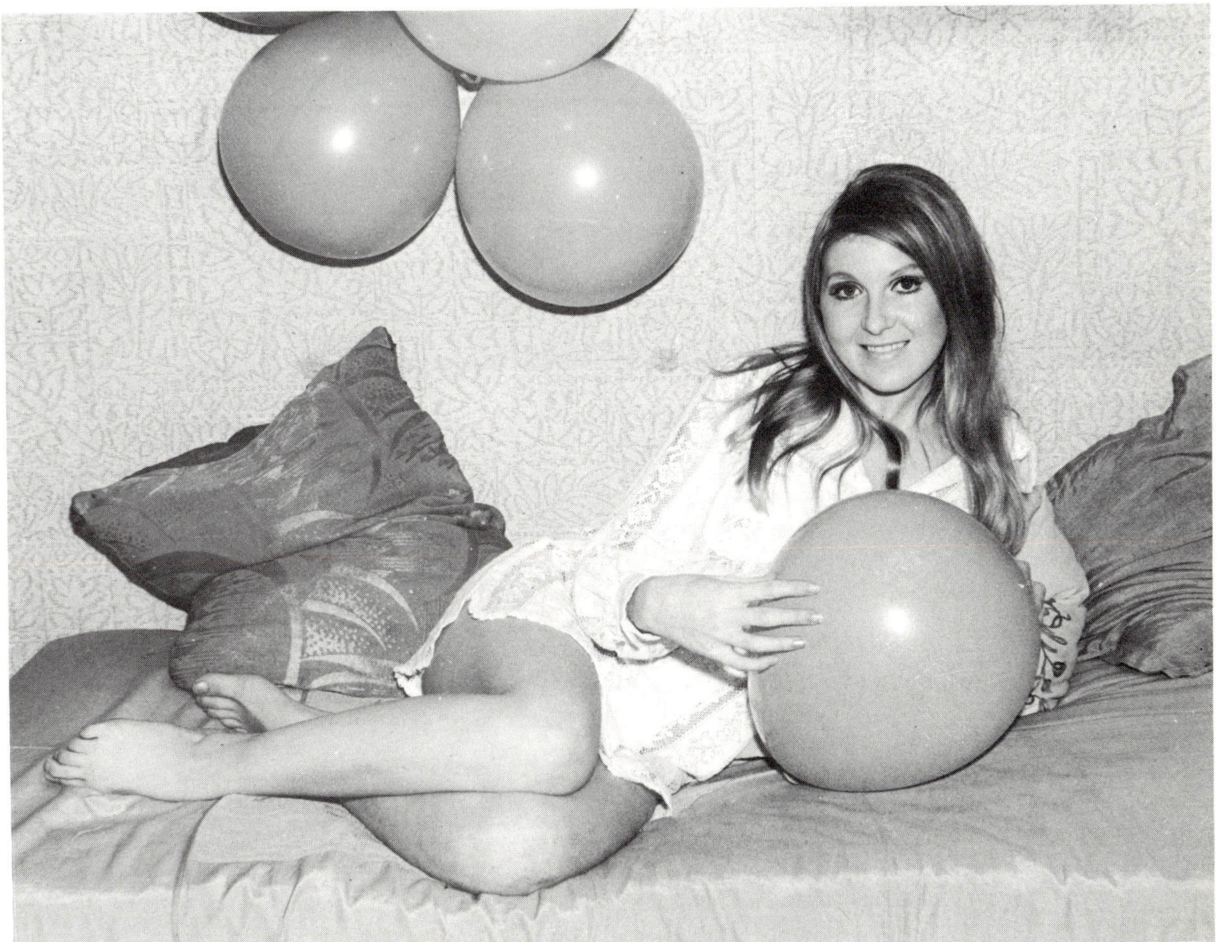

ONE LAMP 'BOUNCED'. Many movielights can be turned 90 degrees upwards so that the light shines up to the ceiling and is reflected or 'bounced' back onto the subject. This gives very soft lighting with hardly any shadows at all, and is pleasant for the subject as there is no glare. Naturally, there is a loss of intensity, which depends mainly on the height and whiteness of the ceiling. Typically, bounce lighting needs about a three f-stops wider lens aperture than the same subject with direct lighting, but of course the exact increase depends on distances and surroundings.

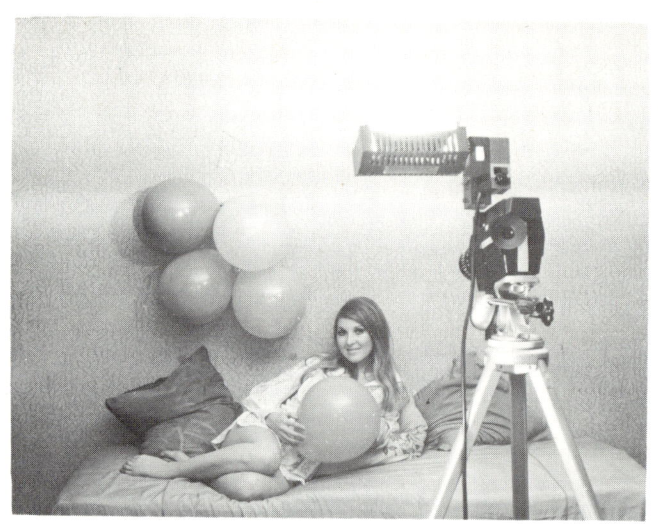

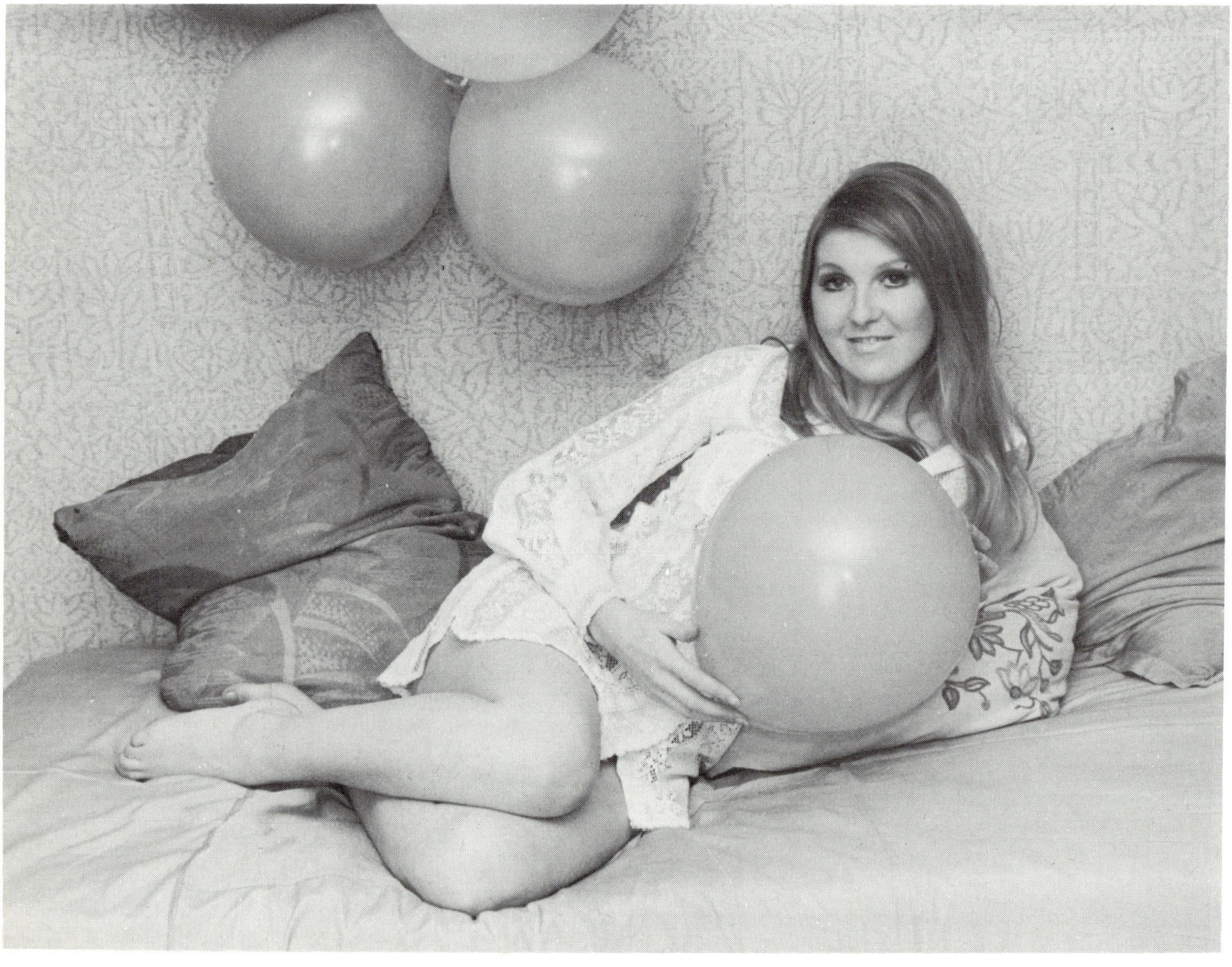

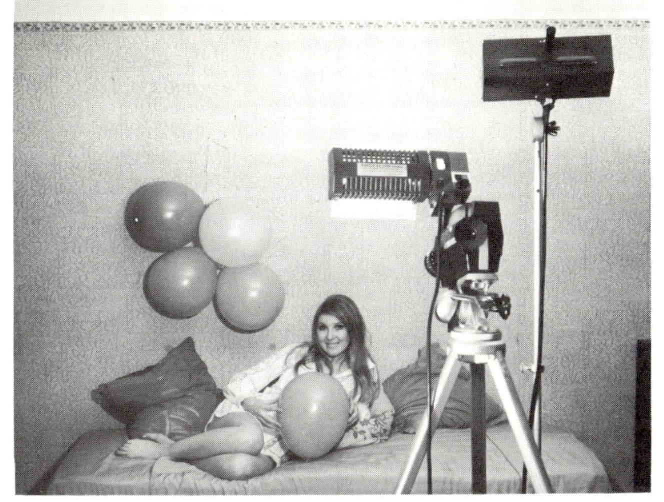

ONE LAMP DIRECT AND ONE BOUNCED. Here we have one movielight on the camera shining directly on the subject and a second of about the same power bounced off the ceiling. The bounce light serves two purposes. First it lights up the room well and eliminates the glare caused by the small and bright direct light, thus making life pleasanter for the subject. Secondly it helps — though only marginally — to soften the effect of the direct lighting. Best results are obtained by using a bounce light of greater power than the direct light.

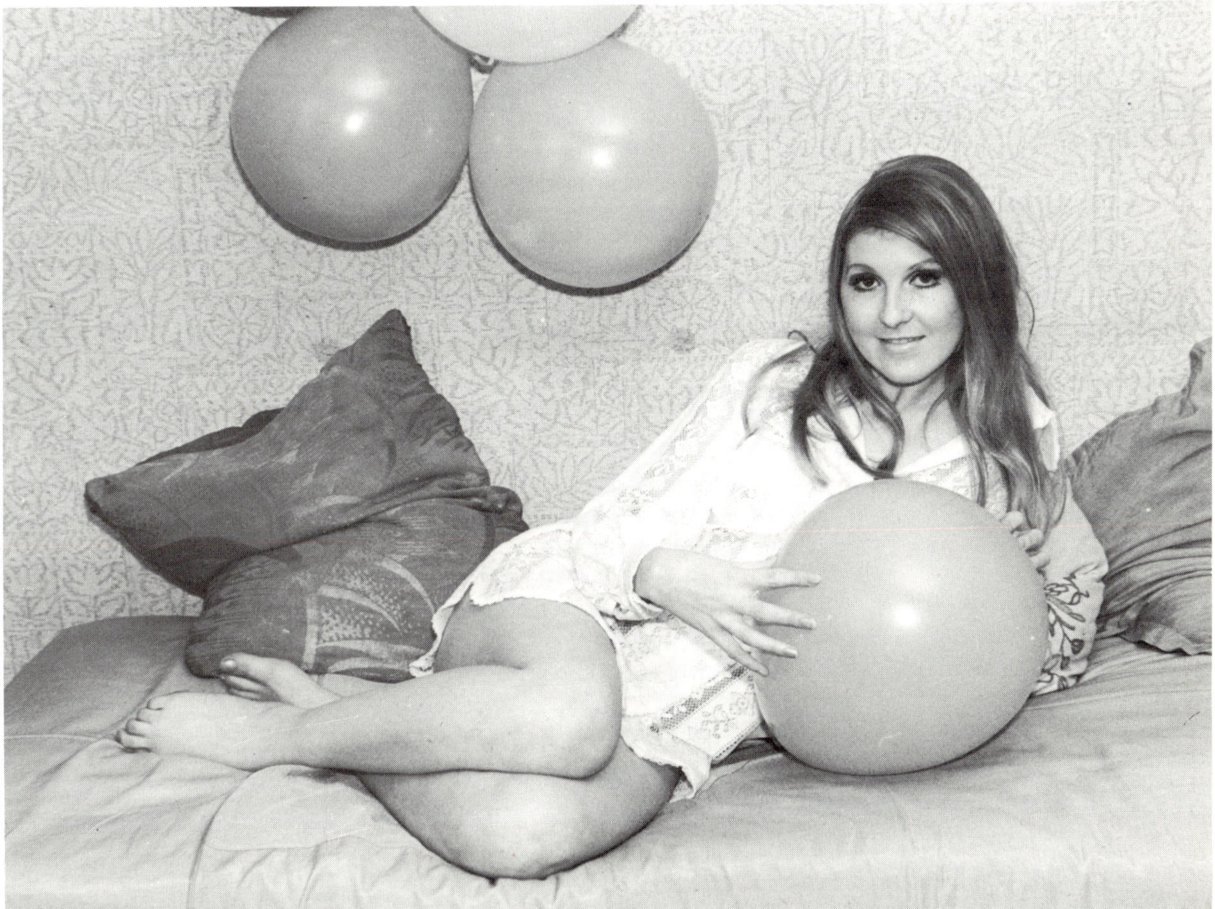

TWO LAMPS DIRECT. With a second lamp unit
shining directly on the subject, more interesting
lighting effects become possible. In this typical set-
up the off-camera lamp provides 45-degree lighting
on the subject, while the on-camera movielight
fills in the shadows. By adjusting the distance of
the off-camera lamp contrast can easily be altered.
Best results are achieved by having it appreciably
closer than the on-camera lamp. This is particularly
true for black and white filming which benefits
from higher contrast.

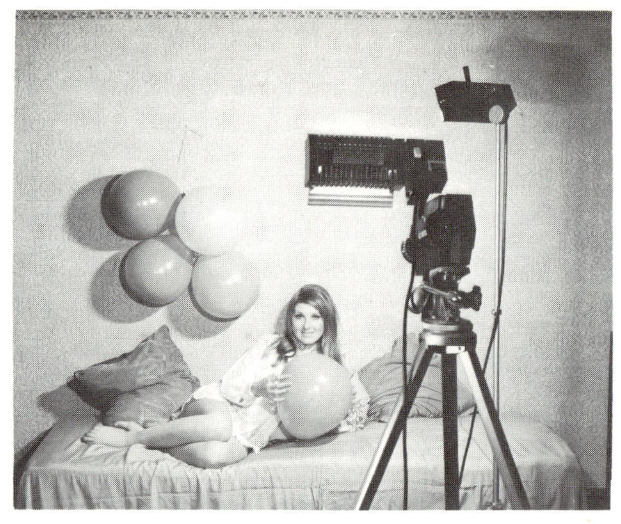

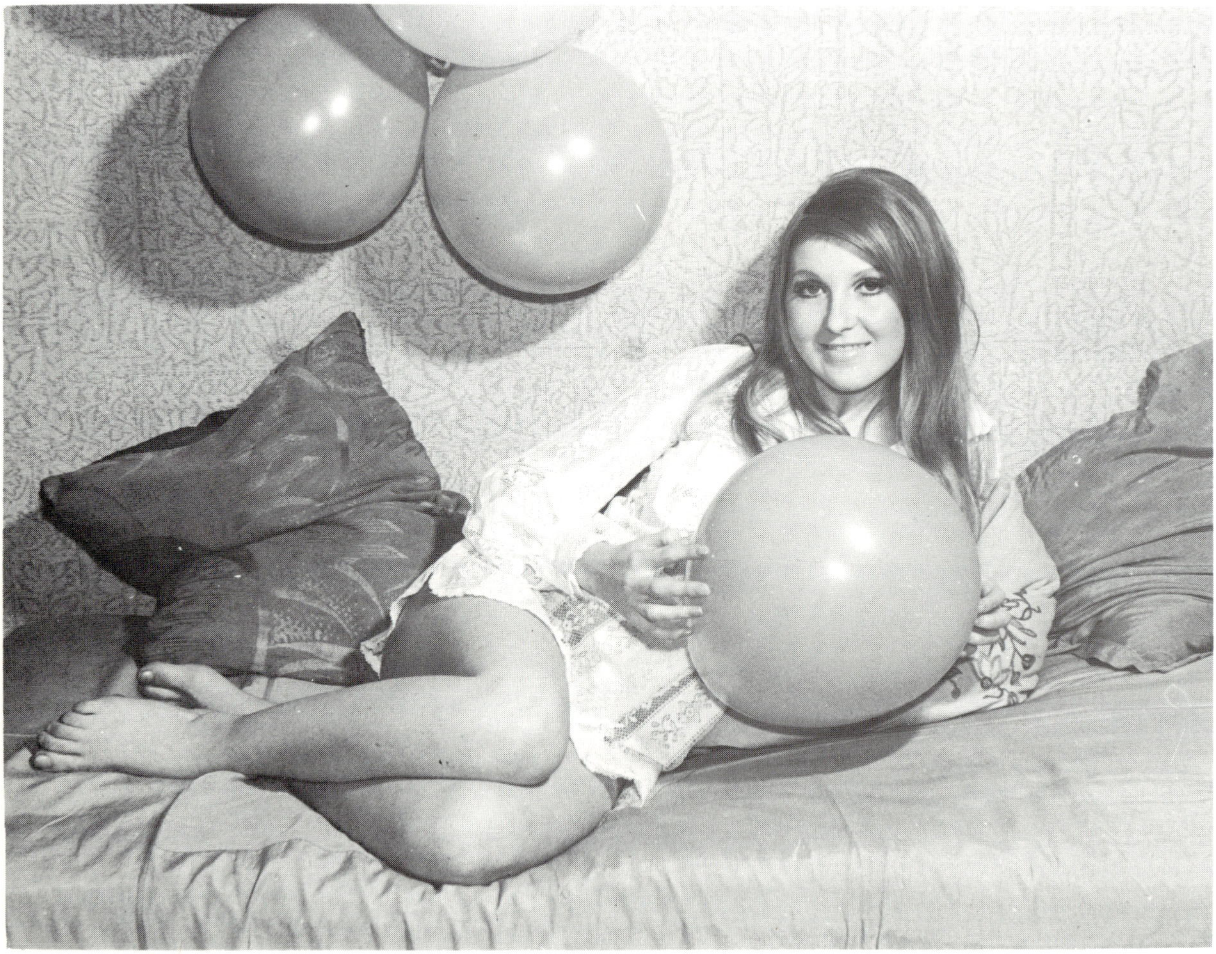

Because the light from a spotlight is concentrated into a beam, its intensity falls off much less sharply than that from a Photoflood or movielight and hence it can be used effectively at a greater distance from the subject. Moreover, it will produce sharply defined shadows when required whereas the shadows from any form of floodlight are always diffused.

The extra control provided by a spotlight makes it ideal for backlighting the subject whereas with a flood-light directed towards the camera there is always a danger that some of the light may spill onto the lens and fog the film. And a final advantage: you can clip coloured filters or diffusers in front of a spotlight lens for special lighting effects.

Spotlights come in a great variety of sizes, taking lamps from 100 watts right up to 20,000 watts. The very small ones are used mainly for table top photo-graphy and the giants are found in feature film studios. For normal domestic use, something in the 500 to 1,000 watt range should prove adequate.

No matter whether you use Photofloods, movie-lights or spotlights — or some of each — you will need stands to support them. Again there are many different types to choose from but you should make sure that you have at least two sturdy ones that can be extended to a height of about eight feet and will not fall over when you breathe on them. Additionally, you may like to invest in one or two clips or clamps that can be used for attaching lamps to furniture or hanging them from picture rails.

So much then for the equipment. Now let's consider the three main methods of tackling an indoor lighting job.

1. On-camera Lighting

The first essential, of course is simply to ensure that there is *enough* light on the subject to give an adequate exposure. And the easiest, not to say the crudest, possible way of doing this is to have a lamp (or two) attached to the camera.

The advantages are obvious. Each time you move your camera position, your lighting set-up moves along with it. No lengthy preparations are required and no assistants to lift lamp standards around. So you can work quickly and with a minimum of fuss.

On the other hand, the results are not very good. The direct frontal lighting gives a flat, uninteresting and unreal appearance to the scene — rather like a still photograph taken with on-camera flash. Shiny surfaces, such as spectacles or paintwork, reflect the light straight back into the camera lens. Worse still, because the level of illumination depends on lamp-to-subject distance, even exposure can only be achieved when the subject is all in one plane; people close to the camera tend to be over-exposed, while those in the background are under-exposed.

Hence on-camera lighting can only be regarded as a makeshift for filming actual events, such as wedding receptions or parties, when you have no control over the action and are compelled to work in a hurry.

Due to its simplicity, however, manufacturers regard this as the method most likely to appeal to amateurs. Hence, when the super 8 system was devised, it was decided that the camera's built-in daylight conversion filter should be automatically removed by the action of fitting a lamp to the top of the camera.

Traditional Lighting

At the opposite end of the scale is the traditional studio lighting method whereby at least four different light sources are used to light every scene and each source serves a specific purpose. Thus:

First, there is the *key light,* representing the main source of illumination, which gives depth and modelling to the scene. The actual lamp used would naturally depend on the scale of the scene but if we assume a straightforward medium close-up, the key light could well be a small spotlight or reflector Photoflood. It is normally positioned above and slightly to the left or right of the camera.

Next, there is the *fill light,* which serves to 'fill' or soften the shadows caused by the key light, bearing in mind that the contrast range which can be accom-modated on films is less than that which is acceptable to the eye. This could well be a Photoflood and is positioned on the opposite side of the camera to the key light. It can be taken nearer to or further from the subject to reduce or increase contrast.

Thirdly, there is the *background light* which, not surprisingly, is used to light the background. The point about this really is that it serves to eliminate unwanted and distracting shadows from the back wall. Again a

Photoflood will serve, and it should be positioned somewhere towards the rear of the 'set', behind the area where the action is taking place. Care must be taken, of course, to avoid getting a 'hot spot' on the wall that will draw attention to itself and away from the foreground action.

Lastly, there is the *backlight* which is directed onto the character or characters in the scene from the rear — in other words towards the camera. This has no effect on exposure and its purpose is to create a rim of brightness around the actors, thus separating them from the background; in Hollywood it is known as a 'liner'. To give the right effect, the backlight must be a directional type of lamp (in other words a spotlight) and it must be positioned high up as well as to the rear so that it does not shine into the camera lens. This is easy enough in a film studio where you have plenty of headroom but not so easy in an ordinary domestic interior where the ceiling is liable to get in the way and where it may not always be possible to find furniture and drapes that will hide the lamp stands.

In fact, I have intentionally kept my description of traditional studio lighting methods on the short side because — although it's useful to know about them — they are virtually impossible for the average amateur to apply. The only way, if you want polished results is to stylise your interiors, scripting them so that the entire action is broken down into close-ups and medium close-ups. As soon as you try to work on a larger scale, you will find that you have to compromise and this can be frustrating. Better, perhaps, to seek a different method entirely.

Naturalistic Lighting

It is worth remembering that the 'rules' — or perhaps we should call them the conventions — of traditional studio lighting were established at a time when most movies were shot in black and white. At that time there was a definite need for the lights to emphasise the solidity of the characters in the scene and separate them from their backgrounds. But now that colour is almost universal — in the amateur field at least — the whole situation has changed.

Colour in itself defines the shape of things and provides separation between foreground and background. People, unless their clothes happen to match the wallpaper, stand out naturally. Hence we can afford to use a more naturalistic form of lighting, reducing the contrast between highlight and shadow and trying not to make the scene look 'lit' at all.

The way to achieve this is to make extensive use of reflected light. In other words, instead of directing the lamps straight at the subject, you 'bounce' them off reflecting surfaces. White ceilings and light coloured walls make good natural reflectors but if the walls happen to be dark or if there is a lot of dark furniture in the room, you may have to resort to artificial means. Sheets of white card or paper will do, providing of course that they are kept outside the picture area.

For simulated daylight in a smallish room, I have found that one fairly powerful direct light (a thousand watt movielight) to represent the window and two reflected lights to fill the shadows provides sufficient illumination for 25 ASA colour film. However, this is a matter for experiment.

One of the main advantages of the reflected light method is that once you have arrived at a satisfactory set-up, you don't have to change it every time you alter the camera position.

There may be times when you want to make use of the actual daylight coming through the window or indeed to include part of the window in the picture area. Normally, this can't be done owing to the colour temperature problem mentioned in Chapter One; the daylight and hence everything seen outside the window will appear unnaturally blue when photographed on artificial light colour film.

However, there is a solution. For a few shillings, you can purchase sheets of amber gelatin which are approximately the same colour as a Wratten 85 filter and stick these over the window glass. In this way the colour temperature of the daylight will be brought into line with that of the lamps inside the room.

Before we leave artificial lighting, there is one last point, often ignored by amateurs, that is worthy of a special note. When you have a shot of someone entering or leaving a room, remember that the area on the far side of the door must be lit as well. Otherwise, you will create the impression that the person concerned is emerging from or disappearing into a cupboard.

Chapter Nine

THE MECHANICS OF EDITING

Some people say that the most thrilling phase in the production of a film is viewing the 'rushes' — the newly processed rolls of film as they are returned from the laboratory. But for me the enjoyment of this particular activity is always tempered by my anxiety to cut the shots apart and put them together again in their proper sequence.

No matter how pleasing it may be photographically, the material only comes to life in editing.

The creative joys of editing, however, can only be savoured to the full when you have mastered the mechanics of the business. These are simple enough to understand but effortless work does depend on having the right equipment and learning to use it in a logical and orderly manner. So let's begin by running through the items you are likely to need and see how they function.

The Splicer

The splicer — or film joiner — is the basic editing tool. It is a small metal instrument with two hinged clamps and register pins which hold the two pieces of film to be joined in correct alignment with each other.

There are two main types of splicer on the market: one for making cement joins and one for making tape joins. In the more traditional cement type, the two film ends are slightly overlapped and are placed on the register pins with base (shiny side) downwards. A scraper — usually built into the splicer — removes a narrow strip of emulsion from the left hand film end and the film base, thus exposed, is coated with a colourless liquid called film cement.

The right hand film end is then clamped down on top of this and the cement temporarily dissolves the film base so that the two pieces of film become firmly welded together. After a few seconds the splice will be set and the film can be safely removed from the splicer.

When a tape splicer is used, the film ends are not overlapped but are butted together and covered on both sides by a patch of thin, transparent adhesive tape. Sometimes separate tape patches are used but the better models carry a roll of tape, each patch being cut to size automatically by a guillotine action that also punches out the sprocket holes.

The cement type splicer is preferable for editing a reversal original that is intended for projection as the joins are less visible on the screen. On the other hand, a tape splicer is more convenient to use for running repairs, should a film happen to break during projection.

Tape again is better for editing a cutting copy because the butt join does not involve the loss of a frame on either side of the cut. So if you trim a shot too tightly, you can always lengthen it again by stripping off the tape and splicing in a few more frames.

For editing a 16 mm original that is to be used purely as a source of future copies cement splices are always used.

The Animated Viewer

In order to be able to edit efficiently, you must be able to see clearly what you are doing. Hence it is virtually essential to have an animated viewer — an instrument which is designed to stand on a bench or table top and through which you can wind the film backwards and forwards, while viewing the moving picture on a small ground glass screen. This enables you to locate the exact point where you want to make each cut.

The viewer is usually mounted between two geared rewinders with spindles to fit ordinary film spools, so that you can wind the film from right to left or left to right — and switch into high gear for extra speed when the film is not laced through the viewer. In the case of 8 mm, the rewinders and the viewer are generally sold as a single unit — the complete assembly being known as an 'editor'.

When purchasing one of these all-in-one gadgets,

make sure that the rewind spindles will take spools of
the same size as your projector and that they are not
too close to the viewer for ease of operation. Also try
to select a viewer with the minimum number of
sprockets and rollers; this makes threading quicker
and reduces the danger of scratching the film.

Some animated viewers have a built-in 'notcher'
for marking cutting points. Having located the frame
where you wish to cut, you press a lever that makes
a notch in the edge of the film. This is a reasonable
arrangement but I prefer the type of viewer which
gives you access to the film without removing it from
the gate. You can then mark your chosen frame —
much more visibly — with a chinagraph pencil and
then check it again before actually making the cut.

Editing Accessories

Apart from your splicer and animated viewer, there are
a few smaller items that should always be near to hand
on your editing bench. These are:

1. A pair of scissors for cutting the film.
Ordinary straight-bladed ones will do nicely.

2. A chinagraph pencil for marking up cutting
points as mentioned above. If you change your
mind, chinagraph marks can easily be rubbed off
without harming the film. These pencils are available in red or yellow, the red being easier to see
when you are looking *through* the film in a viewer
and the yellow being easier to see when you are
handling the film and looking *at* it.

Incidentally, if you are having fades or dissolves
added to a 16 mm film at the printing stage, the
length of these can be indicated by drawing chinagraph lines on the cutting copy. These will show
on projection and thus give you a good idea of
whether or not the timing is right.

3. A bottle of film cement — if you are using a
cement type splicer. This is very inexpensive but
it evaporates quickly and should always be capped
when not in use — even between splices. In some
cases you will find that the bottle stopper has a
plastic rod attached to it, the idea being that you
should use this for applying the cement to the film.
Take my advice and ignore it. If you want clean
splices, it's a much better idea to use . . .

4. A small brush as used in water colour painting. This will enable you to apply just the right

amount of cement — enough to cover the scraped
area completely but not so much that it spills over
onto the adjacent frames where it can cause dis-
colouration and buckling.

5. A clean duster to wipe away surplus cement
and emulsion dust after making each splice.

6. Last but not least, a pair of white cotton
gloves. These should always be worn when handling
original film which may otherwise be disfigured
by sticky finger prints.

Editing Procedure

Breaking a film down into its component shots, re-
grouping them and finally sorting them into a logical
sequence is a job that can extend over weeks or
months of spare time work. Obviously it will become a
nightmare unless you use some form of filing system
which will enable you to put your hand on any
required shot in a matter of seconds and ensure that
nothing goes astray.

Two alternative methods are available to the
amateur. One is to coil the shots up and stow them in
small containers — usually a series of numbered pill
boxes glued to a sheet of hardboard or plywood. The
other is to hang them on a pin rack.

The pill box system is adequate for a short film
and probably more convenient if you have to do your
editing on the kitchen table or some other place where
you are liable to have to pack everything away at
short notice. However, given a room or the corner of
a room which can be permanently devoted to editing,
there is no doubt in my mind that the pin rack method
makes for faster and more efficient work.

All you need is a wooden lath about three feet long
with headless panel pins spaced along it at regular
intervals and numbered from, say, 1 to 30. You hook
your shots on by means of the sprocket holes and they
then hang side by side for easy inspection. The rack
can be hung in front of a light coloured wall and, to
prevent the ends of the shots from trailing on the
floor, a bin or large cardboard carton placed under-
neath it.

If you really want to go to town, you can emulate
the professionals and make up a proper film bin with a

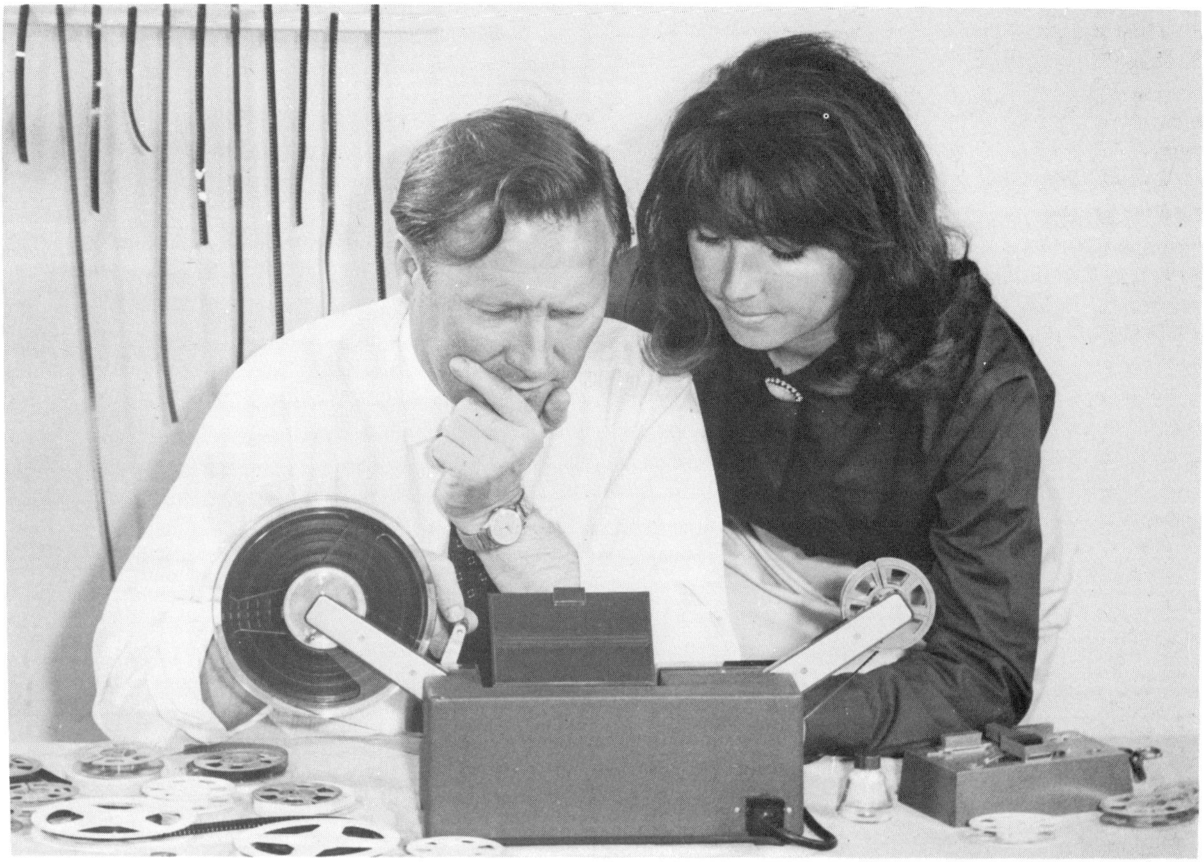

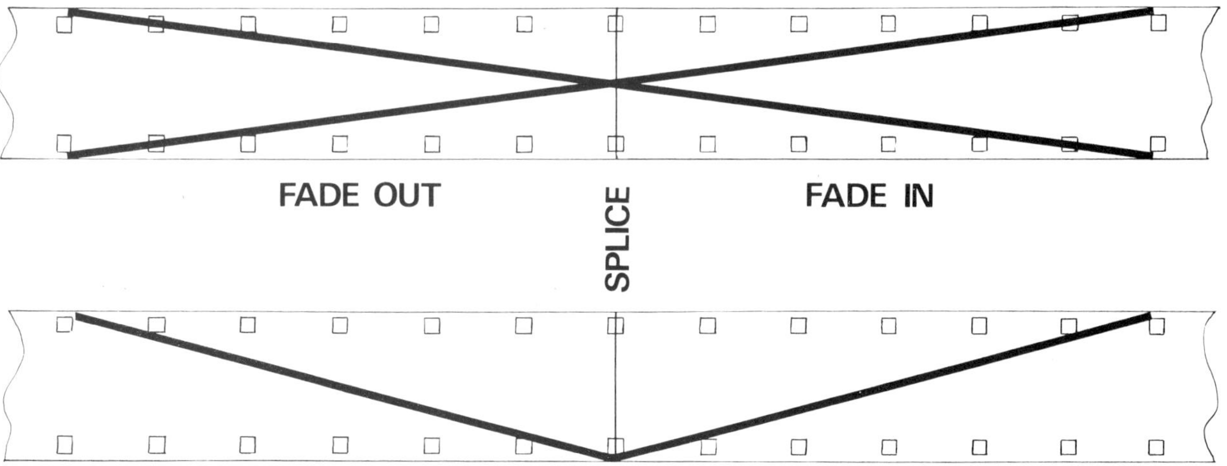

EDITING 8 mm FILM on an animated viewer. This invaluable instrument enables you to wind the film backwards and forwards while viewing the picture on a ground glass screen, before deciding where to make each cut. The small spool on the right (the operator's left) contains unedited film just as it is returned from the processing laboratory, while the edited film is building up on the larger spool. Notice also the pin rack in the background where shots can be hung up and arranged in sequence before being spliced together.

WHEN FADES AND DISSOLVES are required in a 16mm print, the editor marks up the cutting copy with a chinagraph pencil to indicate to the laboratory the position and duration of each of these optical effects. The thick lines in the above diagrams are the conventional signs used for this purpose. The length of the chinagraph lines can be varied according to the duration of the fade or dissolve required and these lines show on the screen when the cutting copy is projected, so that some impression of the final effect can be obtained in advance.

built-on pin rack and frosted glass panel, illuminated
from the rear. As a matter of fact, if you are working
on 16 mm, such a gadget is well worth having because
the frames are large enough to see with the naked eye,
and by looking along the row of shots you can begin
to visualise them as a sequence before you actually
join them up and run them through the viewer.

However, I am running ahead of myself. The first
task is to group the shots into easily manageable
sequences. If you are working to a tight script, this is
no problem. Every shot will have a script number
and in professional practice this is recorded at the
time of shooting by photographing a number board
on two or three frames at the beginning of each take.

If no number board was used, you will have to
identify the shots by reference to the script and then
write the number on the first frame of each with
your chinagraph pencil. Then you can cut the shots
apart and put, say, number 1 to 20 on pin number
one, 21 to 40 on pin number two and so on.

If the film was shot off the cuff without any
script at all, now is the time to write one in retro-
spect. In other words, make a list of all your shots in
chronological order and then re-group them on paper
into logical sequences under appropriate subject
headings. In the case of a holiday film, for example,
you might have one group headed 'Beach Activities',
another 'Sightseeing', another 'Eating and Drinking'
and so on.

You may find that no major re-arrangement is
necessary and that the film can be best presented in
the order in which it was shot. But in my experience
this seldom happens and you can nearly always get
more effective results by forgetting the actual
chronological order of events.

In the course of a seaside holiday, for example, you
may have taken several different boat trips and on each
occasion you may have secured two or three good
shots. On the screen each episode will appear fragmen-
tary and incomplete but put them all together and
you could have enough material to construct a satisfying and smoothly flowing sequence. You can call this
'cheating' if you like but that is what film editing is
all about.

The point is that you can never hope to achieve a
literal transcription of what actually happened on your
holiday but you can do something more interesting —
and that is to give an artistic impression of what it was
like.

Sequence Building

Having sorted your shots into groups, you will have
anything up to, say, twenty shots on each pin. Before
proceeding to the next stage, you must clear the pin
rack by taking each group of shots, apart from the
first, off its pin. Fasten the individual bundles together
with elastic bands, then coil them up and stow them
away in large envelopes or spare film cans with
appropriate labels.

Now you can spread the first sequence out along
the rack, putting each shot on a separate pin. If you
are working to a script, the order will be pre-
determined, of course. If not, you can arrange and re-
arrange them as often as you like before joining them
together with your splicer.

Incidentally, a friend of mine, Gordon Rowley,
has a method of dealing with unscripted films that you
may like to adopt at this point. He uses a stack of
plain postcards and makes a little sketch of each shot
on a different card with a brief note of the action
contained in it. Then, by laying the cards out on a
table, he can shuffle them around until he arrives at
the most lucid sequence. Not a bad idea if you are in
any doubt.

When you have spliced together all the shots from
the first sequence, you can tackle the second sequence
in the same way, and so on right through the film —
although whether everything will go onto one spool
naturally depends on the amount of material at your
disposal.

In any case, having assembled your shots in a more-
or-less logical sequence, you can proceed to the next
step — which is to project the film and make a note
of anything that needs to be removed because it is
technically sub-standard. There may be badly exposed
shots, others out of focus or poorly framed and so on.

When these obvious faults have been removed, you
can begin to pay attention to more artistic matters:
continuity of movement, colour matching, the timing
of cuts on action, the overall tempo of a sequence and
so on. Whatever happens, don't attempt to hurry the
editing process. Whittle away at it a little at a time
and project it often, for your animated viewer —
useful as it is — will not show up all the snags that
become evident on a big screen.

The further you get into it, the more rewarding
editing becomes. Each time you trim out a few

redundant frames, the film moves better, becomes
more sleek and muscular, more fit for public
exhibition.

Using a Cutting Copy

However careful you may be, conscientious editing
does involve the film itself in a certain amount of
wear and tear. That is why, if you are working on
16 mm and can afford the extra cost, it is worth while
investing in a cutting copy.

If you shoot on negative, your cutting copy will
be a print and if you shoot on reversal film, it will be
a duplicate copy. In either case this copy will suffer
all the hazards of the editing bench and you can chop
it about without undue caution, knowing that the
original is still intact. When editing is completed to
your satisfaction, you cut the master film (or order the
laboratory to do this for you) precisely to match the
cutting copy. From the cut master, clean and splice-
free prints are made for exhibition.

Cutting the master to match the cutting copy is,
of course, purely a mechanical job and it is eased by
the fact that most master material has edge numbers
printed along it as intervals of one foot outside the
picture area.* These numbers are, of course,
reproduced on the cutting copy, so that all the cutter
has to do when matching the master is to place the
two strips of film in a two-way synchroniser with
identical edge numbers adjacent to one another and
then wind on until he reaches a splice.

Nevertheless, master cutting does require conditions
of extreme cleanliness plus care and attention to
detail. So you may think it worth while to employ the
services of a specialist in the laboratory — particularly
if you are going to take advantage of the A and B roll
printing method.

A and B Roll Printing

The A and B roll system was originally introduced to
permit the making of good quality dissolves and other
superimposition effects at the printing stage.

The master material, instead of being joined into
one continuous roll, is made up into two rolls of
identical length in the following way. All shots pre-
ceding the first dissolve are spliced into Roll A while

*It is worth checking that your film stock is edge numbered
before you start shooting. If by any chance, you should use
stock that is not edge numbered, you can get your laboratory
to stamp the numbers on after processing and, at the same
time, stamp a duplicate set of numbers onto the cutting copy.

an equivalent length of blank, opaque film (known as
'spacing') is spliced into Roll B.

Roll A now ends with the outgoing shot of the
first dissolve and spacing is spliced onto this. The
incoming shot of the dissolve is spliced into Roll B,
the spacing having been trimmed back so that the two
shots are 'overlapped' by a pre-determined number of
frames — usually 16, 24, 32, 48 or 64 — depending on
the length of dissolve required.

Ensuing shots are spliced into Roll B until the next
dissolve is reached, whereupon the picture is switched
back to Roll A, and so on.

A further refinement of the A and B Roll system is
to employ what is known as 'chequer-board cutting',
whereby consecutive shots are spliced alternately into
Roll A and Roll B. In this way, every shot is joined to
spacing at either end and by making each splice so
that the picture overlaps into the spacing (and *not* the
other way around) splices are rendered completely
invisible in the finished prints.

Finally, it is worth noting that, should you require
multiple superimpositions, it is possible to extend the
A and B Roll system to include a C Roll, a D Roll and
so on.

Marking Up the Cutting Copy

In order to avoid the possibility of mistakes when
cutting the master, the cutting copy must be marked
up carefully with a chinagraph pencil to indicate the
positions and durations of dissolves and other effects.
Conventional signs are used for this purpose and these
are illustrated in the accompanying diagrams.

While working on the cutting copy, it is quite
possible that you will sometimes cut a shot too short
and then decide to extend it by splicing in a few
extra frames. Each of these 'unwanted' joins must also
be marked (by drawing two short parallel lines across
the splice) to make sure that they are not reproduced
in the master.

Shots that are to be linked by a dissolve in the
finished film will, of course, be cut to the mid-point
of the dissolve in the cutting copy. But the portions
that are trimmed away must be carefully preserved
and their length checked at the marking up stage.
The point about this, of course, is that it's no good
marking up a 48 frame dissolve unless you know for
sure that there are at least 24 'spare' frames available
from each shot to allow for the overlap.

Chapter Ten

CONTROLLING TIME AND SPACE

When the curtain goes up on a stage play, we can be fairly sure that the action we are about to witness will take place in real time and real space.

If the play calls for an actress to wash her hair or ice a cake, she will have to go through the whole process of doing these things before our eyes and they will take as long on stage as they would in real life. If a lapse in time is to be suggested, or if the characters are to be transferred to another location, this can only be accomplished by lowering the curtain or dimming the lights and the mechanics are so cumbersome that we are immediately aware of what is happening.

In a film, however, the situation is quite different. Thanks to the flexibility of the medium, the time and space elements are under the control of the film maker. He can decide moment by moment how long any given action is to run on the screen. Hair washing and cake icing, if they are merely incidental to the story, can be condensed into a few seconds and this can be done so unobstrusively that nobody in the audience will notice that anything is missing.

The same location can be made to represent many different places on the screen or, alternatively, the best features of many different locations can be combined to form one ideal and purely imaginary place.

Because a film consists of photographic images, we tend at first to think of it as a transcription of reality. But in fact it is nothing of the kind; reality only provides the raw material — the little snippets of real time and space that we record each time we press the camera button. What we do with this raw material is entirely up to us; we can use it to create a representation of reality or fantasy or what we will.

However, before we consider the more remote possibilities, let's think how we can save film and keep the audience awake by condensing time.

Life Without the Boring Bits

It has been said that art is like life with the boring bits left out and I suppose that to some extent we must all be instinctive artists. At any rate, when it comes to filming some tedious and repetitive action such as washing a car or painting the side of a house, few of us feel inclined to keep the camera running throughout the entire operation.

What we probably do is to shoot the beginning and the end of the action, just enough to tell the audience what has happened. The snag is, of course, that at the instant of transition from the first to the second shot, there is an obvious jump forward in time; the dirty car suddenly becomes clean or the side of the house suddenly gets covered in paint. The simple way to avoid this kind of jump cut is to insert a shot of some related subject (often an onlooker) so that the attention of the audience is momentarily diverted from the main action.

Fortunately, when we are watching a film we lose all sense of real time so that the inserted shot — known as a cut-away — can be much shorter than the unimportant or repetitive action which it replaces. Thus we can be made to believe that we have seen an entire football match in, say, ten minutes of screen time, providing that a dozen or so cut-aways of spectator reaction are inserted at strategic points.

Naturally, however, there are limits to credulity and making a single cut-away bridge *too* great a gap in time may invite derision. Jerry Lewis, indeed, does this intentionally by way of an 'in joke' in one of his comedies: a bell-boy (played by Lewis himself) is shown setting out two chairs in a huge auditorium, then after a brief cut-away, we are shown the auditorium again with row after row of chairs filling the entire floor space.

It is important, of course, that the cut-away scene

should be clearly related to the main action. Otherwise, there may be a danger of confusing the audience. I can remember being puzzled by one beginner's movie in which shots of empty landscapes cropped up from time to time for no apparent reason. When I questioned their significance, I was told with some dignity that these were cut-aways.

Cutting Away and Cutting In

Most subjects will suggest their own natural cut-aways but in case of difficulty — or for the sake of variety — it is worth remembering that cut-ins will serve the same purpose just as well, if not better. As the name suggests, a cut-away is taken with the camera turned away from the main subject while a cut-in is taken when the camera is moved in close so that just one detail of the main subject fills the screen. This concentration on detail again distracts the attention of the audience and allows them to believe that any action they didn't actually see took place outside the frame area.

The two alternative techniques are illustrated in the picture sequences showing a young man setting out some skittles. This whole action would take about two minutes of real time — not very long perhaps but long enough to be tedious on the screen. In the first example we show him starting to set out the skittles, cut away to a clearly related subject (the girl waiting to throw the ball) and then cut back to him as he finishes the job. Total screen time: about fifteen to twenty seconds.

Now look at the second example. We start with the same establishing shot, then cut-in to a close-up of the young man's face as he continues the action, and notice that in this shot we lose sight of the pattern of skittles on the paving stones. So when we cut back to show the whole scene we can show the pattern complete without revealing that part of the action has been omitted. Again two minutes of real time are condensed into less than half a minute of screen time.

The cut-in method is actually more subtle and more convincing. Because the camera never leaves the main subject, the audience will be forced to believe that they have actually witnessed the complete action — providing of course that the cuts are carefully made so that the young man's position does not change

obviously from the end of one shot to the beginning of the next.

To make a perfectly matched cut on action (I shall be dealing with the technique in detail later) is not easy unless you are able to control and direct the action. So when you are filming actual events or trying to do your editing in the camera, it is obviously safer to rely on the more elementary cut-away method.

Stretching the Action

While the need to condense time is a constant preoccupation of the film maker, the need to expand it is rare. Nevertheless there may well be times when you want to give the audience a chance to examine in detail some process or event that happens very quickly in real life — too quickly, perhaps, for the human eye and brain to apprehend.

Action can be stretched mechanically, as we know, by slow-motion photography and this technique is often used in instructional films to observe and analyse the movements of athletes, or the workings of high-speed machinery. But a whole episode can be expanded in a much more subtle way — and without any apparent loss of pace — by means of cut-aways and cut-ins.

The classic example of this, I suppose, is the famous Odessa Steps sequence from *Battleship Potemkin.* Here Eisenstein was reconstructing an historical event — the massacre of civilian demonstrators by a contingent of White Russian soldiers. But a straight reconstruction would not have served his dramatic purpose. The action would have been over too quickly to make anything but a momentary impact and indeed so much would have happened in so short a time that the audience would have seen nothing clearly.

What he did, therefore, was to establish the scene as a whole and then break it down into its component parts, using a series of cut-ins to pinpoint individual tragedies — bearing in mind that what happens to individual people is always more emotionally stirring than what happens to a crowd. Actions that were simultaneous in real life were thus shown on the screen one after the other and the time element was expanded. Yet the cutting from one shot to another was so rapid that the feeling of pace and violence was sustained throughout.

*CUTTING AWAY is the technique
most commonly used to condense
time, and thus avoid boring the
audience by showing repetitive and
unimportant action in full. Here,
for example, we start with a shot
of the young man beginning to set
up the skittles and hold this just
long enough for the audience to
see what is going on. Then we cut
away to a clearly related subject —
the shot of the girl waiting to bowl
her ball at the skittles. Lastly we
cut back to show the young man
setting up the last skittle and
completing the pattern. Thus two
minutes or so of real time are
condensed into about fifteen
seconds of screen time without
letting the audience know that
anything has been omitted.*

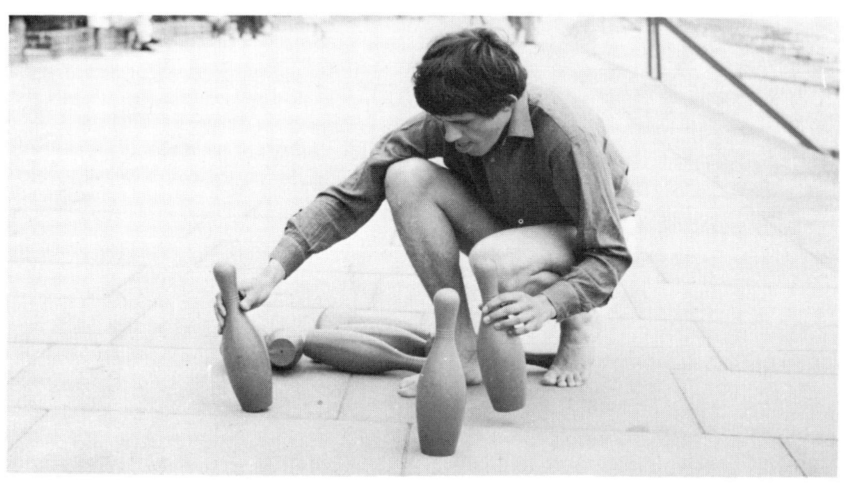

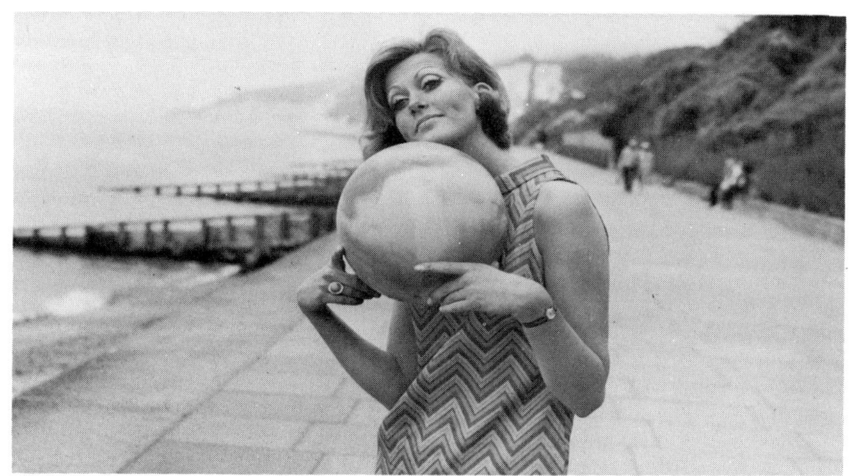

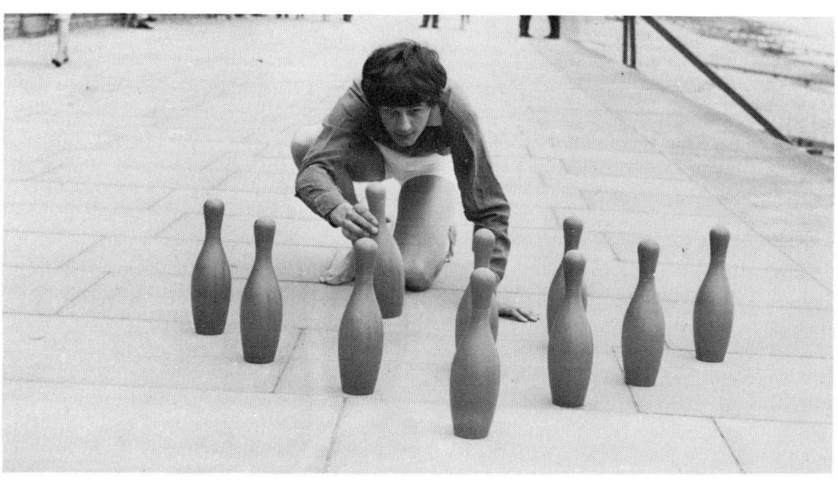

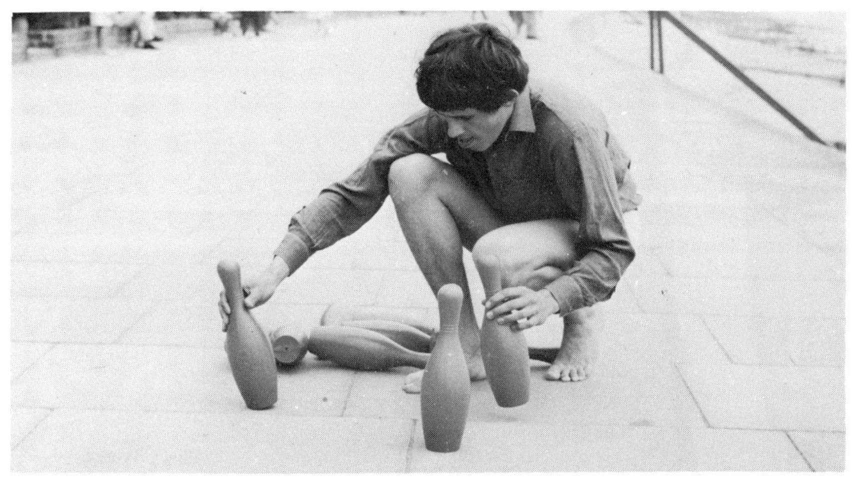

CUTTING IN is an alternative and
perhaps rather more subtle method
of condensing time. Here we start
with the same establishing shot of
the young man beginning to set up
his skittles, then cut in to a low-
angle closeup of him continuing
the action, then back to a medium
shot as he completes the pattern.
The low angle of the closeup
temporarily prevents the
audience from seeing how many
skittles have been set up — and it's
a safe bet that they won't keep
count. So, providing that the
position of the actor is carefully
'matched' from the end of one
shot to the beginning of the next,
the audience will believe that
they have witnessed the entire
action. Yet real time will again
have been converted into much
briefer screen time.

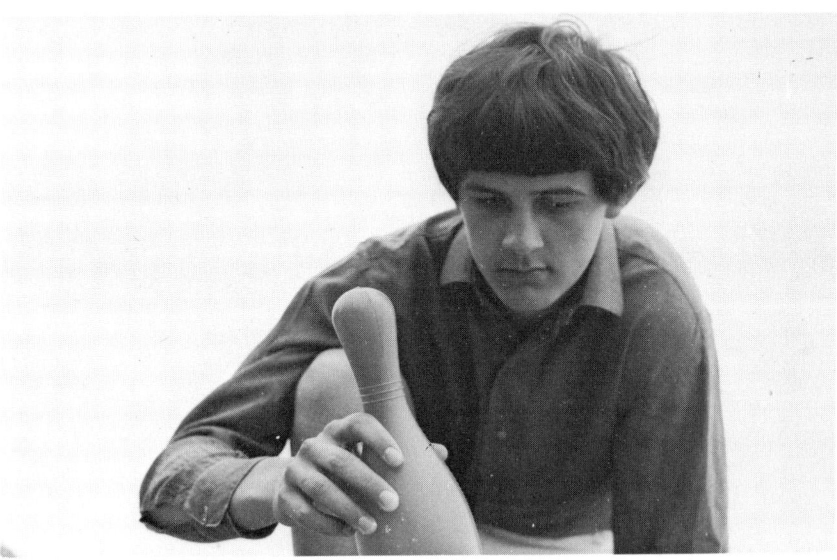

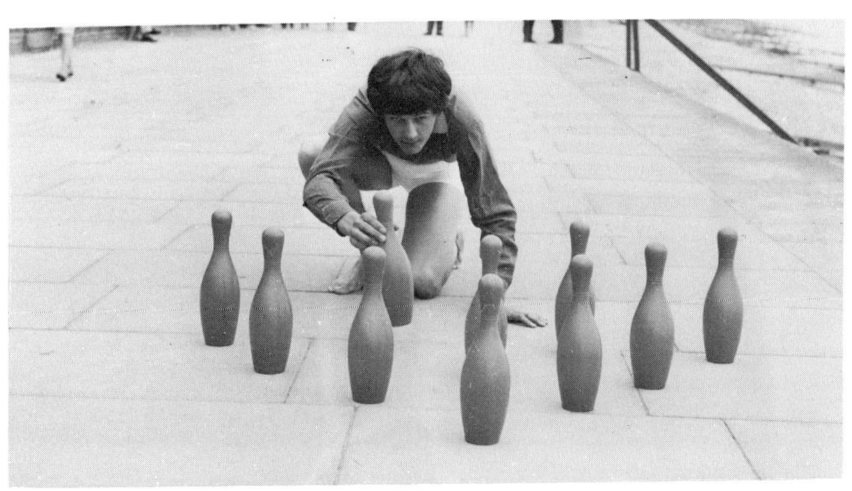

EXPANDING TIME. *The cut-away technique may be used to expand as well as to condense time. This may be done in order to give the audience a chance to apprehend in detail some very swift series of actions that would be confusing in real life. Alternatively, it may be done, as here, simply to prolong a moment of suspense and joy. All that happens is that the girl rolls the ball and knocks over the skittles: two or three seconds of real time. If portrayed in one shot, it would all be over too quickly to mean anything. But we have stretched it by showing simultaneous parts of the action one after the other. 1. The ball leaves the girl's hands. 2. It rolls towards the skittles. 3. The girl 'wills' it to hit the skittles. 4. The moment of impact. 5. The girl's delighted reaction. 6. The fallen skittles. All these shots would, of course, be cut quite short so that, although the incident is actually prolonged, the impression of pace would be sustained.*

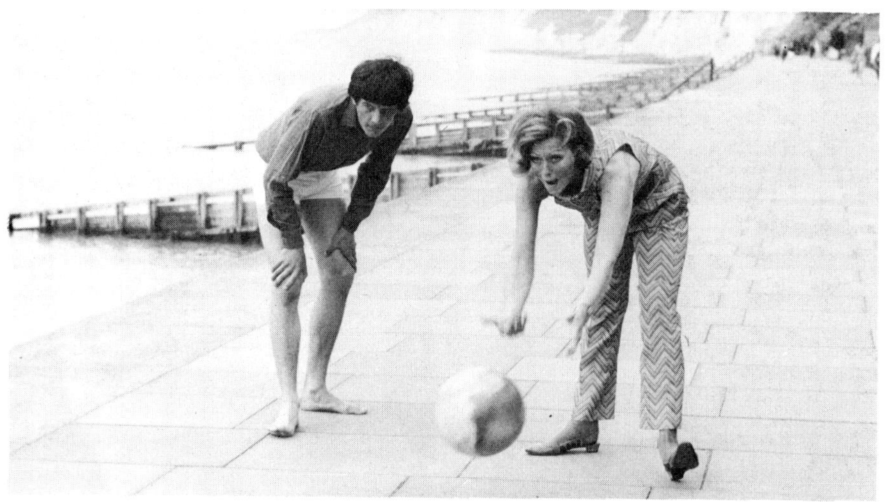

1

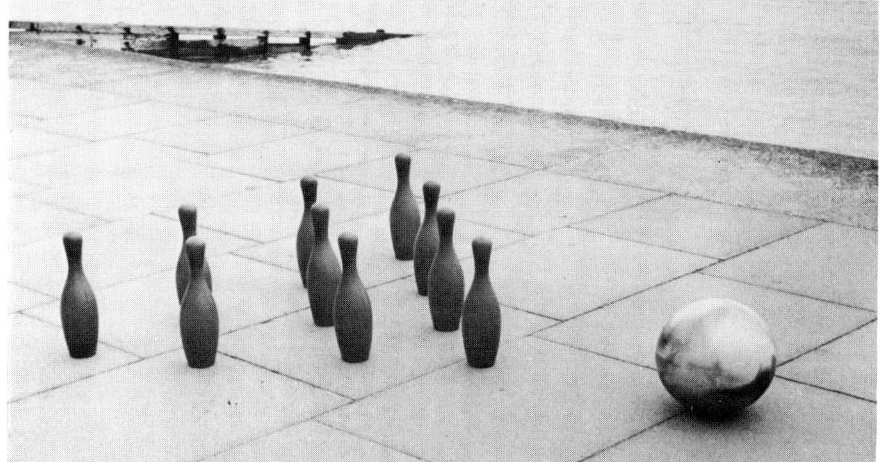

2

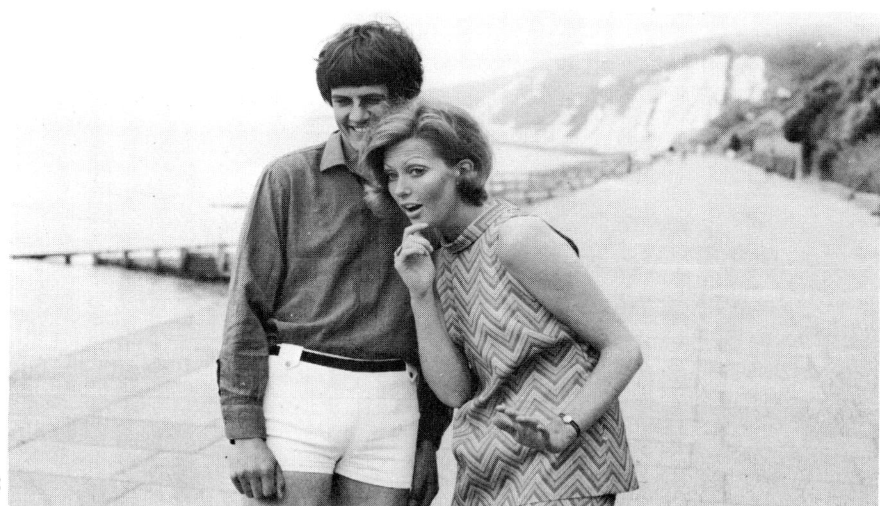

3

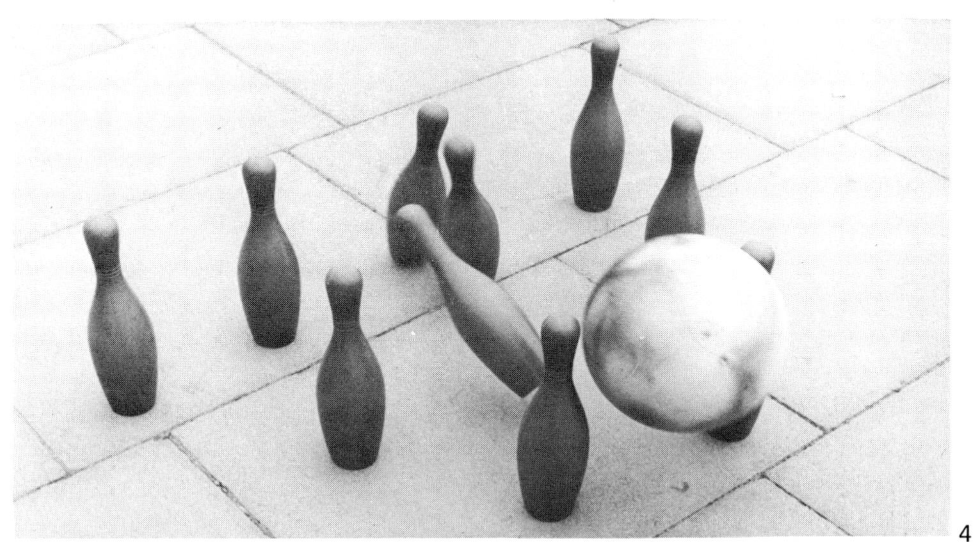

4

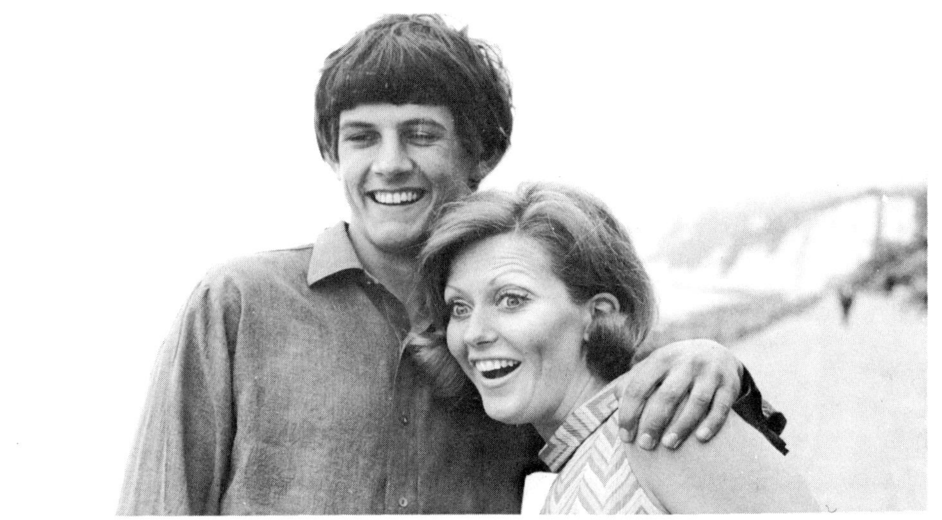

5

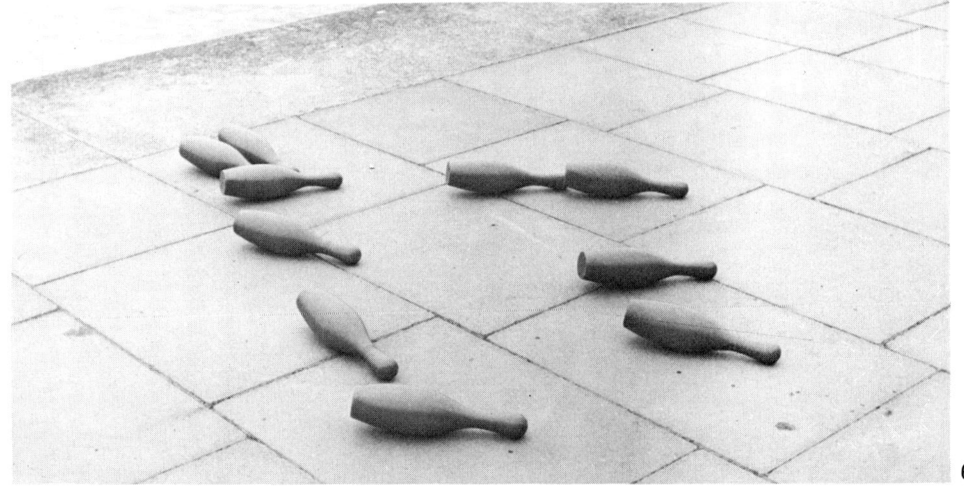

6

My third picture sequence shows how the same principle might be applied to a simple holiday film situation. Here the girl rolls the ball at the skittles, scores a direct hit and reacts with pleasure as they tumble over. In real life this would happen in about two or three seconds and if the complete action were covered in one shot we wouldn't be able to take it all in. But by using separate shots of the skittles falling and the facial expressions of the girl and her boy friend, we can be sure that both will register clearly and at the same time prolong the moment of joy without seeming to drag it out.

Conquest of Space

In film making practically anything is possible once we can free ourselves from the confines of actuality and realise the immense freedom that the medium gives us.

This is surprisingly difficult to do. After twenty years of movie making, I still find myself wrestling with problems that would disappear in a flash if only I could bring myself to think in purely filmic terms, rather than in terms of concrete reality.

Quite recently I wanted to film a short sequence in which two characters recline in deck chairs beside a swimming pool with a private house in background. After a bit of casual by-play they were to get up and dive into the pool.

Not being the owner of a private pool, I spent several weeks combing the district for a suitably opulent location that could be 'borrowed' for the occasion. But no luck. The private pools were either badly placed in relation to the houses or their owners proved inhospitable.

So I was forced to think again and realised at once that the solution was to make two locations serve as one by a simple bit of editing. The man and girl were filmed in their deck chairs on my own front lawn with the house in background. The girl got up, threw off her bathing wrap and hopped out of picture left. This cut to a reverse angle shot taken at a public swimming pool (early in the morning to avoid crowds) in which the girl simply hopped into picture right and plunged into the water.

By trimming the ends of the two shots, the two hops were converted into one continuous movement and it is now virtually impossible for an audience watching the picture *not* to believe that the girl jumped straight from the lawn into the pool.

A movement link of this kind is one way to condense space and make up your own geography. An even easier way is to exploit the old 'look and see' rule. Remember that if one shot shows a character looking out of the picture, the audience will automatically assume that the next shot shows what he or she is looking at. Thus you could take a shot in, say, Kensington Gardens of a girl looking in an upward direction, follow this with a shot of the Eiffel Tower and, unless there were some clearly recognisable landmark in the background of the first shot, the audience would certainly accept that the girl was in Paris.

On screen the world is what we make of it. Given a splicer, a bottle of film cement and a little imagination, we become the masters of time and space.

Chapter Eleven

CUTTING ON ACTION

As we already know, the classic way to break down any incident into a series of shots is to imagine the camera lens to be the eye of an observer watching the action in real life.

In Chapter Three we applied this theory to Lumier's *Watering the Gardener* and discovered that the episode which was originally filmed in one continuous shot, could be made more vivid by frequent changes of camera viewpoint. The observer sees the boy's foot pressing on the hosepipe (we take a shot). The observer shifts his glance to the other end of the hose-pipe where the jet of water dwindles and the gardener is puzzled (we take another shot). The observer glances back at the boy to find out what he will do next (we take another shot). And so on.

It so happens that in this particular episode there is a very simple chain of cause and effect, linking one shot to the next. Each part of the action arouses the observer's curiosity and compels him to glance in a different direction — to the left or to the right, up or down. Hence at every cut there is a complete change of subject matter.

Not every episode, of course, can be broken down in the same way. Very often, instead of turning his head, the observer will be compelled to scrutinise more closely some detail of the scene that he is already watching. By the same token as before, this means that we must move the camera lens closer to the subject — or switch to a lens of longer focal length.

In other words, instead of cutting away, we must cut in — and this is a little more difficult because it involves the risk of a jump cut.

Let's suppose, for example, that the observer is watching a girl walking through the park and sitting down on a bench. As she sits down, he notices that she is an attractive girl and naturally he wants to look at her more closely. This is our cue to cut from medium long shot to, say, medium close-up.

On screen the transition from one shot to the next will be instantaneous but, in fact, there is bound to be an interval of a few seconds at least while we move the camera physically or change lenses or perhaps just alter the zoom setting. And during this brief interval anything may happen to the subject. The girl may turn her head or raise a hand to pat her hair. More likely, a passer-by who was not present in the first shot may suddenly appear behind her or one who was present may suddenly disappear.

Unless we take measures to counter them, any one of these small discrepancies will show on the screen as a jump cut and the audience — however non-technically minded they may be — will notice the visual disturbance and be dimly aware that something has gone wrong.

What can be done about it? The most obvious solution, I suppose, is to ask the person or persons in the scene to 'freeze' at the end of the first shot and remain frozen until we are ready to start taking the second. But this is seldom practical and it tends to produce self-conscious behaviour unless you are dealing with trained actors.

Changing the Angle

A much safer and less irksome method is to remember to change the camera angle when you change the distance. In other words, when you move the camera in for a closer shot, don't take it straight in but move it slightly to one side or up or down. This will alter the composition of the picture so that any slight change of posture will almost certainly pass unnoticed. You will get the idea if you study the pictures of the couple sharing an umbrella on pages 74 and 75.

However, a word of warning is in order here. Don't change the angle so drastically that you bring a completely new and unrecognisable background into view. This can be as visually disturbing as a jump cut and may make the audience feel temporarily 'lost'.

The best technique of all — and this should always be combined with an angle change — is to cut on action. In other words, shoot a second or two of 'overlapping' action from both camera viewpoints so

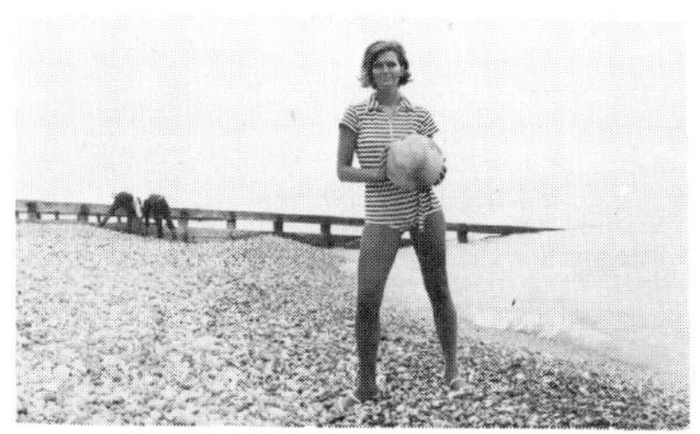

OVERLAPPING ACTION from the end of one shot to the beginning of the next is the best way to ensure a smooth cut on action. Here, for example, the long shot of the girl ends with her throwing the beach ball. So, having set up the camera for the medium closeup, we asked her to start by repeating the same action. This gives a choice of cutting points at the editing stage. By running the two shots in a viewer (or actually examining them side by side if you are working on 16 mm) it is possible to locate a frame in each where the position of the subject matches precisely — the ideal place to cut and splice. In this case the portion of the long shot above the dotted line would be joined to the portion of the medium closeup below the dotted line, so that on the screen the action would flow on continuously. Needless to say, if these were actual movie shots there would be many more intermediate frames than we can show here.

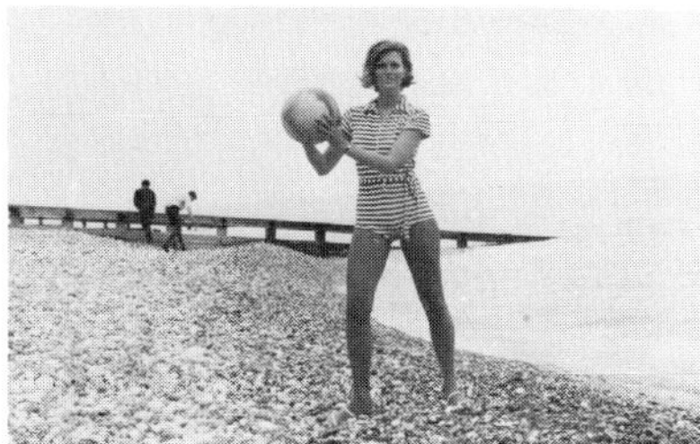

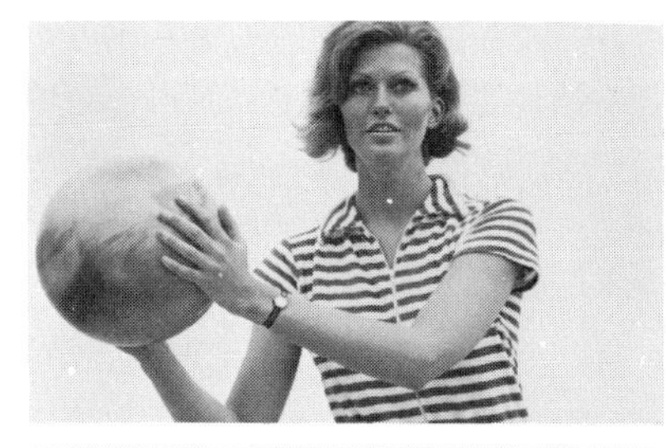

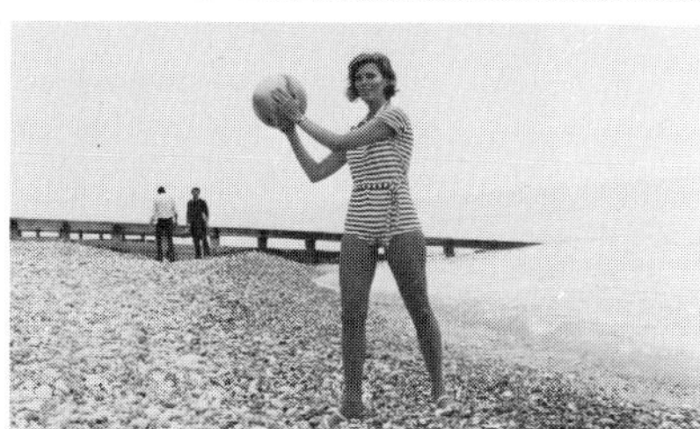

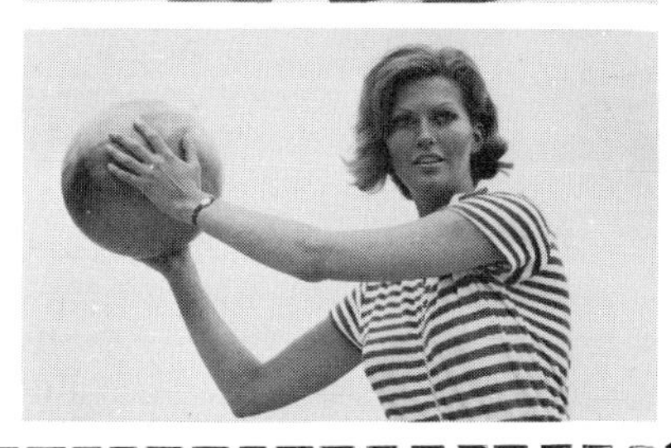

◄ CUTTING POINT

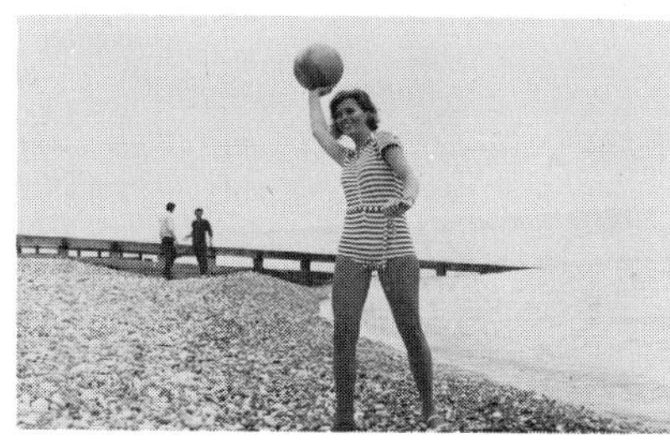

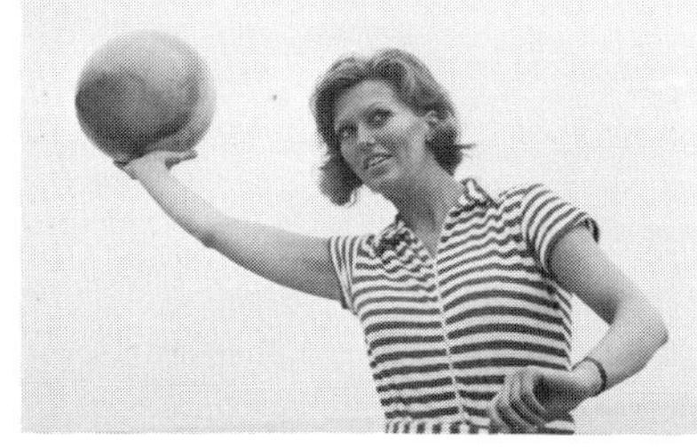

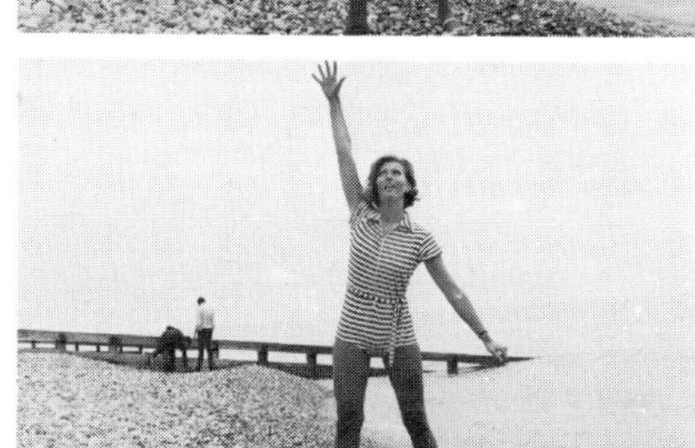

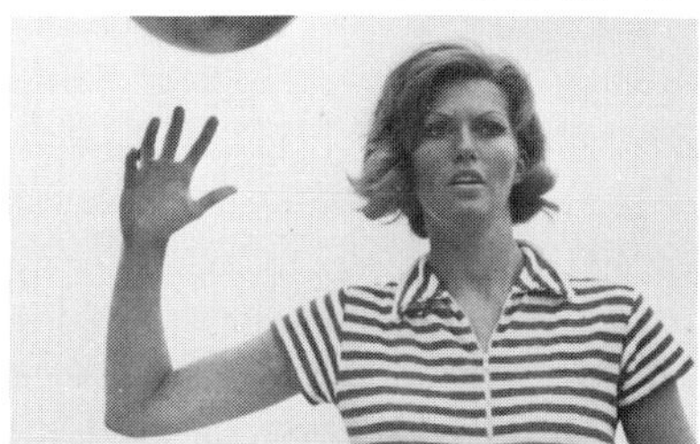

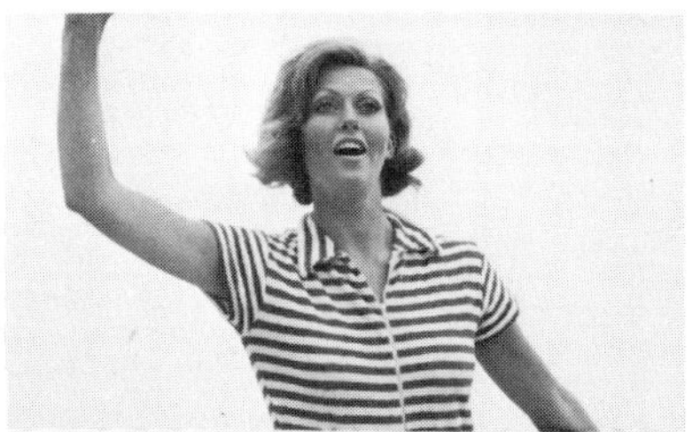

that you can make your cut during a definite movement which will start in one shot and continue into
the next.

Admittedly, this calls for a certain amount of
advance planning. It usually means that you have to
ask the people in the scene to repeat part of the
action from the end of one shot at the beginning of
the next but this is far less difficult than 'freezing'
and the results certainly justify the means as we shall
see presently.

Meanwhile, it is worth noting that even when the
subject of the film is not under your control, you can
still shoot material that will cut together on action by
taking advantage of ritual movements, such as bowling
in cricket or serving in tennis, that are repeated at
frequent intervals.

Invisible Cuts

Now let's pause for a moment to consider the special
advantages of cutting on action. As we know, movement on screen is so arresting that it overrides all
other considerations; providing the movement flows
naturally from shot to shot, the audience will follow
this and have no chance to register any minor discrepancies at the cutting points.

We can go further than this and say that when a
cut occurs during movement, the cut itself is far less
noticeable than it would be if the subject were static.
And, of course, the real hallmark of good cutting —
as of any other technique — is unobtrusiveness. Only
the ham actor draws attention to the fact that he is
acting, and similarly when every cut in a film hits the
audience between the eyes, it is a sign of ham direction
or ham editing or both.

To be sure there are times when a shock cut is
dramatically justified but these rare, spinechilling
moments will be all the more effective if they are used
sparingly and if the cuts in between glide past
unnoticed. Professional film makers are naturally well
aware of this and, except when cut-aways are needed
or when shock cuts are intended, arrange for most of
their cuts to take place on action.

The result is that the ordinary filmgoer simply
absorbs the story and is blissfully unaware of the fact
that his thoughts are being guided and re-directed by
constant changes of camera viewpoint; of the five

hundred or so cuts in an average feature film, he probably will not notice more than a dozen. The rest
will be virtually invisible to him.

As a matter of fact, it is quite a useful exercise when
visiting the cinema, to sit through the opening
sequence of a film for a second time making a mental
note of each cut and analysing the story-telling purpose
of each new camera viewpoint. Even better, if you can
get hold of an 8 mm or 16 mm print of a well-made
film, run it through on an animated viewer at home
and analyse the cuts; you'll need to keep your wits
about you not to miss any of them.

Cutting in Camera

As I have mentioned before the essential craft of film
making is editing and by 'editing' I mean the arrangement of a series of shots in a meaningful order. In
this sense, of course, editing need not involve the
physical act of cutting and splicing film at all.

Indeed, it is possible to edit an entire film in the
camera. And when you are working on an 8 mm
original that has to be used for projection, I must
admit that there is some practical advantage in keeping the number of splices to a minimum. For even a
well made splice tends to make an audible 'click' as it
passes through the projector gate.

Personally, I have only once attempted to cut a
film 'in camera' and that was a short demonstration
piece about two children in a playground which I did
for the B.B.C. Television series, *Making Home Movies*.
At that stage in the series we had not demonstrated
splicing so the producer insisted, quite rightly, that
we should play fair with the viewers by showing the
film exactly as shot.

This meant filming in sequence and judging just
the right moment to start and stop the camera for
each shot. It proved easy enough so long as I was using
cut-aways and relatively simple when I allowed one of
the children to go out of frame at the end of a shot
and come in at the start of the next one. Cuts on
action, however, were decidedly more tricky. Being
apprehensive, I only attempted three and only one of
them turned out just as I intended; the other two
could certainly have been improved by trimming away
the few frames of 'overlapping' movement.

No doubt, with practice it would be possible to
improve on this performance but I doubt whether the

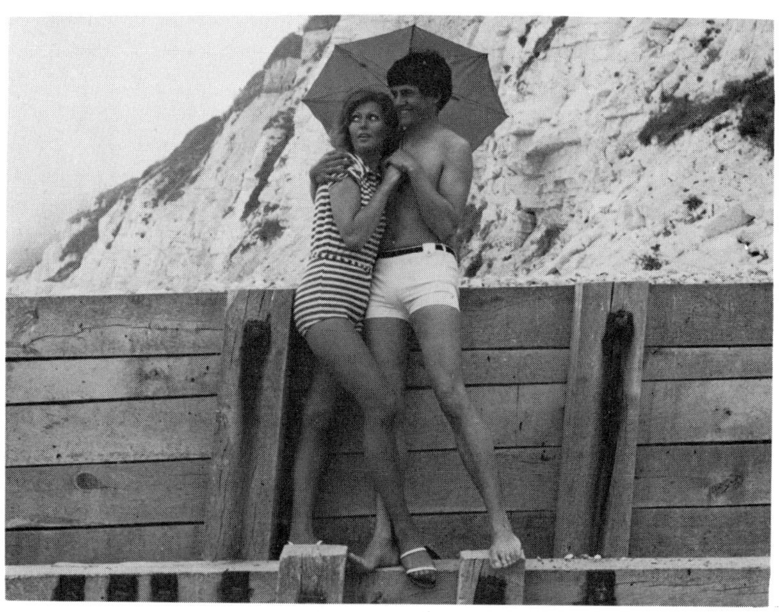

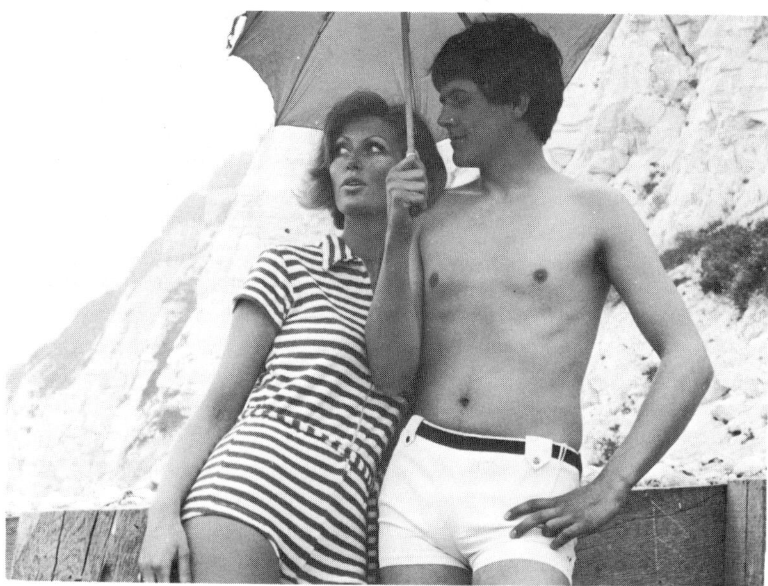

MOVING STRAIGHT IN when you are cutting to a closer shot will immediately reveal any change in the position of the characters and — unless you are working with trained actors — such changes are always liable to take place while you are shifting the camera. Here, for example, it is obvious that the young man has switched the umbrella from one hand to the other while the girl's arm has fallen to her side in the closer shot. These discrepancies would show as a jarring 'jump cut' on the screen.

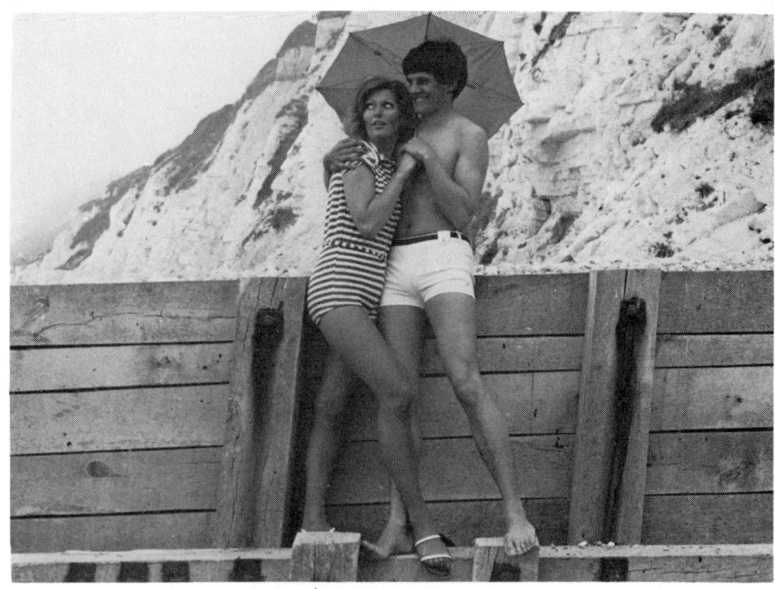

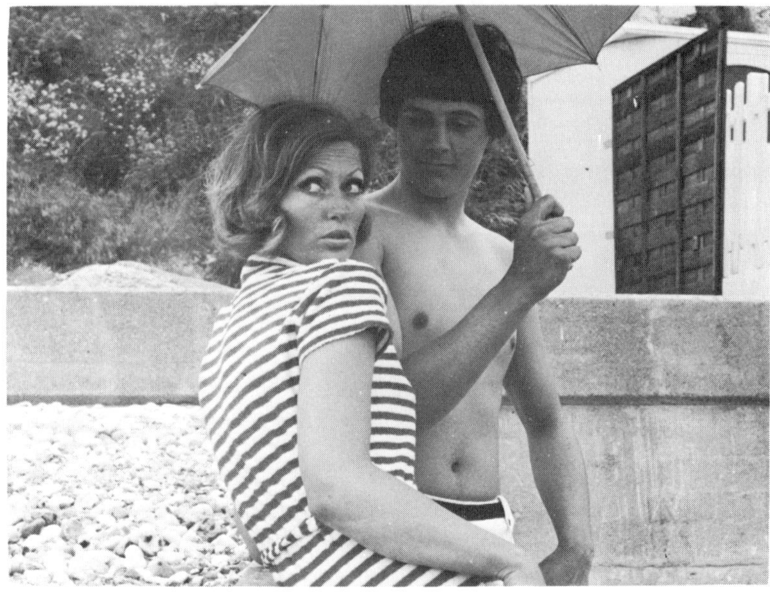

CHANGING THE ANGLE of the camera when you move in for a closer shot will not eliminate the possibility of a jump cut but it will provide a useful degree of 'camouflage'. Here the positions of the young man and the girl have changed just as much as in the first example, but the fact that we are looking at them from a different angle makes comparison more difficult and distracts attention from the 'jump'. Another good idea — impossible to illustrate with stills — is to start the incoming shot with a sudden movement.

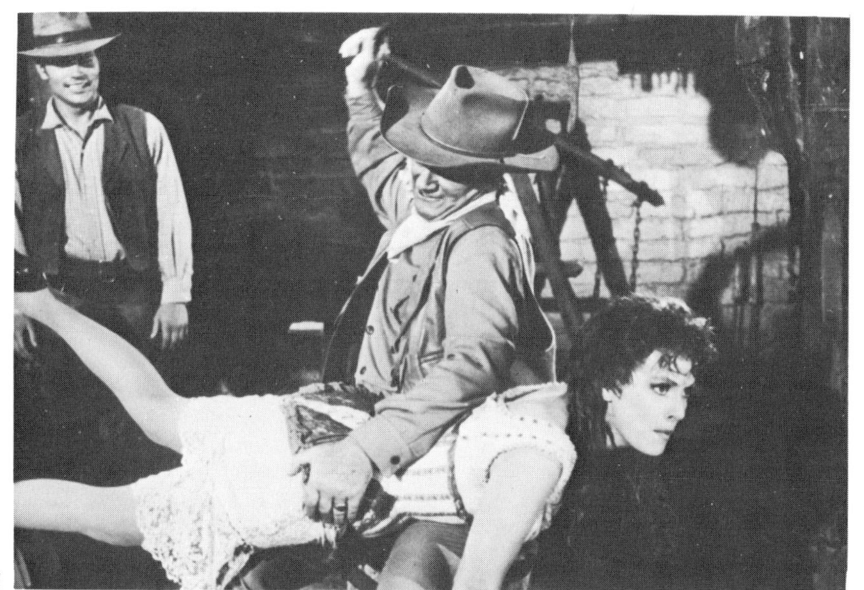

1

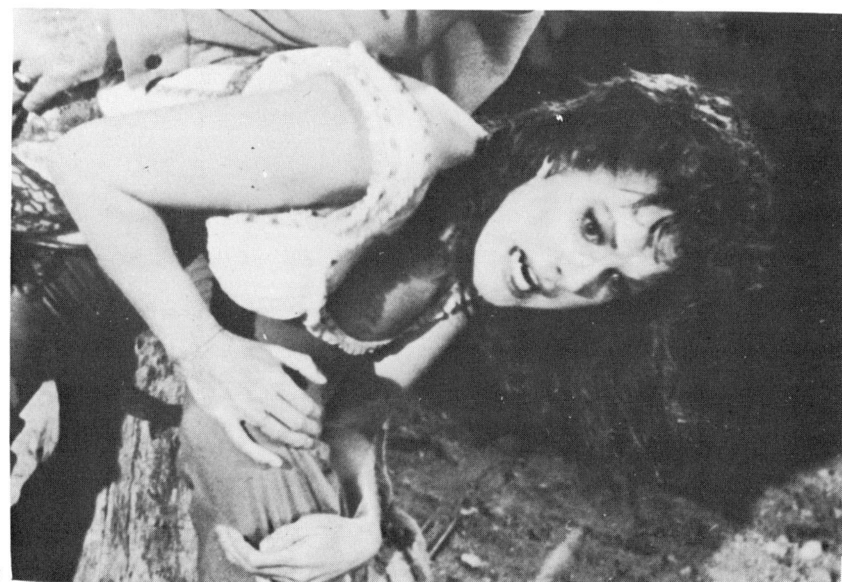

3

VIOLENCE CAN BE SIMULATED without anyone getting
hurt by filming parts of the action separately and then cutting
them together so that they appear to be continuous on the
screen. Here, for example, Shot 1 establishes that the lady is
about to be spanked, but by cutting to closeup (Shot 2) when
the man's arm is half way down, the actual moment of contact
is avoided. With the lady out of harm's way, the spanking
action can now continue in Shot 2. A cut to another closeup,
showing the victim's anguished reaction (Shot 3), adds to the

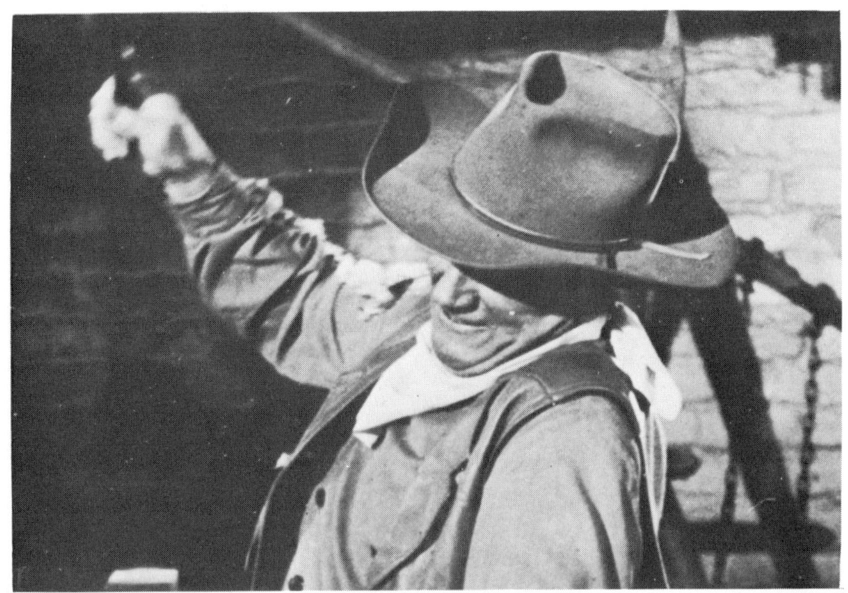

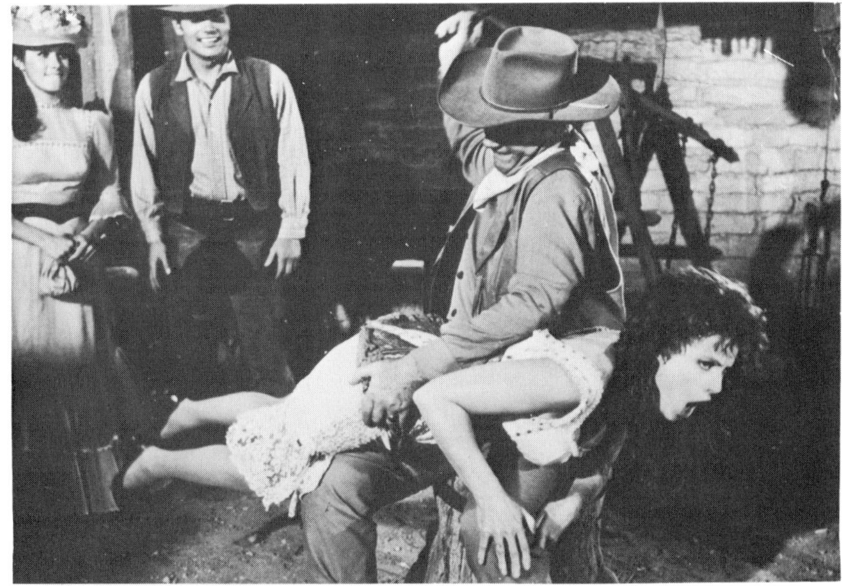

effect while allowing the audience to imagine that the action is still going on outside the frame area. Finally, the illusion is completed by cutting back to a re-establishing shot of the whole scene (Shot 4) when the man's arm is travelling up. The same technique, often elaborated, is used in fight sequences and it is worth noting that a fight filmed in separate fragments and then cut together on action is always much more convincing than one in a live television production which has to be shot continuously. (Stills from McClintock *with John Wayne and Maureen O'Hara.)*

small advantage of avoiding a splice would really justify the effort and anxiety involved. An effective cut on action depends on absolute precision and this can only be achieved by shooting overlapping footage. This gives you the chance to run the two shots backwards and forwards on your animated viewer and decide at leisure the best possible cutting point.

Movement Across the Splice

Given precision, movement across the splice is so compelling that it can even hold together scenes taken in different locations — a fact that was ably exploited in the opening sequence of *On the Town* in which three sailors dance literally all over New York. Here similar dance steps, leaps and gyrations were performed by the actors in different parts of the city and then the various shots were cut together on action so that the dance appears to be continuous while the backgrounds change as if by magic.

An early experimental film in which this idea was illustrated is the late Maya Deren's *Study in Choreography for Camera* which you can hire on 8 mm or 16 mm from the British Film Institute Library at 42/43 Lower Marsh, London S.W.1. The technique obviously has many applications outside the dance field.

A variation on the same theme, also explored by Miss Deren, is to cut together repetitions of the same movement so that they appear as one. For example, she has a shot of a dancer leaping into the air against a neutral sky background. Before he starts to descend she cuts to a second closer shot of his legs travelling horizontally across frame against a similar sky background. Again the shot is cut before he starts to descend and is followed by a third longer shot in which he starts travelling horizontally and finally comes down to earth. Three actual leaps are thus combined into one gigantic one beyond the limit of human prowess.

Whether your aim is realism or fantasy, drama or slapstick, you will find that the technique of cutting on action, once mastered, yields the most exciting results. And perhaps the best thing about it, from an amateur point of view, is that it involves no special apparatus and costs nothing except a little thought and imagination.

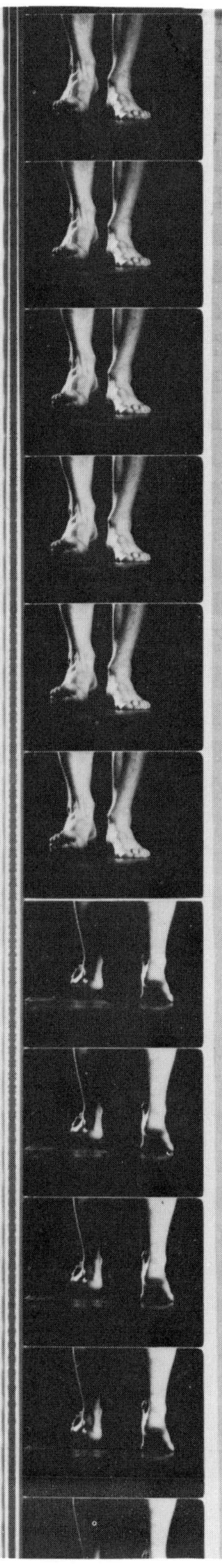

CUT THAT DECEIVES THE EYE. Fundamentally, film editing is the craft of creating an illusion. What looks right and convincing on the screen is often wrong in a literal sense and vice versa. The point is made graphically in this clip from The Body *which shows a cut from a direct front view to a direct rear view of a man's walking feet. On the screen this appears to be a perfectly normal cut on action, but by examining the still frames reproduced here, you can see that it is nothing of the kind. In fact, the editor, Alan Cumner-Price, has matched the position of the man's left foot in the outgoing shot to that of his right foot in the incoming shot — the reason being that both appear in the right hand side of the frame. If he had made a literally correct cut, the action would have appeared to 'jump' from one side of the screen to the other and would have looked wrong.*

Chapter Twelve

THE HUMAN ELEMENT

Get plenty of people in front of your lens and then get close to them!

This is about the crudest and yet the most effective piece of advice that one can offer to any budding movie maker. For no film with people in it can ever be completely tedious, however bad the photography or incompetent the cutting. Conversely, a film *without* people in it needs to have some very special qualities to compensate for the lack of that basic box-office ingredient — human interest.

It was no accident that the very first close-up ever flashed on to a screen was a shot of a human face. Indeed it is probable that the popularity of the cinema, and television too for that matter, rests very largely on the fact that it enables us to observe our fellow men (and women) closely, secure in the knowledge that they can't see us.

We have all been told as children that it is rude to stare but we want to stare and in the cinema we can do it to our hearts's content. Before the movie camera was invented this real human need was catered for to some extent by the live theatre but films added immensely to the piquancy of the staring game in two important ways.

Firstly they were more intimate, the magnification of the image making it possible for us to detect the smallest gesture, the most tentative change of expression. Secondly they had a much broader range; they could bring before us not only actors who are trained to exhibit themselves to the public gaze but also 'natural types' who can do no more than be themselves and are that much more defenceless; they could show us not only simulated emotion but the raw commodity itself.

The live theatre can only operate with trained actors because responsibility for the continuity of the performance rests with them; once the curtain goes up they are on their own. But the people in a film need not be conscious performers at all; as we have already discovered, the film maker builds his continuity from fragments of action recorded at different times and places which may or may not have been related in fact.

When a shot of a child's laughing face is joined to a shot of a monkey in a cage, the audience will believe that the child is laughing at the monkey but he may have been laughing at something quite different without being aware for one moment how his expression was to be fitted into the context of the film.

I think it is true to say that the most gripping and memorable moments in the cinema are provided on the one hand by actors who are so good at their job that they achieve an impression of absolute sincerity and on the other hand, by natural types who are so absorbed in the business of living that they actually are sincere. Unfortunately, most of the people we have to deal with in amateur film making fall somewhere between these two extremes. They are not completely sophisticated, nor yet completely unsophisticated and all are to some extent inhibited by the presence of the camera.

Nevertheless, for practical purposes, it is convenient to divide them into these two broad categories: actors and natural types. The actor, we shall assume, is a conscious callaborator; he knows what the film is all about and understands what contribution he is supposed to make to it; he is prepared to accept the discipline of rehearsals and to project himself into imaginary situations. The natural type is simply someone who will allow his normal appearance and behaviour to be recorded by the camera and is utterly unconcerned with the effect that this will produce on the audience.

Finding Actors

The practical advantage of using actors — even poor ones — is that you can control them and get more-or-less predictable results with a minimum of film wastage. So when you are making a film with some kind of story line, involving sustained characterisations, it is expedient if nothing more to use actors in the main parts.

The question is: where to find them? People with

acting ambitions seldom attach themselves to cine clubs. They are much more likely to join amateur drama groups where they can enjoy the satisfaction of playing a part straight through from start to finish and, what is more, of feeling the direct response of an audience to their efforts. Nevertheless, given the chance to see themselves on the screen, they will probably jump at it all too willingly.

Recruiting talent from the local stage can, of course, be rewarding. It worked very well, for example, in the case of Dover Film Society's *Ancient Liberties* and High Wycombe's *The Stray* not to mention Peter Watkins' *The Forgotten Faces.* But if you expect a dramatic society to provide you with a team of fully-fledged film actors able to adapt themselves to any role you have dreamed up beforehand, you will be in for a nasty shock.

The only advantage that you can reasonably expect from a stage actor, as opposed to any chance acquaintance, is that he will be keen to succeed and possibly rather well endowed with self-confidence. On the debit side, you will find that he has acquired the habit of exaggerating his gestures and reactions so that they can be clearly seen by people sitting in the back row of the auditorium and you will have the job of convincing him that this kind of magnification is not needed when the camera is only a few feet away.

Deep down, the craft of acting — of thinking oneself into the mind of a character — is the same, whatever the medium. But the surface techniques of stage and screen are very different and the novice actor, who only knows the surface techniques, is inclined to cling to them tenaciously.

On balance, therefore, I would not set great store by stage experience. Given the choice between a man who looked right for the part and one with a theatre background, I would go for the looks every time. In most films we are only given a few minutes in which to get to know the people on the screen and in that short time appearances are bound to count for a very great deal.

Fortunately, most people can be made to act, or appear to act in a film, with careful direction and editing. But there are the exceptions who just seem to be allergic to the camera and turn to ice when confronted with a lens. In ordinary conversation they may appear to be quite sure of themselves and often they fail to recognise their own weakness. So to avoid embarassment it is always sensible to arrange some kind of dummy run — call it a camera test if you like — before inviting an untried newcomer to take part in one of your movies.

Handling Actors

Much of the action in any film is routine stuff — walking from point A to point B, sitting down, standing up, opening a door, taking a drink and so on. Thus much of a film maker's time is spent in persuading his actors to do consciously and deliberately the kind of things that they do every day without thinking about them. Which is not as simple as it might seem.

Even the simplest actions must be performed in a neat and disciplined way if they are to register clearly on the screen and yet they must not appear stilted. For a start they must be fitted into the rectangular frame of the viewfinder. Next each one must be isolated and clear-cut, rather than slurred together as actions tend to be in real life. Finally, despite these artificialities, they must be performed with apparent ease.

Let's suppose that you were going to shoot the following scene:

M.S. Camera pans with Bill as he walks through the park. He stops at a bench, sits down and picks up a newspaper that is lying on the seat. After studying a paragraph in the paper (Insert C.U. of weather forecast in newspaper, indicating thunderstorms) he looks up at the sky.

It looks straightforward enough on paper but a rehearsal will inevitably reveal several problems — not least that of co-ordination between actor and cameraman. So let's tackle this mechanical side of the business first. The cameraman has to pan with Bill and then stop panning as he stops by the bench. There is a natural tendency here to pan too far and then come back a little to adjust the framing which always looks ragged and amateurish. The actor can help, however, by slowing down a little before he stops and this will permit the camera to come to rest smoothly. Again when Bill sits on the bench the cameraman will want to tilt down with him for the sake of a more pleasing composition and this movement will appear more polished if the actor lowers himself gradually rather than suddenly flopping.

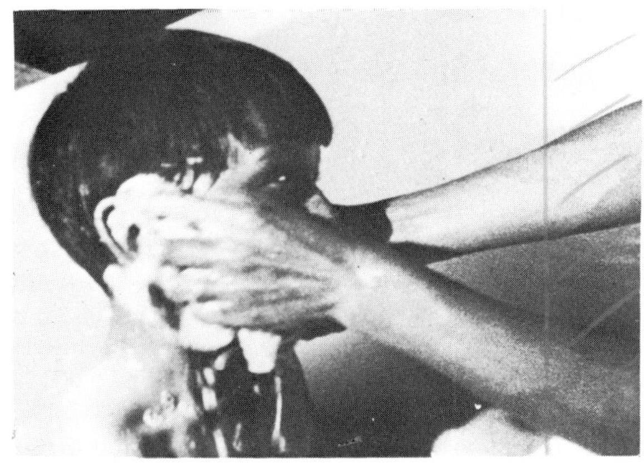

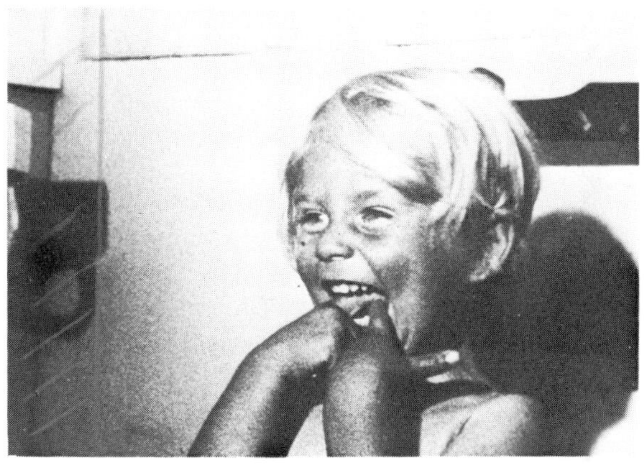

Even when there is no camera movement in a scene, the cameraman's requirements can't be ignored. In close shots, for example, movement is obviously very restricted. Simply by shifting his weight from one foot to another, an actor may hide the face of someone else in the background or find that half his own face is cut off by the edge of the frame. When there is movement towards camera, focus may be critical and one step too many will produce a blurred image on the screen.

You can often help an actor to arrive at his correct position by providing 'anchorage' — arranging furniture, for example, so that he finishes his walk with his leg touching the corner of a table or the arm of a chair. If that is impossible, you may resort to chalk marks on the ground or strips of adhesive tape on the floor.

All this, of course, is mainly common sense and one or two rehearsals will ensure that the scene works mechanically. The trouble then is that it often looks mechanical and your next task is to restore to your actors the appearance of naturalness that you have carefully drilled out of them.

This is mainly a matter of getting them to think of the particular scene in hand in relation to its story context and, if necessary, running through the action in a series of 'thought stages'. Bill's way of walking through the park, for example, will obviously be conditioned by what has gone before and the content of the previous scene in which perhaps, he had a quarrel with his girl friend and must be in his mind as he walks. Without the thought the scene will have no positive edge.

It is no good the actor thinking: 'Now I have to walk to the bench. Now I pause. Now I sit down. Now

I look at the newspaper. That must be long enough. Now I look at the sky'. The result, at best, will be negative and characterless. Rather he must try to think: 'I'm just about ready for a sit down. Ah! there's a paper; perhaps that'll take my mind off things. Blimey thunderstorms — that's all I need'. If he can do this, his movements will resemble those of a normal human being and he will begin to contribute something positive to the film.

Actors, of course, differ in the way they take direction. Some like to be guided along and given a thought appropriate to each action while others prefer to work things out for themselves. The latter need to be treated gently and given a fair chance to show what they can do before you make alternative suggestions. What they offer may not match your conception but there is just the chance that it might be an improvement!

Handling Natural Types

The actor's performance emerges out of conflict between opposing forces: on the one hand there is the need to perform his actions in a controlled and artificial way so that they may be effectively recorded by the camera and, on the other hand, there is the need to make them appear natural. But where natural types are concerned there must be no such conflict and therefore the method of handling them is entirely different.

As soon as the natural type becomes aware of technical restraint he loses his biggest asset — spontaiety. So, instead of arranging the action to suit pre-determined camera positions and camera movements, you have to provoke the action and then depend on agile camerawork to cover it as best you can. What you lose in polish and clarity, you can hope to gain in warmth and realism.

As an elementary example of this catch-as-catch-can technique, perhaps I may refer again to my own experience with three small children and a dog in *Good Clean Fun.* Although I went to the trouble of preparing a detailed shooting script, this was more honoured in the breach than the observance. I soon found the happiest results were obtained by organising the action rather like a game and shooting as and when the opportunity arose.

In one key sequence the children were supposed to capture the dog and give it a bath on the lawn. Here my direction consisted simply of saying: 'Here's the bath and there's the dog. Let's see if you can get him into it'. A friend and I then covered the ensuing action with two cameras — one on a tripod for the long shots and one hand-held for close-ups. The resulting footage was admittedly a bit chaotic but it contained some splendid material — including a shot of one small boy clinging desperately to the dog's tail which could never have been manufactured in rehearsal.

Having rough cut this, it was a fairly simple matter to decide where cut-aways and extra shots were needed to smooth out the continuity and these were taken later under relatively controlled conditions.

When it comes to close-ups of facial reactions, an actor may be asked to switch on an expression to order but the natural type must be given something to react to, although the stimulus need not of course have anything to do with the film. Thus for a later scene in *Good Clean Fun* I wanted a close-up of a little girl howling with laughter at her two brothers being scrubbed in the bath. To provoke the required expression, I had to conceal myself in the empty bath and bob up over the rim uttering weird noises while my colleague pressed the camera button.

Getting the semblance of a performance from a natural type often involves doing a good deal of ham acting yourself behind the camera but when it works the satisfaction is tremendous. You know that what you have got on film is a bit of genuine human emotion and the best professional actor in the world can't give better than the real thing.

Chapter Thirteen

THE MECHANICS OF SOUND

If you are thinking of making a sound film — however unpretentious — it's not a bad idea to start with a clear understanding of the way that professionals tackle the job. After all, they have been at it since about 1928; so you can be fairly sure that if there were an easier or cheaper method of obtaining acceptable results, they would be using it by now!

First of all, it's important to realise that very little of the sound you hear in the cinema is recorded at the time of shooting. Most of it is added after the picture has been edited. The one exception is dialogue — and that only in scenes that can be filmed inside the studio under ideal conditions.

The walls of the studio are lagged acoustically to keep out unwanted noise and prevent echo. The floor is covered with soft material to eliminate footsteps. The camera is housed in a soundproofed 'blimp' to kill the sound of the mechanism — and it is also electrically synchronised to the recording machine. The microphone is suspended from a long, swinging boom so that it can be kept as close as possible to the actors, without actually appearing in the picture.

Separate Tracks

In fact, every effort is made to ensure that the voices — and only the voices — are recorded. The reason for this is that incidental sounds, such as footsteps, can easily be added later but if they are included on the same recording as the speech, their volume cannot be altered independently to give a proper 'balance'. It is much more convenient to have them on a separate track.

When dialogue is recorded on location it is virtually impossible to eliminate other sounds and — except in the case of newsreels when speed is the overriding factor — such recordings are generally used only as 'guide tracks' to help the actors re-record their dialogue in time with the projected picture. This is known as post synchronisation.

For singing and dancing sequences an opposite method is used. The music and songs are pre-recorded and the actors mime to playback while the camera is, of course, synchronised to the playback unit.

Normally, sound is recorded directly onto magnetic film — separate from the picture film but matching it frame for frame in length. The well known clapper board provides a reference point for synchronisation at the beginning of each take.

Sometimes tape recorders are used for location recording because of their smaller size and weight. In this case synchronisation is maintained by recording a pulse from the camera onto a second track of the tape. It is important to realise, however, that the tape is only used as a temporary measure. The sound from it is transferred on to perforated magnetic film before editing begins.

When the picture is edited, the speech track is of course edited along with it. The end result is an edited picture and a sound track of exactly the same length, consisting of dialogue sections interspersed with long blank spaces. In other words, you might say that the sound editor is in a very similar position to the amateur who wants to add sound to a silent film. And it is perhaps worth adding here that the majority of professional documentaries contain no dialogue so that work on the sound track only begins after the picture has been shot and edited.

Sound Editing

Now there is one vital difference between picture and sound editing. The picture consists of shots joined one after the other in sequence but in the finished sound track many sounds occur simultaneously: speech may be heard over effects and effects over music and so on. To allow for these overlaps, the sound editor, who compiles the track, must be able to work with the various component sounds on separate rolls of magnetic film which can all be run parallel with the picture on the editing bench.

Whatever the original source of sound — it may, for example, be a tape recorded on location or obtained from a library — it has to be transferred onto

magnetic film before editing, or 'track laying' as it's
called, can begin. Now the strips of magnetic film
can be laced into an editing machine such as the
Picture Sync — a kind of animated viewer with four
sprockets mounted on a common shaft, one for
picture and three for sound. Once a particular sound —
a door slam for example — has been placed opposite
the appropriate picture frame and spliced into position,
it is held in sync by means of the sprocket. Hence the
great importance of working with the sound on perforated film.

Volume controls on the editing machine make it
possible to listen to one track at a time in conjunction
with the picture — or indeed all three at once — and
of course one can wind them backwards and forwards
any number of times to check that everything is
correct. Incidentally, on an ambitious film there would
be many more than three tracks but this number is
usually considered sufficient for the average 16 mm
documentary.

Mixing the Tracks

When the separate sound tracks have been edited
in sync with the picture they are taken to a dubbing
theatre and laced up into a bank of sound track
reproducers. These reproducers are all coupled
together synchronously with each other, and with
the projector showing the picture, so that they can
be re-recorded or 'mixed' on to a final magnetic
master sound track. At the rear of the dubbing theatre
is a large console with volume and tone controls for
each reproducing channel.

The sound mixer, who operates the console, works
from a dubbing chart provided by the sound editor.
This is divided into columns, showing the sequence of
sounds on each track with footage numbers to
indicate where each sound begins and ends and where,
if necessary, it should be faded in or out. While the
film is running an illuminated indicator under the
screen shows footage numbers equivalent to those
on the chart.

The mixer's job, therefore, is to fade in the various
sounds on cue to an appropriate volume level in order
to achieve clarity and a proper artistic balance. He
does not have to worry about synchronisation as this
has been taken care of by the sound editor during
track laying.

Once the master sound track has been recorded,
it is a matter of routine to transfer this to an optical
track which is then printed with the picture master
onto a single roll of film in indestructable sync.
Alternatively, of course, the picture can be printed
mute and the sound transferred on to it by means of
magnetic stripe.

Now let's consider the main points that the amateur
can learn from professional procedure:

1. *Synchronisation between the camera and the
recorder is only necessary for dialogue scenes. And
bearing in mind the danger of takes being spoiled
by extraneous noise, it is arguable that post
synchronisation — with or without the aid of guide
tracks — may prove the best solution here.*

2. *For freedom and control in editing it is
essential to have the sound separate from the
picture and also to have the various sounds that
will be used simultaneously separate from each
other.*

3. *To maintain synchronisation during editing
it is a great help to have the sound on perforated
material.*

4. *The re-recording or mixing process allows
the volume levels of the various component sounds
to be adjusted relative to each other after they
have been synchronised to the picture.*

5. *The final film must have picture and sound in
indestructable sync and the obvious method is to
have both on the same film.*

Contrary to popular belief, a sound film consisting
entirely of lip sync dialogue is relatively easy to make
from a technical point of view. Indeed Bell & Howell's
Filmsound 8 system reduces it to a simple press-
button operation — providing you are content to do
without editing. And even the more flexible methods
of synchronising cameras with tape recorders are quite
easy to handle, so long as one member of the production team is free to concentrate exclusively on sound.

Live Recording Problems

The difficulty of live speech recording arises not
from synchronisation but from the intrusion of
unwanted sound and the nervousness of untrained
actors who fluff their lines. These twin hazards make
for a far higher proportion of wasted film than is
normally accepted when shooting mute. Sufficient
reason, perhaps, why amateur dialogue films will

always be in a minority and why dialogue — when it does occur — should be confined to a few brief 'inserts', interspersed with longer passages of narration, music and effects.

Whether or not such dialogue inserts are to be used, the main task of compiling the sound track to fit the picture lies ahead. Those 16 mm users who can afford it may, of course, follow the professional procedure outlined above. The rest of us, including all 8 mm users, have to settle for some kind of compromise.

As it is impractical to edit the component sounds on separate strips of film, the best alternative is to record them on separate tracks of the same tape, using a ¼-track tape recorder with facilities for play-ing back two tracks together. Thus commentary can be recorded on one track and music on another with appropriate lowering of the music volume where the two overlap. Ideally, one would like a third track for effects but as only two tracks are available, the solution is to use a second tape recorder — possibly one of the portable battery types used for collecting sound effects on location.

A two-way mixer is now required and this may be part of the master tape recorder or an additional unit. One input takes the music from a turntable and the other the effects from the second tape recorder and these are recorded together on to the track of the master tape which is not occupied by commentary.

While the various component sounds are being added to the tape in this way, synchronisation has to be maintained and several different devices for syncronis-ing projectors with tape recorders are available — some electronic and some mechanical. A mechanical type, such as the Synchrodek, is more convenient for editing or compilation purposes as it permits the pro-jector to be stopped and re-started without risk of losing sync.

Re-recording

Incidentally, when a second tape recorder is available, it is quite usual to record all the commentary sections 'wild' so that the commentator can concen-trate on his delivery without having to worry about cues. Then these sections can be re-recorded on to the commentary track of the master tape, using the pause control on the second recorder to bring in each one to synchronise with a visual cue from the projected picture.

The underlying principle in all this is that the amateur uses re-recording, instead of physical cutting and splicing of the sound track as his main editing method.

As I said, it is a compromise and does not permit the same degree of precision and complexity that professional methods permit. However, where 'spot effects' such as door slams and gun shots are required, it is possible to employ a simplified form of track laying with perforated tape taking the place of magnetic film.

Perforated Tape

Because film and tape run at different speeds, it is rather less convenient to edit picture and sounds side by side. But it is possible to obtain perforated tape in which the number of sprocket holes for any given duration of sound is the same as the number of sprocket holes in 8 mm film for the same duration of picture. Hence the exact point where a spot effect needs to be spliced into the tape can be determined by counting sprocket holes and, as I write this, new editing equipment is coming onto the market which will make it possible to run tape and film in interlock which should simplify the procedure considerably.

As there is no equipment available for playing back several perforated tapes simultaneously in sync, you will have to content yourself with one edited track to accomodate all the really vital synchronous sounds. When this is complete you can play it back in sync with the projected picture by using a projector synchroniser such as the Synchrodek — and at the same time dub in other less critical background sounds and music from a second tape recorder.

In this way you finish up with all your sound on a perforated tape that can be played back in sync every time the film is projected or, more conveniently, it can be transferred onto a magnetic stripe on the film itself.

Finally, it is perhaps worth adding that a sound track can be recorded directly onto stripe by speaking into a microphone supplied with the stripe projector while the film is running and feeding in music from a turntable. This works well enough for a simple track but is obviously hard on the film if repeated erasure and re-recording should be necessary.

Chapter Fourteen

USING SOUND

Of all the subjects I have dealt with in this book sound is the one I approach with most trepidation. It worries me because I know full well that to make proper use of the sound track we must have the means to edit it independently and, at the same time, to synchronise it precisely with the picture. I mean precisely to the frame.

Without this technical facility — which at present is enjoyed only by a small minority of amateurs — much of the advice that I would like to offer about the use of sound is worthless. Well, perhaps 'worthless' is too strong a word; shall we say that it is of academic interest only?

Let's begin, therefore, by trying to understand why exact synchronisation is so important.

Although we know what cinema historians mean when they refer to 'the silent era', the term is really rather misleading. For films have never been shown in silence. It is on record that even the first Lumière programme of the 1890's was accompanied by music and sound effects. Later every local fleapit had its pianist and the big cinemas had full orchestras playing music that was specially composed or arranged for important feature films.

A New Medium

At worst, these sound accompaniments served the purpose of drowning extraneous noises such as coughs and scuffles in the auditorium. At best, they played a much more positive and sophisticated role. Nevertheless, they were only accompaniments and the arrival of the synchronised sound track in 1929 made all the difference in the world.

The obvious difference that everyone noticed was that the characters on the screen began to talk but that wasn't the whole of it or even the most significant part of it. The key point was that control of the sound as well as the picture now passed into the hands of the film maker; instead of being a garnish that could be added more or less at the discretion of exhibitors and showmen, it became an integral part of the film.

The film maker could now decide not only what music should be played but how it should be played and just exactly where each note should fall in relation to the action on the screen. He could bring in the sound of a creaking door slowly over a close-up of the heroine's eyes dilating or he could crash it in at full volume on a cut to the door itself. The ability to *combine* sound and picture in harmony or in opposition to each other vastly extended his range of expression — and this ensured that the film medium would never be the same again.

'Pure' Cinema

Because film production is a business, the artistic possibilities of synchronised sound naturally caused less excitement than its commercial possibilities. The obvious, commercially exploitable fact was that words could now be fitted to the lip movements of actors and dialogue subjects became a viable proposition. Successful stage plays and musical shows could be transferred to the screen with a minimum of creative effort.

Reacting against the stress of all-talking, all-singing drivel that followed, some critics suggested that the art of the cinema had died with the 'silent' film. But their theorising about 'pure cinema' was pure eyewash; there was nothing wrong with the new medium only with the way that it was being used and the novelty of talk for talk's sake soon wore off. Certainly no film maker of real talent and imagination has ever refused to take advantage of the synchronised sound track with its vast range of creative possibilities.

Unfortunately, for technical reasons outlined in the last chapter, very few amateurs have ever had the opportunity to explore these possibilities fully for themselves. The exceptions are those who work on 16 mm and somehow afford to use professional methods, plus a few 8 mm fanatics who manage to achieve almost the same results by expending about ten times as much effort.

In due course it may be that better technical facilities will become available to us all but meanwhile many of us have to be content with sound that accompanies the film, rather than forming a fully integrated part of it. And here I should like to add that films of this type are still perfectly valid; they still win prizes in international competitions and there is still much more satisfaction to be had from making a good one than from making a sound film that fails to achieve its purpose.

The important thing always is to realise your limitations and then work sensibly within them.

Let's consider, therefore, the various types of sound that may be used to accompany a film and the different ways in which they can be treated when forming part of a synchronised track.

Commentary

The basic purpose of most commentaries is to inform and it follows that the information they offer should add interest to the picture rather than repeating what is obvious or distracting attention from it.

To say 'The Mayor arrives in his Rolls Royce' over a scene of him doing just that is redundant and rather irritating. On the other hand, to say 'Grateful rate-payers provide the Mayor with a Rolls during his term of office' is relevant yet oblique to the picture; it says something that couldn't very well be explained visually and is therefore worth including.

A comment of this kind will make sense whether it precedes or follows the action to which it refers — providing of course that the variation is not more than two or three seconds either way. So it is safe to use in a tape accompaniment.

A good example of non-sync commentary is the narration provided by Andrée Clements for her 8 mm Ten Best winner, *October Country*. Here an old man speaks his thoughts as scenes from his life in retirement pass on the screen. The words are very important insofar as they give a deeper meaning to the visuals but they are tied to whole sequences rather than particular shots and the visual continuity is complete without them.

Only once does the producer tempt providence and this is in a sequence where the old man has a heart attack and collapses in the street. The commentary here gives way to gasps and groans — an effect of sudden immediacy that can really only be depended on to work in a synchronous sound film.

Essentially, non-sync commentary is something added to a film that is already capable of standing on its own feet. But a film designed for synchronous commentary need not — and indeed should not — make sense without the words. Thus a holiday film might start like this:

1. The family sitting in front of the fire, pouring over a travel agency brochure.	*Months ago on chilly winter evenings our thoughts were already turning . . .*
Cut to:	
2. The same family lazing on the beach.	*southwards to sunny Spain.*

This is a cliché example of the way that a few words carefully timed in relation to a cut can prepare the audience for a leap forward in time that would be unacceptable in vision alone. Used sensibly, this kind of device can save footage and make for a speedier form of narrative.

More interestingly, perhaps, an actual rapport can be established between the commentator and the people in the film. They can be made to react to his words or follow his instructions. He can not only talk *about* them but also *to* them and even *as* them.

I recall an amateur comedy film of many years ago called *How to Catch a Burglar* which made admirable use of these variations. It started with a burglar entering a house at night and starting to break open a desk. He drops something on the floor and we cut away to the bedroom where a woman sits up in bed with a startled expression on her face. The commentator speaks to her: 'Look, I don't want to scare you lady but this situation calls for a man. Have you got one handy?'

The camera now pans over to the other side of the bed where a man is sleeping. (Commentator: 'Oh! good.') The woman's hand comes into picture and jabs the man in the back. (Commentator now speaking as the woman in a stage whisper: 'Charles, Charles! Wake up Charles.') The man continues to sleep and we cut back to the woman looking exasperated. (The commentator now speaking to her again: 'Well, either he's hedging or you've got the name wrong. Try Joe.')

Music

Practical considerations first. When it comes to the choice of music for his films, the amateur is somewhat bedevilled by the laws of copyright.

Nothing, of course, can prevent you from playing any gramophone record while you are projecting a film in your own home — or indeed in a public hall, providing that the hall in question holds an appropriate licence. Unfortunately, however, you are not permitted by the law to re-record (or dub) music from a gramophone record onto tape or film and a specific warning to this effect appears on the label of every disc on the retail market.

Commercial film and television companies use mood music discs which are produced specifically for the purpose of dubbing and fees for the use of their contents are paid to the publishers through the Mechanical Copyright Protection Society. These records, however, are supplied direct to trade users and carry no purchase tax; they cannot be bought from retail shops.

The M.C.P.S. operates a scheme in conjunction with the Institute of Amateur Cinematographers whereby amateurs can obtain a blank licence to dub from certain records on payment of an annual fee and details are obtainable from the Secretary of the Institute, 63 Woodfield Lane, Ashtead, Surrey.

In addition, Fountain Press have issued a selection of mood music on various long playing records. Each disc has its own dubbing licence which covers 'public performances organised by amateur cine or tape recording clubs, providing that admission charges (if any) are devoted to club funds or other non-profit making purposes'.

Music, even when it is only used as an accompaniment, can obviously help to establish mood and atmosphere. It can give flow to a sequence when the editing of the visuals is not, perhaps, quite as polished as it might be. It can stress tempo and underline an emotional climax.

Music also has its story-telling properties. A tune can be associated with a particular character (as was the famous Harry Lime theme in *The Third Man*) and can be used to hint at his off-screen presence.

A melody, established early in a film as part of some happy incident, can be repeated later under sadder circumstances and will immediately suggest that the characters in question are thinking back nostalgically. Intentionally inappropriate music can make its own humorous comment on the action. And so on.

Given a synchronous track, the correspondence between music and action can, of course, be much closer. In a comedy cricket match, for example, a bowler might be made to deliver a ball to a roll of drums and the wicket fall to a crash of cymbals. Sometimes an existing piece of music may dictate the editing of a complete sequence — or even a complete film. Generally, as we know, in a well edited film the cuts are unobtrusive and music can make them even more so. Conversely, however, a bit of rhythmic, staccato editing can be given greater impact by making the joins coincide precisely with the beat of appropriate music.

Cutting the music track itself to fit the picture may be regarded as artistic sacrilege where serious music is concerned. But mood music is not exactly sacred; Steve Race, who has composed a lot of it, calls it 'musical wallpaper', implying that anyone who follows the pattern can cut it with impunity. The main point to watch when removing a section of music is that you should work in units of complete bars, taking care also to avoid a change of key and instrumentation at the cutting point.

Effects

In a tape accompaniment general or continuous effects, such as birdsong, rushing water or the whirr of machinery, may be used to assist atmosphere or suggest a particular location. But they need to be treated with discretion and kept in the background as too much realism will lead the audience to expect spot effects (footsteps, opening doors and so on) that coincide with the action — and nothing is better calculated to destroy dramatic tension than a gunshot which is heard three seconds *after* the victim has fallen to the ground, writhing in agony.

In a sound film, of course, every minor spot effect *can* be cut in to match its appropriate action but this is a laborious and unrewarding task. With care many unimportant sounds can be 'lost' under music or general effects, leaving you free to concentrate on the essential ones and those that have real story-telling significance.

Just like commentary and music, effects used

creatively, can add something to the picture aside
from realism. If a shot of a car going along the road
is accompanied by the sound of the car engine, then
the track is merely repeating the visual statement.
But suppose we have a shot of a woman waiting on a
street corner and we know from what has gone before
that she is waiting for her lover who may or may not
have deserted her; now if we bring up the sound of
the car engine while the camera stays on her face,
the combination of sound and picture will say
something that cannot be conveyed by vision alone.

This, if you like, is a crude example but once you
grasp the idea that sound, in whatever form, should
complement and enrich the meaning of the picture —
rather than duplicate it, you will be on the way to
making full use of the sound track.

Chapter Fifteen

STORY INTO SCRIPT

The veteran Hollywood director, Howard Hawks, once remarked that 'audiences remember scenes but they don't remember plots'.

For any one person who can tell you the story of *Ben Hur*, there must be a thousand who can recall the chariot race in vivid detail. Everyone who saw Hitchcock's *North by North West* can call to mind a picture of Cary Grant being chased through a cornfield by a low flying aircraft but how many can remember the complex sequence of events leading up to this situation? Very few, I would guess.

Moreover, it's not only the big, spectacular action sequences that stay in the mind; for who could ever forget Charlie Chaplin eating his boots in *The Gold Rush*? Sometimes, indeed, the most memorable moment may be embodied in a single shot such as the close-up of the young soldier's hand reaching out for the butterfly at the end of *All Quiet on the Western Front*.

If we look for the common factor in these diverse scenes, we find that they are all visually expressive or, if you like, eloquent beyond words. Putting it another way, they all belong essentially to the film medium and were conceived with that medium in mind.

Thinking in Pictures

This brings me to the first point I want to make about writing a film script. It is no use simply thinking of a story and then thinking afterwards how you are going to turn it into a film. It must be imagined right from the start in terms of moving pictures.

I know that existing stories are sometimes successfully adapted for the screen but in that case the original story only provides source material. It has to be re-thought and re-imagined as a movie. The discovery of the story represents the beginning and not the end of the creative process.

It is all too easy for the amateur script writer to fall for an ingenious plot, forgetting that the value of a plot — from a film maker's point of view — must be judged by the opportunities it provides for creating visually effective scenes. That is why the majority of amateur fiction films get bogged down in their own plots; they are all explanation and no action.

Amateur comedies, in particular, tend to stake all on the kind of twist ending that may be acceptable in a spoken anecdote which takes thirty seconds or so to tell but is poor compensation for sitting through twenty minutes or so of screen stodge.

The Raw Material

How then should you begin to write your first film script? If you sit down at the typewriter and wait for inspiration to strike, it probably never will. A much more promising way is to think of your material resources: the available locations, the people you know who can be persuaded to 'act' or at least appear in front of the camera. Even a prop can start a train of thought.

You can begin, if you like, by making a list of these items — the tangible raw material of your film. Sometimes the material itself will suggest the outline of a story, just as a sculptor can sometimes look at a block of stone and 'see' the shape of his statue waiting to be carved out of it.

If you are not inspired in this way, there are certain 'rules' of construction that will help you to organise your thoughts. These are not sacred rules, remember, but generalisations based on practice, rather like the rules of composition in still photography. It is useful to know them, even though you may discard them deliberately later on.

For example, it is generally accepted that every film should have a beginning, a middle and an end — even though the French director, Jean Luc Godard, has declared that they need not necessarily come in that order! Let's consider, therefore, how this three-part structure might be applied to the very simplest kind of film — a holiday record for family viewing:

1. *Beginning.* The family prepare for a picnic. They set off and arrive at the beach.

2. *Middle.* They go swimming, eat and drink, lie in the sun and play games on the sand.

3. *End.* They pack up and make their way home as the sun sets.

Now that is not exactly a masterpiece of creative writing but at least it has a certain satisfying 'wholeness'. Just because the action is confined to one day and events are presented in a logical sequence, it would make a more satisfying film than the random collection of snippets that many camera owners bring back from their holidays and subsequently inflict on their nearest and dearest.

Three-Part Structure

Moreover, there are several points worth noting about this simple three-part structure — and worth remembering when you come to deal with more complex and ambitious subjects. Note, for instance that Part One should introduce the characters and establish the setting, also that it should not occupy more than about one third of the film's total running time. Note that Part Two should contain all the main action and occupy most of the remaining running time. Finally, note that Part Three should be relatively very short and yet set a seal on everything that has gone before.

These are classic proportions that can be applied to almost any film, fact or fiction. But when we come to think of the story film in particular, there is another element to consider — an element of conflict, giving rise to suspense, something that will make the audience wonder what is going to happen next.

In an orthodox construction Part One would establish the conflict situation and build up suspense to a point where something decisive happens (the first major climax) that will motivate the main action of the film. In a murder story, for example, this could be the discovery of a body which will lead to the tracking down of the criminal.

At the beginning of Part Two suspense is allowed to slacken off and is then gradually built up again to a point where something even more decisive happens (the second major climax) which resolves the conflict situation. In other words, the criminal is caught by the detective or gets killed while trying to escape.

In Part Three (the very short part, remember) suspense falls away rapidly as the detective explains how he solved the mystery and the end title comes up.

You may find it helpful to plot the 'line of tension' in the form of graph which would look rather like a lop-sided letter 'M' with the base line representing the running time of the film. Starting from zero, the line of tension slopes up to a peak one third of the way along the base line. It then dips sharply, curves round and slopes up again to a second and higher peak before falling almost vertically to reach zero again at the end of the base line.

Needless to say, few film stories will conform precisely to this orthodox structure and in a long film there will almost certainly be various minor peaks and valleys along the way. Nevertheless, it is a shape that has been evolved through practice over the years and has proved serviceable. It won't enable you to become a brilliant script writer overnight but it will save you from making gross structural errors like taking too long to get to the point of allowing the end sequence to meander on pointlessly after the audience has lost interest.

Moreover, you should not make the mistake of thinking that sound construction is only important when you are dealing with stock melodrama such as the murder story mentioned above. It can equally well serve the mildest of domestic anecdotes.

Consider, for example, the little movie I made some years ago and which I have mentioned in earlier chapters, called *Good Clean Fun*. This was produced for Kodak Limited as an example of the very simple type of story film that anyone can make at home without having to go outside the family circle for actors or technical assistants. It runs for about six minutes; there is no dialogue and the sound consists only of a loosely synchronised musical accompaniment:

1. The scene is the back garden of a medium sized house in the country. A large dog is sunning itself on the lawn and nearby three children are filling a tin bath with water. There are two boys, aged five and seven, and a little girl of three. As they run into the house and back with a watering can and other recepticles which they empty into the bath, the dog eyes them suspiciously. Finally when the bath is full they advance stealthily on the dog and then suddenly make a grab for it. Galvanised into action, the dog evades their grasp, and disappears through the garden gate, hotly pursued by the children.

2. The children chase the dog up hill and down dale, over a ploughed field and finally through a shallow stream where they all get plastered in mud. A passer-by catches the dog and hands it over to the children who drag it back home, and, after a protracted struggle, land it in the tin bath. They

FROM SCRIPT TO SCREEN. When you have control over the action, it is always a good idea to plan your shots in as much detail as possible. But when you are writing for an unknown location — as in the case of a holiday film — you must be prepared to make alterations as you go along. Here we follow the evolution of a sequence from A Place to Call Your Own, a T and R Film directed by the author for Mediterranean Villas Ltd.

SCRIPT EXTRACT. The typescript was written before leaving England. The hand-written alterations were made after inspecting the location in Ibiza. In fact, two locations were used, although they appear as one on the screen.

8. Close shot of window in villa. The shutters are thrust open and man in pyjamas looks out. He inhales with satisfaction. Pan or cut to...

[handwritten: One shot] [Comes] [Use French windows.]

9. Door of villa. Woman comes out onto terrace wearing swimsuit under bathrobe. Man we have just seen comes out and joins her. Arm in arm they stroll out past camera.

[handwritten: 9. Edge of terrace — out left. 9A. Lower steps in right — out right]

10. Beach with sea in background. Man and woman stroll in from foreground, then turn and look back at...

[handwritten: IN LEFT]

11. L.S. of villa attractively framed by trees.

12. As 10. Man and woman looking back. They smile at each other, then walk on to water's edge. As she starts to take off bathrobe, cut on action to...

[handwritten: run]

13. M.S. Woman takes off bathrobe and throws it aside. Man takes off pyjama jacket. Camera pans with woman as she runs into sea. She dips under water, then beckons to him.

*[handwritten: * Lose man here.]*

14. From sea (low angle). Man runs to join her.

15. Reverse angle. Woman in water. Man runs in from foreground, plunges into water and both swim out to sea.

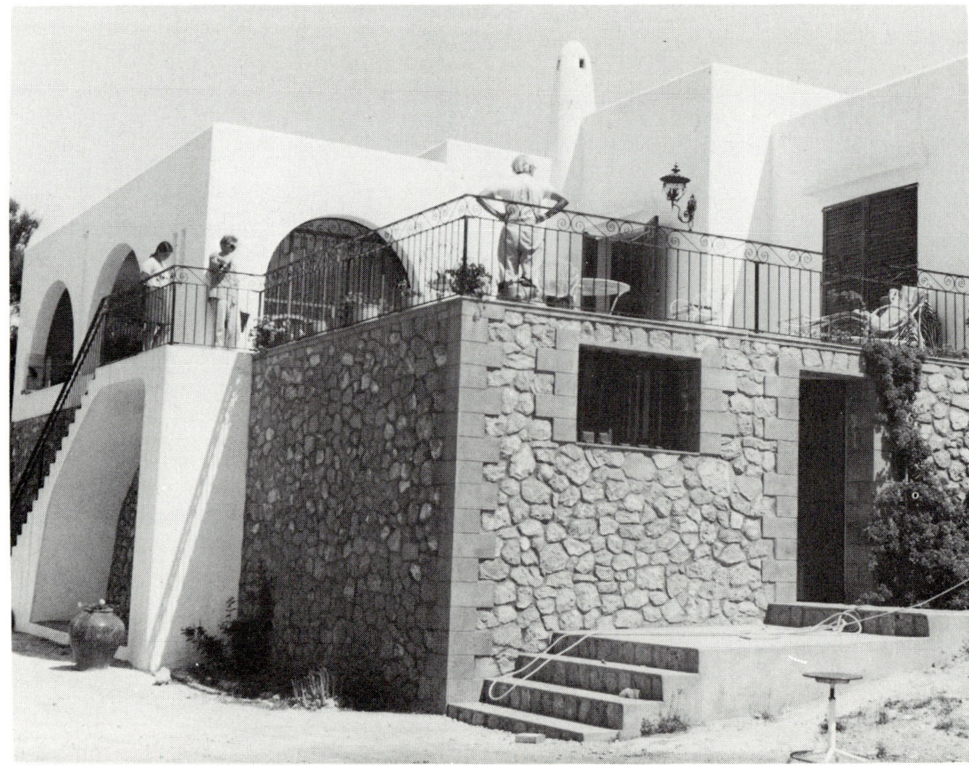

LOCATION. As the main purpose of the film was to illustrate the joys of a villa holiday, the villa itself was the key location. This one was chosen for its photogenic possibilities and here the director and cameraman are revising the action and camera angles to show off its best features. Its geographical situation in relation to the beach didn't conform with the script but this was unimportant as the beach and villa never appear in the same shot.

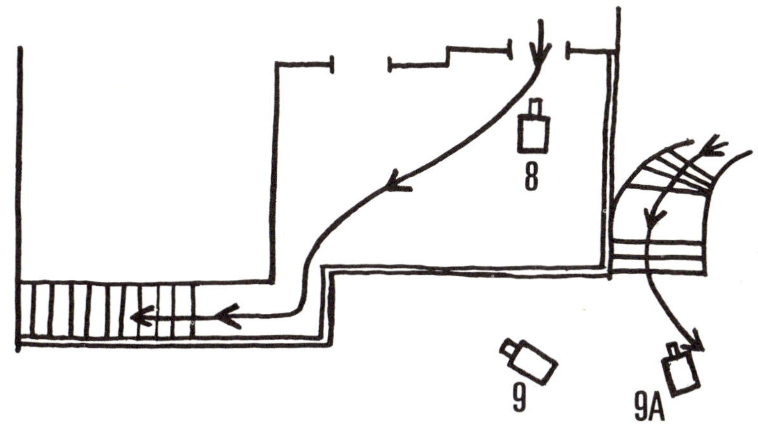

PLAN VIEW of the villa shown in the photograph opposite, with the three camera positions indicated. The arrowed line represents the movement of the 'actors'. On screen, Shot 9A appears to be a direct continuation of 9, although this was actually 'cheated' by transferring the action to the second flight of steps on the right which were better lit.

FINISHED SEQUENCE. Notice how the two locations are combined into one by the action link from Shot 9A to 10 and again by the look back at the end of Shot 10 which is followed by a shot of the villa, apparently from the view-point of the couple.

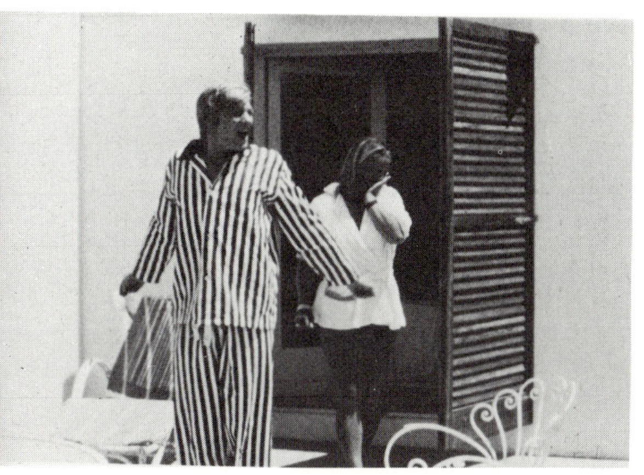

8. Villa. MLS of French windows. The shutters burst open and young man in pyjamas comes out followed by girl. He yawns and walks out left. Camera holds girl.

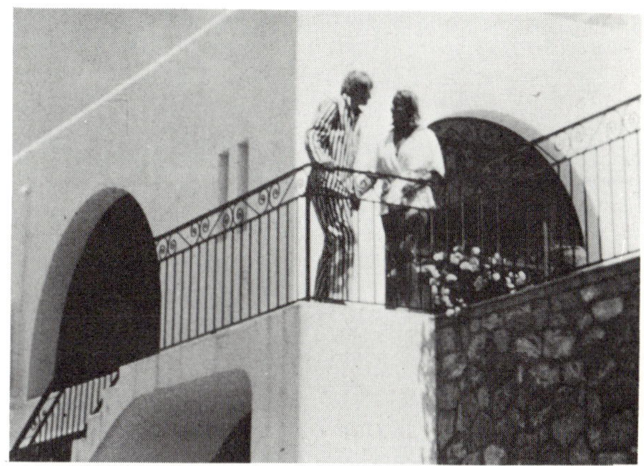

9. Villa. LS of young man leaning on ballustrade at edge of terrace. Girl comes in from right and they go out left down steps.

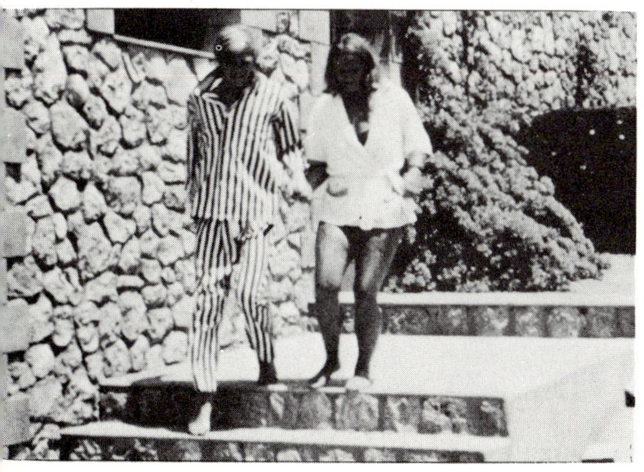

9A. Villa. MLS of lower flight of steps. Young man and girl come in from top right and go out past camera right.

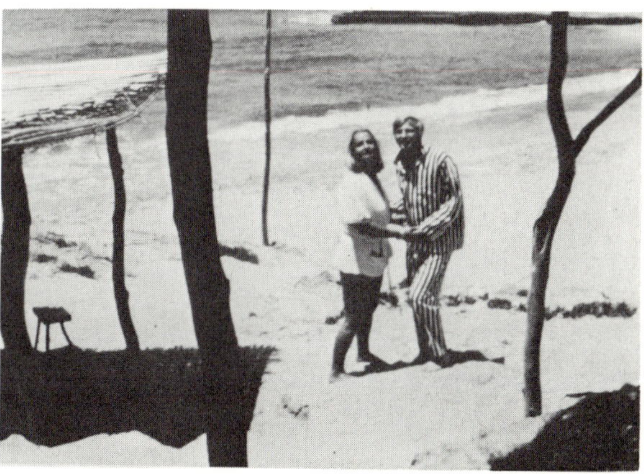

10. Beach. LS from high angle. Young man and girl come in from left foreground, pause and look back.

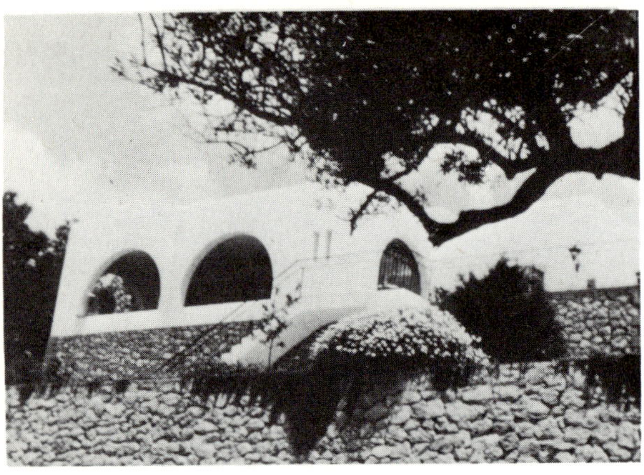

11. *Villa. LS from low angle to simulate viewpoint of couple in previous shot.*

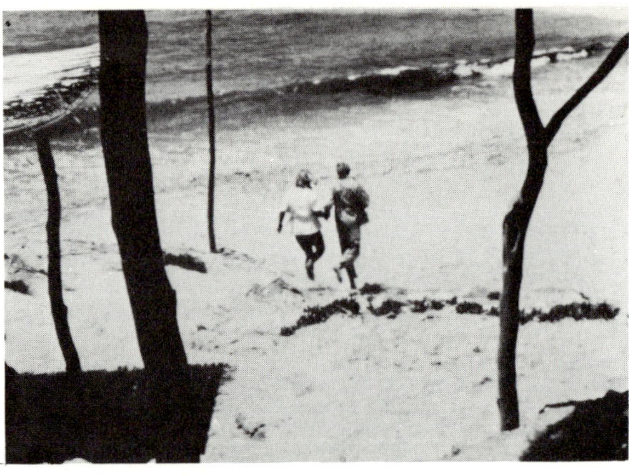

12. *Beach. As 10. Man and girl still looking back, they smile at each other, they run on to water's edge. As she starts to take off bathrobe, cut on action to . . .*

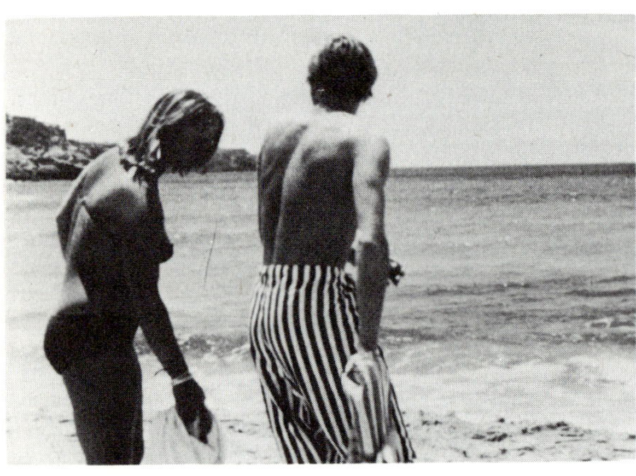

13. *Beach. MS of couple as girl finishes taking off bathrobe and then moves to right, camera panning with her . . .*

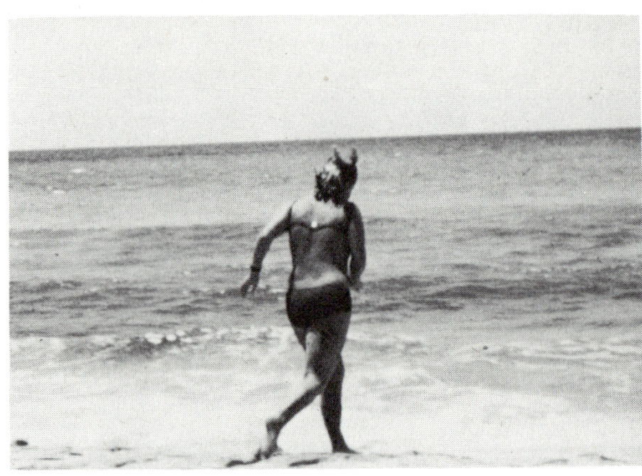

13. *(Continued). Camera continues panning with girl until man is out of picture. She runs into sea, dips under water and looks back at . . .*

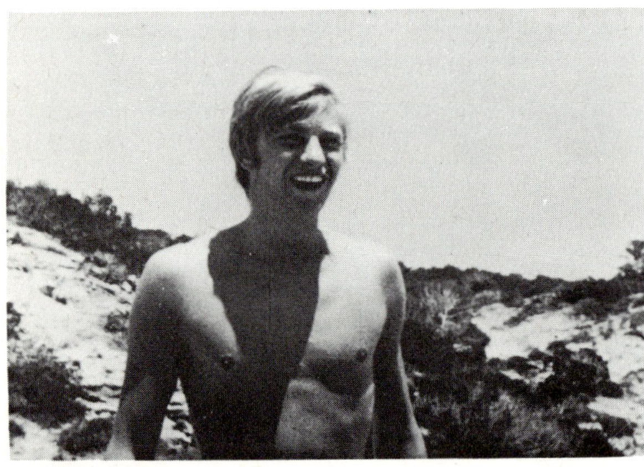

14. *Beach. MCU of young man who smiles at her, then runs out right.*

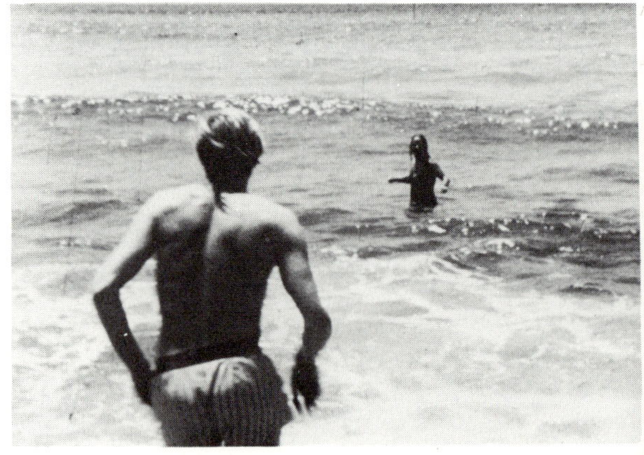

15. *Beach. LS of girl in water. Young man runs in from left foreground and both swim out to sea.*

*are all scrubbing the dog gleefully when their
mother glances out of the kitchen window and
spots their dishevelled appearance. Whereupon,
of course, the tables are turned: the children are
hauled into the bathroom and Mother does the
scrubbing.*

*3. Once again the dog is sunning itself on the
back lawn when the little girl, still naked from her
bath, runs out into the garden, clutching a flannel.
The dog takes one apprehensive look at her and
bolts, disappearing rapidly into the far distance.
Fade out.*

In such a very simple story the three-part structure
stands out fairly obviously. You will notice that Part
One introduces the main characters and also establishes
the conflict situation: children want to bath dog but
dog doesn't want to be bathed. This ends when something happens (the dog escapes from the garden)
which precipitates the main action of the film in
Part Two: the cross country chase culminating in the
recapture of the dog. The bathing of the dog and the
children provides the climax which resolves the
conflict situation. And Part Three ends the whole
affair briefly on a light note, suggesting that this is
where we came in.

Visual Treatment

The story outline I have given here, which is a
slightly abbreviated version of my original 'treatment',
obviously has no literary merits. But it does have the
cinematic merit of being completely visual. The story
is unfolded entirely in terms of action without any
need for spoken explanation. It is also practical in the
sense that the children are not required to do any
dramatic acting but simply to be themselves and
exhibit natural high spirits.

Personally, I always find it helpful to write a treatment — that is a description of the story as it will
appear on the screen — as a preliminary to the actual
shooting script. It enables me to visualise the film as
a whole and decide whether it is going to 'work' before
getting involved with detail. Moreover, it can be read
and understood by 'actors' and others who may not
be familiar with the technical language of film making.

Such a treatment can be as brief or as full as you
like but when writing it you should be on your
guard against the literary phrase that may read well
but does not conjure up any picture to the mind's eye.
Thoughts and feelings, remember, can't be photo-

graphed until they are translated into action. 'John is
so depressed that he begins to contemplate suicide' is
unfilmable but 'John picks up a revolver and points
it at his forehead' is a practical if somewhat crude
expression of the same idea.

Having completed the treatment, I think it is a
good idea to select the cast and the locations and then
write the script around them, bearing in mind that the
features of a landscape — as well as the features of the
people who are going to appear in front of the
camera — can greatly influence the way that a sequence
is shot.

Shooting Script

Writing a shooting script is basically a matter of
breaking down the story into a series of long shots,
medium shots and close-ups. But, of course, this is
not done in an arbitrary way. It is a matter of thinking back to the principle of the changing camera
viewpoint, as described in Chapter Three.

Remember our old friend, the attentive observer.
How would he observe the action in real life? When
would he want to take a broad view of the scene as a
whole and when would he want to concentrate on
a detail? What would he wish to look at next? If you
can answer these questions, you will find that shooting
script writes itself — after a fashion.

I say 'after a fashion' because there are many
different ways of observing a sequence of events and
the most obvious way is not always the most effective
from a story telling point of view. Sometimes, it's
true, the nature of the action is so compelling that
we all watch it in the same way — as for example at a
tennis match when the heads of all the spectators
swing from side to side in unison. But often the
action is less compelling and less simple than this,
allowing us a degree of freedom in what we choose
to look at from moment to moment.

By exercising this freedom in script writing, we are
able to express our individuality and, if we do it
thoughtfully, heighten the enjoyment of the audience.
For example, in real life we generally take in the
broad expanse of a scene before we become interested
in the details and so it would have been logical and
orthodox to start the script of *Good Clean Fun* with a
long shot, showing the whole garden with the dog
lying on the grass and the children filling the bath all
in frame together. But it seemed to me that this
would give away too much of the story too quickly.

So I decided it would be better to start with a close-up to arouse the curiosity of the audience and then, in subsequent shots, reveal the situation a little at a time. Here, then, is the shooting script for the opening sequence:

EXTERIOR — GARDEN

1. *C.U. of tin bath with water pouring into it. Camera tilts up to show Adam (the older boy) pouring water from watering can.*

2. *M.S. continuing action. As Adam empties the can, we see Mark (the younger boy) coming from door of house in background carrying a saacepan of water which he empties into the bath.*

3. *M.C.U. of dog lying on grass and apparently watching the operation with interest.*

4. *As 2. Brigitte (the little girl) comes from house carrying a tea cup and carefully adds her small contribution to the water in the bath.*

5. *As 3. The dog is still watching with interest.*

6. *M.L.S. The boys pick up the bath and advance with it, Brigitte bringing up the rear. Camera pans slightly with them, bringing the dog into picture. They put the bath down on the grass.*

7. *C.U. of dog looking wary.*

8. *C.U. of Adam looking down at dog. He turns in the direction of Mark and puts finger to his lips, indicating caution.*

9. *C.U. of Mark looking towards Adam. He nods in assent, then turns in the direction of Brigitte and repeats Adam's gesture.*

10. *C.U. of Brigitte, deadpan.*

11. *M.L.S. from low angle with dog (rear view) in foreground. Adam, on the left, and Mark, on the right, advance in an encircling movement. Brigitte is standing by the the bath in centre of picture.*

12. *C.U. of dog (front view) looking to left.*

13. *M.C.U. from low angle (dog's viewpoint) of Mark moving towards right stealthily. He looks left towards Adam.*

14. *M.C.U. from low angle of Adam moving towards left. He looks across right at Mark, then down left at dog.*

15. *C.U. of dog looking up from side to side.*

16. *M.S. of Mark moving left to right. He stops, looking down at dog (which is out of picture).*

Adam moves across in foreground from left to right and also stops, looking down. Suddenly they both make a lunge.

17. *M.C.U. Dog jumps up and runs out past camera as Mark and Adam lunge into picture, just missing him.*

18. *M.S. Dog running away from camera and through garden gate, followed by the children.*

On first reading, you may well find this section of the script over-elaborate and even confusing. Why take eighteen shots to cover such a very simple piece of action when half a dozen would surely be adequate?

There were, in fact, several reasons. Firstly, you must remember that when you are dealing with non-actors, such as young children and dogs, it is very difficult to sustain and co-ordinate group action. Very naturally, they can't accept the discipline of rehearsals and the more people there are in any one scene, the more chances there are of something going wrong.

The alternative is to break the action down as far as possible into close-ups so that the director (in this case myself) can concentrate on one character at a time and the 'performance' need only be sustained for four or five seconds at a time. There must be *some* group scenes, of course, to establish the relative positions of the characters and let the audience get their geographical bearings but I kept these to a minimum — Shots 6 and 11 — and I may add that these were by far the most difficult to organise.

Another reason for the fragmentation of the action into so many short shots is that it allows more latitude for the adjustment of timing at the editing stage. The key moment in the whole sequence, for example, is when the dog jumps up and just escapes the boys as they try to grab him. If this had been filmed all in one shot, the chances are that the boys would have slowed down, knowing that the dog had to get away, and this would have looked unconvincing. Or they might have actually caught him in which case there wouldn't have been any story!

As it was, the boys were able to make a very determined lunge in Shot 16 and for Shot 17 I started the camera running when the dog's owner (somewhere out of picture) called him. I then waited until the dog was actually moving before signalling the boys to repeat their lunge. Later, of course, on the editing bench, it was a simple matter to trim back the beginning of Shot 17 so that the lunge appears to be one continuous movement and the dog's evasive action is impeccably timed.

Finally, take another look at Shots 11 to 16 — a passage that appears needlessly complicated on paper, but, I believe, works on the screen. What I was doing here was to let the audience see the encircling movement from the point of view of the dog so that one boy is moving right to left and the other left to right. The inter-cutting of these opposing movements does create a certain visual tension which was fully deliberate. I wanted a big build-up — the suggestion of an elaborate military-type manoeuvre — collapsing abruptly when the dog, which remains immobile until the last moment, simply gets up and runs away. The more complex and prolonged the build-up, the bigger, I hoped, would be the laugh at the end of it.

As it happened, I was able to shoot this opening sequence almost exactly according to plan. The result is that it looks a little stiff and formalised with the children appearing somewhat ill at ease. Fortunately, however, this works in the particular story context because here it was natural that they should look as if they were 'acting out' a prepared plan and not be too sure of carrying it through successfully. There is, if you like, an element of nervousness built into the situation.

Later in the film, when I wanted much more freedom and spontaneity of action, I had to change my approach completely. For the final bathing sequence, as I mentioned in Chapter twelve, the script was virtually abandoned; the action was organised rather like a game that the children could enjoy and covered newsreel fashion.

You could say, in fact, that it was a waste of time to write a detailed shot-by-shot script of this sequence in the first place. And you could be right. For certain types of subject a script can be inhibiting and you may find it easier to work with a general outline of the action in mind, improvising your camera set-ups as you go along.

This is very much a matter of choice and tempra-ment. Personally, I like to work out a detailed script beforehand, even when I know that I shall probably depart from it at the shooting stage. I don't look on it as a sacred document but rather as a form of insurance; when everything else fails, I can always go back to the script.

Chapter Sixteen

GETTING ORGANISED

In many ways, making a movie is like having a baby. The infant may be conceived in a spirit of gay abandon but patience and fortitude are needed to carry you through the long period of gestation and the birth pangs that inevitably follow.

Unlike a baby, however, a film often has more than two parents and — while it is intended to minimise labour — this arrangement is always the cause of additional problems. In fact, it is probably true to say that the bigger the cast and the bigger the unit, the greater is the danger that the film will die in embryo and never see the light of the projector.

When an ambitious amateur production comes to grief in this way, the people concerned tend to blame each other — and often with good cause. Somebody is over-zealous. Somebody else is lazy, people are like that and when they join forces on any group enterprise, you can be sure that the clash of egos will be heard for miles around.

Joy Through Planning

Strife is unavoidable. It is a part of the climate and a part of the excitement of film making. But what you must ensure is that the heat engendered by it is used creatively, rather than destructively and this depends on two important conditions.

Firstly, you need a man who knows exactly what the finished film ought to look like and who is capable of communicating his ideas and his enthusiasm to those around him. Call him the inspiration man — the director. Secondly, if more than three or four people are involved, you need another man who will take care of the business side of production — working out how much the picture will cost, how long it will take to shoot, ensuring that actors are on tap when and where they are needed, providing props and transport as required. Call him the organisation man — the producer if you like.

Now you may be thinking that all this seems a bit too much like hard work, bearing in mind that most of us take up movie making for the simple purpose of having fun. But, believe me, there is very little fun to be had from getting involved in a half-hearted production and nothing more depressing than to arrive at some distant location, only to find that half the members of the unit have gone somewhere else and the man who was supposed to bring the tripod has left it at home.

No, unless you are prepared to work completely on your own, some kind of administrative planning is essential. And if it is handled efficiently, it can form the basis of real, lasting pleasure.

Writing a Treatment

Before planning can begin, there has to be a script and before there is a script there ought to be a 'treatment'.

This treatment, as I indicated in the last chapter, is simply the film 'story' — and a story can of course be either fact or fiction. In other words, it is a plain description of the action that will take place on the screen with indications of commentary or dialogue if any.

There are several advantages in using this free form of composition before attempting a shot-by-shot script. For one thing, it can easily be read aloud and digested at a single sitting so that all concerned will be able to understand the writer's intention and judge the overall effect without getting bogged down in technical detail.

At this stage the story can be torn apart and re-shaped with a view to making the plot more credible or the characters more convincing — and also with a view to simplifying the practical production problems. Parts of the action may be telescoped to avoid repetition and minor characters deleted if they have no vital role to play.

Because the work involved in preparing a treatment is relatively small, the writer will be more inclined to accept constructive suggestions than he would be after investing the greater time and effort demanded by a shooting script.

A treatment may be vague about locations and interior settings but these must all be decided upon before the script is written so that the action can be arranged to fit the geography. Key parts should be cast too as a known personality can influence the way the script is written, just as a known lack of acting ability can be compensated for by breaking the action down into shorter shots.

Rationalising the Script

To show how a treatment is converted into a shooting script and how it gets rationalised in the process, perhaps I may quote the opening sequence of a short film I made called *Hot Dog*. This is how the treatment begins:

A fine morning on the upper reaches of the Thames. Two boys are making their way down stream in a canoe — one paddling lazily, the other scanning the banks through field glasses. From his viewpoint we see the banks drifting by — an occasional swan, fishermen dotted along the towpath.

Outside a house on the far bank a man is putting up a notice on his fence. The boy with the field glasses signals to his companion to slow down, then he reads the hand-lettered sign: LOST. BLACK LABRADOR PUPPY. £1 REWARD TO FINDER.

A group of children, walking along the towpath, also stop to read the notice. As they get the message, their expressions brighten. A boy on a bicycle stops to read the notice too and hails his companions who come wheeling up. A group of girls who are skipping abandon their rope to join the crowd.

The boys in the canoe continue their way down stream, the one with the field glasses scanning the banks with renewed interest.

Now let's see how this looks in the shooting script:

LOCATION — RIVER NEAR COOKHAM (Camera in boat throughout)

1. *Wide-angle shot. Tracking along narrow back-water with both banks in picture, we glide beneath overhanging branches and a small bridge, then out into the main stream.*

2. *M.L.S. still tracking, with camera looking back at two boys in canoe which is facing slightly to left of picture. Boy at rear is paddling. Boy at front is taking it easy; he glances through field glasses which are hanging around his neck, looking left.*

3. *C.U. Boy with field glasses. He raises and lowers them several times.*

4. *Various shots of river bank, fishermen etc. to intercut with Scene 3.*

5. *As Scene 2. Boy with field glasses gestures to his companion to stop paddling and as the canoe continues to drift forward he peers intently at . . .*

LOCATION — DOWNLEY, OUTSIDE FLAGMORE COTTAGE

6. *M.L.S. (zooming in slowly to simulate movement of boat). Man tacking notice on garden gate. He finishes, goes through gate and closes it behind him so that we can clearly read the notice: LOST. BLACK LABRADOR PUPPY, £1 REWARD TO FINDER.*

LOCATION — RIVER NEAR COOKHAM (Camera in boat)

7. *As Scenes 2 and 5. Canoe is now stationary. Boy with field glasses excitedly hands them back to the other boy who looks through them and sees . . .*

LOCATION — DOWNLEY, OUTSIDE FLAGMORE COTTAGE

8. *M.S. Gate with notice on it. A child walks into shot and stops to read. He then beckons to someone out of picture and another child comes in and studies the notice. Then another and another until the gate is hidden from our view by a crowd of excited children.*

LOCATION — RIVER NEAR COOKHAM (Camera in boat)

9. *As Scenes 2, 5 and 7. Boy at rear of canoe puts down field glasses, picks up paddle and swiftly propels canoe out of picture left.*

No doubt, you will have noticed at once that two different locations (actually about ten miles apart) are used here to represent one in the film. Hence the two boys in the canoe are never seen in the same shot with the garden gate or the other children who stop to read the notice. At first glance, this may seem needlessly complicated but, in fact, it simplified the production of the film immensely. Let me try to explain why.

Firstly, if you have ever tried directing two young actors who are dividing their attention between acting and manoeuvring a canoe, you will realise that it is not the easiest job in the world. And it is not made easier if you and your camera are in another boat. Just co-ordinating camera movement with subject movement is enough to keep you busy without having to make allowance for (and organise) more action in the background.

Perhaps with a larger unit I might have attempted it but as I was working with only two colleagues — one to operate the camera and one to steer the boat — I decided to keep it simple and, while filming from the boat, to concentrate solely on the boys in the canoe. Related action on the river bank therefore had to be covered by cut-aways and, once having made that decision, I realised there was no particular reason why the house with the garden gate should be in the same location at all. We didn't even need water; a little tall grass in the foreground would suggest the river bank — and so it did.

The house at Downley was chosen simply because it belongs to a relation of mine and is situated in a quiet spot without passing traffic. To clinch the matter, I knew there were plenty of children in the vicinity who could be converted into film extras at the drop of a sweet.

Preparing the Breakdown

Although it would be nice, from a purely artistic point of view, to shoot a film in natural story sequence — starting with the first shot and going straight through to the last — this is seldom practical. Nobody but a madman, for example, would attempt to take the nine opening scenes of *Hot Dog* in story sequence as this would mean abandoning the actors literally in mid-stream and dashing to a different location for each cut-away. The sensible way, obviously,

is to tackle one location and one set of actors at a time and cut your shots into story sequence at the editing stage.

As soon as the script is complete, therefore, the next logical step is to prepare a 'breakdown'; that is a list of scenes re-grouped in the most convenient order for shooting. To do this you need several sheets of paper ruled off in four vertical columns. Start with the first scene in your script and write down its location or setting at the top of your first breakdown sheet. Write down the number of the scene in the first column, the names of the actors involved in the second column, and the props in the third column. This will leave the fourth column free for notes about any special equipment, costume changes or other production requirements.

Work your way through the script, listing all the scenes that take place in this same location with their relevant particulars. And repeat the process, using a separate sheet for each new location until every scene in the script is accounted for.

The breakdown will give you a pretty good idea of how much work is going to be involved. If there are more than a dozen or so scenes listed under any one location, you may well decide that it is impossible to cover them all in one shooting session. (As a rough guide, I allow twenty minutes for each shot when working out of doors.) That being so, you will have to make a further breakdown, grouping together now the shots that require the same actors — or possibly the same special equipment.

In the case of *Hot Dog*, for example, there were 47 scenes scripted for the main river location and I divided these into four groups, each of which could conveniently be covered on a separate visit. Thus:

> A. 14 shots involving Ian Hawes and Robert Kennedy (the two boys in the canoe) — 11 to be taken from boat and 3 from bank.
> B. 14 shots involving the same two actors plus a dog which had to be accompanied by its owner — all from bank fortunately.
> C. 12 shots involving seven other children — 10 from boat and 2 from bank.
> D. 4 shots involving the dog only and 3 without any cast at all — from boat.

This accounted for a little less than half the complete film which, by the way, ran for about ten minutes. In all there were eight different shooting sessions, each occupying a day or the best part of a day — which may not seem very much until you begin to work out just how much spare time amateurs are willing and able to devote to film making. Which brings me to my next point.

The Time Element

It is comforting to think that time is the amateur's cheapest commodity and that he can afford to spend it as lavishly as the feature film companies spend their cash. Comforting but, I fear, an illusion — at least where group productions are concerned.

Assuming that all your shooting has to be done at week-ends, consider how many fine week-ends constitute the average British summer. Then consider that unpaid actors and technicians have an awkward way of taking their holidays just when it suits *them* and sometimes, quite unexpectedly, they fall sick — or in love with someone who is not a member of the unit.

All these eventualities must be taken into account when you are drawing up your shooting schedule — that is allotting tentative dates to each section of the breakdown. The weather, of course, can't be anticipated but if there are interior scenes — or scenes actually requiring rain — then you can have an alternative wet-weather programme up your sleeve.

If the schedule shows on paper that you will complete the film in four weeks, there is a fair chance that you will actually complete it in eight. It is better than not having a schedule at all and just trusting to luck that you will finish one day — and it is certainly more satisfactory for the actors to know well in advance when and where they will be needed.

I mention actors in particular here because they are the major risk in film making. If the cameraman has a fight with the director and walks out, someone else can usually take over at a pinch. But once you have recorded an actor's face on film, you have an investment in him and that investment grows with every foot that's exposed. Like him or not, you must keep him healthy and happy until his last scene is in the can.

Preparing the Budget

Talking of investments brings me finally to the rather tricky question of costs. Amateurs, as we know, work for love but unfortunately the film manufacturers still insist on charging for their wares. So this is a question that has to be faced.

No matter how you finance your film — whether by an allocation from club funds, an informal whip round among friends or a grant from some local sponsor — you will avoid subsequent embarassment, if you can prepare an accurate budget before you begin.

Unless you are working on 16 mm and using professional sound recording services, the major item will amost certainly be film stock and the total expenditure will therefore be in direct proportion to the length of the picture.

While we cannot be arbitrary about this, I think it is reasonable to assume that the average length of a silent film shot (taken at 16 f.p.s.) before cutting is about 2 feet for standard 8 mm (just over 2 feet for super 8 and 4 feet for 16 mm). So, if you allow yourself an average of two takes per shot and you have 100 shots or scenes in your script, you will need 400 feet of 8 mm stock (800 feet of 16 mm). Allow a reasonably generous margin for editing and you can reckon that the running time of the finished film will be in the region of ten minutes.

As the cost of film stock changes quite frequently and usually in an upward direction, there is no point in quoting actual prices here but you can easily convert the quantities I have mentioned into cash.

Oddly enough, where 8 mm is concerned, you can't save very much by shooting on black and white reversal stock, as this costs nearly as much as colour. However, black and white is an interesting economic proposition for the 16 mm user who wants to have several copies of his film and wants to preserve the original from any possible damage. He can, for instance, shoot on negative and have a cutting copy made quite inexpensively.

When the cutting copy has been edited to everyone's satisfaction, the negative (which, of course, is never projected) is carefully cut to match it and becomes the source of blemish-free show copies — which again are relatively cheap.

For a group production where the cash outlay is likely to be small compared with the expenditure of human effort, this system is well worth considering. A similar procedure can, of course, be used with colour but it is very much more expensive and to get good quality, you must shoot on a professional-type colour stock such as Ektachrome Commercial which is made for copying and *not* for projecting.

The Cost of Sound

Sound need not add materially to the budget, providing of course that you are thinking in terms of a purely 'home made' sound track.

However, as I tried to show in Chapter Fourteen there is all the difference in the world between the kind of sound accompaniment that you can get with standard amateur apparatus (I am not talking about special home-made equipment) and a properly edited, properly synchronised sound track. If you want the latter, you must expect to pay for professional facilities and the addition of sound will probably be the biggest item on your budget.

Chapter Seventeen

THE SECRET OF SUCCESS

Film, as I said at the beginning of this book, is a language — and anyone can learn to speak it.

Only a few, perhaps, will ever become poets and authors of the cinema but we can all become literate; we can all learn to express ourselves clearly and economically in this visual medium. The secret of success lies in the realisation that the purpose and meaning of a movie shot is only revealed by its association with other shots.

One good shot by itself is like one good word selected at random from the dictionary. Words only come alive and command our interest when they are arranged in sequence to form coherent sentences and when each new sentence leads us naturally to the next, continually arousing and then satisfying our curiosity. It is the same with shots and it is only when we start to think of them as interlocking links in a continuing chain of narrative, rather than as separate moving photographs, that we really begin to be film makers.

Only Connect

We must remember that an audience is always instinctively seeking a connection between one shot and the next and will often find one where none was intended. Thus shots can be connected in all sorts of different ways. The link may simply be one of visual similarity: a cut from a shot of a man hosing his garden to a shot of a fountain. Or it may be based on contrast: a cut from the smooth face of a little girl to the wrinkled face of an old lady.

The most useful link however — and this is the basis of film grammar — is that between cause and effect or action and reaction. If we see a boy firing a catapult and then we see a window shattering we automatically assume that the second event is the result of the first. Similarly, if we see a girl looking upwards and then an aircraft in flight, we automatically assume that the girl is looking at the aircraft. If the shot of the aircraft is removed and a shot of a seagull substituted, we shall be equally willing to believe that she is looking at *that*.

In Chapter Three we saw how a sequence can be constructed on this cause-and-effect principle by imagining that the camera is an attentive observer who, to see any sequence of events clearly, must constantly shift the direction of his glance. Extending the same idea, we gave our observer wings, enabling him to flit through space and follow simultaneous events in different places — the basis of the parallel action sequence.

The aim and object of the film maker must always be to guide the thoughts of his audience from one part of the action to the next, stressing what is important and omitting what is irrelevant to his purpose. He must strive to do this as smoothly and painlessly as possible and, as we discovered in Chapter Eleven, one way that he can do this is to arrange for a maximum number of his cuts to take place on action.

The Heart of the Matter

Now it is true that movie making has many other facets. Good photography, for example, is obviously an asset. As we found in Chapters Six, Seven and Eight, the knowing use of lenses and lighting can add power and subtlety to the way we express ourselves on film. Yet photography is not the heart of the matter and a good film can triumph despite photography that is only moderate.

Again, as we found in Chapter Twelve, acting and the spontaneous behaviour of natural types can contribute hugely to the success of a movie. Yet acting is not the heart of the matter for fine films have been made without actors and even without people in them.

The use of sound has added a new dimension to our craft as we discovered in Chapter Fourteen. Yet sound is not the heart of the matter for excellent films are still being made in which sound is simply an unobtrusive accompaniment to visuals which carry the whole burden of the story.

The heart of the matter is the arrangement of the images in a meaningful order. This is the one craft that has no existence outside the film medium and the one that makes it unique; it is also the one that no film can do without.

Unfortunately, the only word we have for this central process is 'editing' which to most people means cutting and splicing. But the arrangement of images can, of course, be planned in detail before shooting begins by writing a script, or, it can be done off the cuff at the time of shooting, or, it can be done after shooting with scissors and film cement. Usually, of course, the process is spread out over all three stages of production, ideas being altered or refined as we go along.

Growing Ambition

The amateur who works completely on his own is fortunate in a way because he has absolute control over the images and their arrangement from first conception right through to the physical assembly of strips of film on the cutting bench. On the other hand, of course, he is severely restricted in his choice of subject matter. He is restricted too by the range of his own talents for it is a rare man who would claim to be equally good at writing scripts, operating the camera, lighting, sound recording and cutting.

With growing ambition there is a natural tendency for most of us to call on the help of other people. We willingly sacrifice direct control over each and every aspect of the film in exchange for the expertise of specialists. One man with a good speaking voice is persuaded to deliver the commentary, a lettering expert offers to prepare the title cards and so it grows.

When actors come into the picture we probably find it difficult to give them all the attention they need while concentrating on the details of composition, exposure and focus. So, reluctantly perhaps, we hand over the operation of the camera to someone else and before we know what has happened we have become film directors with nothing at all to do — except to control and co-ordinate the work of other people.

The Director's Role

The role of film director is much coveted by those who imagine that it consists of sitting in a canvas chair and shouting directions through a megaphone.

Actually, of course, that is not the full extent of it any more that conducting an orchestra consists of standing on a platform and waving a stick.

Like the conductor, the director has an intangible role which calls for humility as well as strength of purpose. No single sound that is heard in the concert hall can be attributed to the conductor. If he were to do his job badly or if he were to stop doing it altogether, the orchestra would still be able to go on playing and individually the musicians might play just as well.

Similarly, there is no single element in the picture or the sound track of a film that can be isolated and pointed out as the work of the director. The contributions of the actors, of the cameraman of the recordist of the editor are there for all to see and hear. But the director's contribution is invisible and inaudible. He cannot shine independently of his team but only through them and his success can only be judged in relation to the total effect.

If the director does his job well the complete film may be worth a little bit more than the sum of the individual talents that go into it. If not — and this is sadly true of many films — it will be worth a great deal less.

Collective Discords

Individually, the musicians in an orchestra may play well and yet collectively produce a terrible noise. Similarly, actors and technicians can all do their own jobs well and yet produce a total effect that is muddled or ineffective.

Inevitably, the specialist will always think of a scene in terms of his particular craft. Let's suppose, for example, that we have a scene in which one of the characters is nervously awaiting a crucial telephone call. The actor playing the part will devise his own way of conveying tension — perhaps by drumming with his fingers on a table top and occasionally tightening his facial muscles. If he thinks of the camera at all, he will think of it only as a mechanical instrument for recording his performance.

The cameraman, on the other hand, will instinctively devise pictorial ways of conveying the same message. He may compose the shot so that the telephone is boldly framed in foreground while the

actor paces up and down in the background and then
he may pull focus from the actor to the telephone
to suggest the way the characters thoughts are tending.
If he thinks of the actor at all, he will think of him as
a mobile object which has to be lit and manipulated
within a given space.

The film editor and the sound recordist will again
have their own interpretations of the scene and each
new approach will tend to cancel out or, at best,
muffle the effect of the other. The actor, for example,
having brought the tightening of his facial muscles to
perfection, will be frustrated to find that on screen
he is simply an out-of-focus shape moving about in
the background of a shot dominated by the telephone.

Restoring Harmony

The director, being the only man with no particular
axe to grind, is the only one who can preserve a
proper balance between the various elements. He must
control the movements of the actors to suit the composition of the picture and, at the same time, ensure
that the camerawork supports and enhances the work
of the actors.

Ideally, I suppose, he should be a jack-of-all-trades,
able to employ the skills of photography, acting,
editing and sound recording with equal felicity. In
practice, however, such perfectly balanced individuals
are seldom encountered. The director who is primarily
interested in photography will put the emphasis on
camerawork and subdue the other elements. The man
who has come into films by way of the theatre will
tend to make a vehicle for actors and so on.

A degree of bias is unavoidable and not necessarily
harmful. There are many different ways of interpreting
a subject and it is impossible to say that one way is
right and all the others wrong. So long as the director
decides firmly which is his way and then backs it for
all he is worth, his film will be consistent in style and
good of its kind.

Thinking in Sequence

There is one thing, however, that all directors must
have in common and that is the ability to think in
sequence while shooting out of sequence.

As we know, a film is made up of shots — tiny
fragments of action each lasting a few seconds. As
we also know, it is hardly ever convenient or practical
to take the shots in their natural story sequence and
hence the perpetual problem of maintaining continuity.

The scene of the wife weeping over her husband's
coffin may be filmed before the scene of their wedding.
The shot we take today of the boy leaping from an
open window may be followed instantaneously on
the screen by a shot we took three weeks ago of him
landing on the grass. The woman reacting in horror at
the sight of a street accident may, in fact, be looking
at nothing more moving than a group of technicians
standing round a tripod.

Because filming calls for a high degree of concentration, there is an overwhelming temptation to treat
each shot as a self-contained unit. But the director
must never yield to this: part of his mind must be
dwelling on what came before and what is to come
after. If a character is to walk out of one shot and
into the next, he must ensure that the direction of his
movement across the screen is constant, left to right
or right to left. If the camera is moving in from long
shot to medium shot, he must ensure that the
characters do not change places or alter their positions
drastically at the cutting point, or, indeed, change
their clothes. The direction and intensity of the light,
the colour of the sky, the pace of the action must not
chop and change from shot to shot.

Above all, he must remember that all these mechanical aspects of continuity are only important insofar as
they help to sustain the continuity of idea — the forward thrust of the narrative. In a well made film, the
first shot starts a train of thought in the minds of the
audience. The second shot picks up the thought and
carries it forward, whereupon it is picked up again by
the third shot and so on right through to the end. If
this chain of cause and effect, of action and reaction,
is once allowed to slacken or fall apart, the film will
lose its grip on the audience and the director will have
failed in his task.

Unity of Purpose

Which brings me back to my opening gambit. The
heart of the matter — the essence of the film maker's
craft — is the arrangement of a series of moving
images in a meaningful order. This 'editing', for want

of a better word, begins when a script is written, continues through shooting and reaches its final form when the shots are cut and spliced together.

The lone worker, who copes personally with every stage of production may have little difficulty in carrying his editing plan in his head. But when a group is involved and when, as a result, film making becomes more complex, there is a grave danger that nobody will be able to see the wood for the trees. That is why it is necessary to have a director who — just because he has no detailed and specialised job to do — can restore unity of purpose to the whole enterprise.

DATA

Screen Size and Projection Distance

The following tables provide an easy way of working out the projector-to-screen distance when you want to fill a given width of screen, or alternatively, the screen width when the projector is at a given distance from the screen.

All you need to know is the factor of projection distance, calculated in terms of screen widths. This figure will be a constant for any one focal length of projection lens and film gauge. The tables give you the factors for different lenses on each gauge.

To find the projection distance, multiply the screen width by the appropriate factor, taken from the tables. Example: 25 mm lens on standard 8 mm. Factor from tables is $5\frac{3}{4}$. Screen width is 3 ft. Projection distance will be $3 \times 5\frac{3}{4}$ ft $= 17\frac{1}{4}$ feet.

To find screen width divide the factor (taken from the tables) into the projection distance. Example: 18 mm lens on super 8, and projection distance of 10 ft. Factor from tables is $3\frac{1}{3}$. So 10 ft. divided by $3\frac{1}{3}$ = 3 ft; 3 ft; (approximately).

STANDARD 8 mm

Focal length of projection lens	Factor
13 mm	2·98 (say 3)
15 mm	3·44 (say $3\frac{1}{2}$)
18 mm	4·12 (say 4)
20 mm	4·57 (say $4\frac{1}{2}$)
25 mm	5·73 (say $5\frac{3}{4}$)
30 mm	6·86 (say 7)
32 mm	7·33 (say $7\frac{1}{3}$)
35 mm	8·02 (say 8)

SUPER 8

Focal length of projection lens	Factor
13 mm	2·42 (say 2·4)
15 mm	2·8
18 mm	3·36 (say $3\frac{1}{3}$)
20 mm	3·73 (say $3\frac{3}{4}$)
25 mm	4·66 (say $4\frac{2}{3}$)
30 mm	5·6
32 mm	5·97 (say 6)
35 mm	6·53 (say $6\frac{1}{2}$)

9·5 mm

Focal length of projection lens	Factor
25 mm	2·94 (say 3)
32 mm	3·76 (say $3\frac{3}{4}$)
35 mm	4·12 (say 4·1)
40 mm	4·7
50 mm	5·88 (say 5·9)

16 mm. (Metric focal lengths)

Focal length of projection lens	Factor
25 mm	2·6
35 mm	3·63 (say $3\frac{2}{3}$)
40 mm	4·15
50 mm	5·18 (say 5·2)
75 mm	7·77 (say $7\frac{3}{4}$)
100 mm	10·3

16 mm. (Inch focal lengths)

Focal length of projection lens	Factor
1 in	2·63 (say 2·6)
$1\frac{1}{2}$ in	3·95 (say 4)
2 in	5·26 (say $5\frac{1}{4}$)
$2\frac{1}{2}$ in	6·58 (say 6·6)
3 in	7·8
$3\frac{1}{2}$ in	9·2
4 in	10·5

NOTE:

These figures are approximate, because of the inevitable slight variations due to tolerances in lens focal length and in exact gate width on different projectors. Figures have been rounded off for convenience.

The factors are calculated on the basis of the standard projector aperture sizes, as follows:

Standard 8 mm	0·172 in	(4·37 mm)
Super 8	0·212 in	(5·36 mm)
9·5mm	0·335 in	(8·5 mm)
16mm	0·380 in	(9·65 mm)

Title Sizes and Camera Distances

The following is a simple way of calculating the size of title required for filming at a given distance and with a given focal length of camera lens.

The calculation uses the principle of equal triangles which represent the gate width and lens focal length on one side, and the title size and distance on the other side, thus:

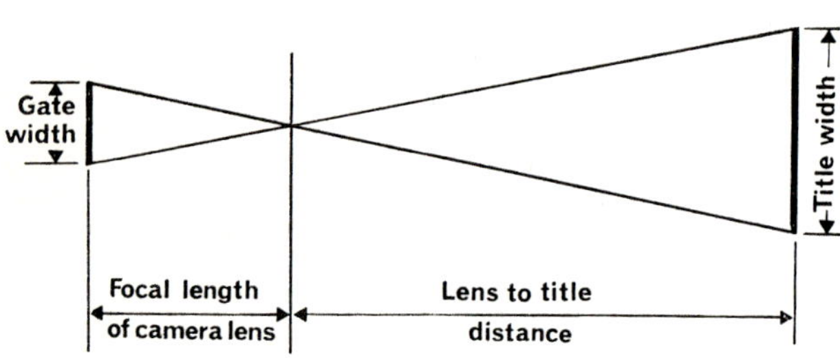

Most beginners make the mistake of getting their title lettering too close to the edges of the title card. It is much better to allow plenty of safety margin of card outside the photographed area, to avoid all risk of 'running off the edge'. The actual title letters should not come too close to the margins of the screen.

This sketch, drawn to scale, shows suggested placing of lettering in the central area of the card, with the filmed area and the slightly smaller projected area around it but not too close. Typical dimensions would be: card, 8 x 6 inches; area appearing on screen when projected, 6 x 4½ inches; title lettering kept within central 4 x 3 inch area, or possibly a little larger, depending on the title design.

Knowing three of the dimensions on the diagram, you can quickly calculate the fourth. Use this basic formula:

$$\frac{Title\ width}{Lens\text{-}to\text{-}title\ distance} = \frac{Gate\ width}{Focal\ length\ of\ camera\ lens}$$

For ease of calculation, however, we can transpose these into two simple formulae:

$$(1)\quad Title\ width = \frac{Gate\ width}{Focal\ length} \times Title\ width$$

or

$$(2)\quad Lens\text{-}to\text{-}title\ distance = \frac{Focal\ length}{Gate\ width} \times Title\ width$$

Note: For gate width, use the dimension for projector gate size, to give the size that will be seen when the film is projected. These dimensions are given below

Example: Standard 8 mm camera, with 13 mm lens, distance (lens-to-title) 19 inches (=483 mm). Gate width (see Table) 0·172 inches or 4·37 mm. What is title width that will be seen on projection?

Use formula (1)

$$Title\ width = \frac{4\cdot37}{13\cdot0} \times 483$$

$$= 162\ mm\ (which\ is\ 6\cdot4\ inches).$$

Title width refers to the actual area that will be seen when the film is projected on the screen. The title card *must* be larger than this, to give a 'safety margin'. Also, the title lettering should come well within the title width.

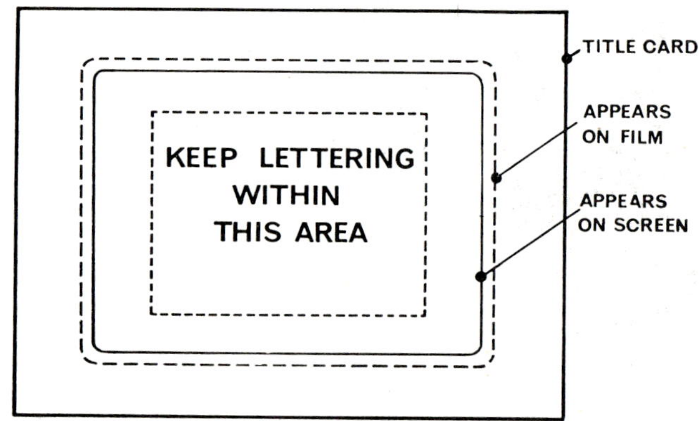

TITLE SIZES

Film Gauge and Lens	Distance	Title Size	
		inches	millimeters
Standard 8 mm Film 13 mm lens	13 in	$4\frac{3}{8} \times 3\frac{1}{4}$	111×83
	19½ in	$6\frac{1}{2} \times 5$	166×125
	26 in	$8\frac{3}{4} \times 6\frac{1}{2}$	222×167
	39 in	$13\frac{1}{8} \times 9\frac{7}{8}$	333×250
Super 8 Film 15 mm lens	13 in	$4\frac{5}{8} \times 3\frac{1}{2}$	118×89
	19½ in	$7 \times 5\frac{1}{4}$	177×133
	26 in	9·3×7	236×177
	39 in	$13·9 \times 10\frac{1}{2}$	354×266
9·5 mm Film 20 mm lens	13 in	$5\frac{1}{2} \times 4\frac{1}{8}$	140×105
	19½ in	$8·3 \times 6\frac{1}{4}$	211×158
	26 in	11×8·3	281×211
	39 in	$16·6 \times 12\frac{1}{2}$	421×316
16 mm Film 25 mm lens	13 in	$4\frac{5}{8} \times 3\frac{3}{4}$	128×96
	19½ in	$7\frac{1}{2} \times 5\frac{5}{8}$	191×143
	26 in	$10 \times 7\frac{1}{2}$	255×191
	39 in	15×11·3	382×287

Title sizes given in the Table have been chosen so that a non-focusing camera can be used with a supplementary lens as follows:

Distance	*Supplementary lens*
39 in	+1 Dioptre ("No. 1")
26 in	+1·5 Dioptres
19½ in	+2 Dioptres ("No. 2")
13 in	+3 Dioptres ("No. 3")

When using a supplementary over the front of the camera lens, measure the lens-to-title distance from the supplementary. British and European manufacturers generally use the above numbering system, but this does not apply to some Japanese manufacturers of supplementary lenses.

Table of Gate Sizes

Width of projector gate aperture

    8 mm 0·172 inches (4·37 mm)

    Super 8 0·212 inches (5·36 mm)

    9·5 mm 0·335 inches (8·5 mm)

    16 mm 0·380 inches (9·65 mm)

The height of the picture (and hence of the title) is three-quarters of the width. In other words, the standard amateur format is always a 3 x 4 ratio.

When calculating title sizes, remember to work in the same units throughout. That is, use either inches, or millimeters. Useful equivalents: 1 mm = 0·039 inches; 1 metre = 39·3 inches; 1 inch = 25·4 mm.

Running Times

The following table converts film footages into running times at the standard projection speeds of 24 frames per second (commonly used for 16 mm sound films) and 18 frames per second.

Feet	9·5, 16 mm sound 24 f p s		9·5, 16 mm silent 18 f p s		Super 8 18 f p s		Standard 8 mm 18 f p s	
	min	*sec*	*min*	*sec*	*min*	*sec*	*min*	*sec*
1		$1\frac{2}{3}$		$2\frac{1}{3}$		4		$1\frac{1}{2}$
2		$3\frac{1}{3}$		$4\frac{1}{2}$		8		9
3		5		$6\frac{1}{2}$		12		$13\frac{1}{3}$
4		$6\frac{2}{3}$		9		16		$17\frac{2}{3}$
5		$8\frac{1}{3}$		11		20		$22\frac{1}{3}$
6		10		$13\frac{1}{3}$		24		$26\frac{1}{2}$
7		$11\frac{2}{3}$		$15\frac{1}{2}$		28		31
8		$13\frac{1}{3}$		$17\frac{2}{3}$		32		$35\frac{1}{2}$
9		15		20		36		40
10		$16\frac{2}{3}$		$22\frac{1}{3}$		40		$44\frac{1}{2}$
12		20		$26\frac{1}{2}$		48		$53\frac{1}{2}$
15		25		$33\frac{1}{3}$	1	0	1	$6\frac{2}{3}$
20		$33\frac{1}{3}$		$44\frac{1}{2}$	1	20	1	29
25		$41\frac{2}{3}$		$55\frac{1}{2}$	1	40	1	$51\frac{1}{3}$
30		50	1	$6\frac{1}{2}$	2	0	2	$13\frac{1}{3}$
40	1	$6\frac{2}{3}$	1	$28\frac{2}{3}$	2	40	2	$57\frac{2}{3}$
50	1	$23\frac{1}{3}$	1	51	3	20	3	$42\frac{1}{3}$
100	2	$46\frac{2}{3}$	3	$42\frac{1}{3}$	6	40	7	$24\frac{1}{2}$
200	5	$33\frac{1}{3}$	7	$24\frac{1}{2}$	13	20	14	$48\frac{2}{3}$
400	11	$6\frac{2}{3}$	14	$48\frac{2}{3}$	26	40	29	$37\frac{2}{3}$
800	22	$13\frac{1}{3}$	29	$37\frac{1}{2}$	53	20	59	$15\frac{1}{2}$